EARLY VIRGIL

Corpore et statura fuit grandi, aquilo colore, facie rusticana, valetudine
varia . . . in sermone tardissimum ac paene indocto similem fuisse Melissus
tradidit.

He was tall and heavy, had a dark complexion, the face of a rustic, and
delicate health . . . Melissus reports that his speech was extremely slow and
like that of a man who is barely educated.

Donatus, Life of Virgil

Early Virgil

WILLIAM BERG

UNIVERSITY OF LONDON
THE ATHLONE PRESS
1974

Published by
THE ATHLONE PRESS
UNIVERSITY OF LONDON
at 4 *Gower Street London* WCI

Distributed by Tiptree Book Services Ltd
Tiptree, Essex

USA and Canada
Humanities Press Inc
New York

ISBN 0 485 11145 4

Printed in Great Britain by
WESTERN PRINTING SERVICES LTD
BRISTOL

GEORGE E. DUCKWORTH

in memoriam

PREFACE

What was ancient pastoral? The present work is designed to answer that question for students of ancient and modern poetry, for poets, and for the educated public. Just as Spenser, Dryden, Burns, Cowper, Herrick—and all the poets who are called 'pastoral' by convention—included Virgil among their sources of inspiration, so Virgil himself, and Theocritus before him, relied for inspiration on his own traditions, some literary, some religious. Chapter I introduces the reader to these traditions, and the essays which follow my text and translation of the *Bucolics* are meant to show how Virgil adapted literary tradition to the needs of his own developing poetics. This process seems to reveal itself most readily in the showpiece of his collection, a poem which celebrates the pastoral hero Daphnis. In later *Eclogues*, Daphnis becomes by turns a Roman hero, a hero of the future, and a hero-lover; his transformations can be followed in the final chapters of this book.

My essays are meant to depart from conventional discussion of the *Bucolics* and to share, even with the 'uninitiated', the fruits of a century of scholarship in Europe and America. Poetry is complicated stuff; the *Bucolics* may be the most difficult poetry to survive from the ancient world. A baldly popularizing work which emphasizes what was already obvious about Virgilian pastoral, which only 'notes the beauty' for those who need to be told that good poetry is beautiful, is of use only to the dullest of graduate students. To speak of the *genesis* of Virgilian poetry, to show how Virgil worked and developed, is a task which requires attention to details which are often inter-related in a complicated way. I have sought, on the one hand, not to conceal these details; and on the other, to present them as lucidly as possible.

A word about the text and translation. Both are new, though I owe much, orthographically and otherwise, to Sabbadini's incomparable edition. The translation does no justice to Virgil, but attempts to reproduce his 'rustic' ingenuousness through a modern American style which matches in its own pedestrian way at least the simplicity of Virgilian vocabulary. I have also tried to approach his rhythms, though perhaps no translation can capture the subtlety of his variations within the ancient metrical scheme. Reproduced in both text and translation are those internal divisions which lent structure to the individual poems; for the most part, I follow the observations of Otto Skutsch on symmetry. A good translation of the *Bucolics* is a life's work; it can never hope to keep abreast of changes in the appropriate modern idiom. This is why I have included the Latin text of these ten short poems which are so precious to our Western literary tradition. Many of us have had the fortune to cross swords with the Latin language; those who have not are encouraged to read the Latin for its sounds alone —they are inimitable.

Finally, a word of thanks to those who made this book possible. George Duckworth, who directed my Ph.D. dissertation on the *Bucolics* in 1966, and to whose memory the present work is dedicated, helped immeasurably by encouraging my thought in its germinal stages. T. B. L. Webster and Otto Skutsch were kind enough to give the final text a careful reading, rescuing it from some of the deeper pitfalls; the latter would have preferred to see the whole section on the *Culex* omitted, and its inclusion is entirely my responsibility. I am grateful to Robert Duncan for so generously giving me permission to reproduce extracts from *The Opening of the Field*. Eric Handley and others contributed valuable criticism; the staff of the Athlone Press have been patient and most helpful; and Stanford University has been generous in granting me both time for the book's completion and financial resources towards its publication. I cannot begin to acknowledge here how much friends, colleagues, teachers and students on the east and west coasts have taught me about poetry. My wife was a source of inspiration for much of what is good here, and of consolation for what is irremediably flawed.

W.B.

CONTENTS

FRONTISPIECE

Museo Nazionale, Naples. The painting was found in Pompeii but apart from its inventory number (9488) no more is known of its provenance. See p. 133.

INTRODUCTION

Lovely their feet pound the solid green meadow.
The dancers
mimic flowers—root stem stamen and petal
our words are,
our articulations, our
measures . . .
Lovely our circulations sweeten the meadow.

Robert Duncan, 'The Dance'

The mind of man has evolved a self-awareness which sets him apart from the rest of nature. In a paradox of double vision, he sees the world, and he sees himself seeing the world. Deriving his physical existence, his body, wholly from nature, man feels himself to be, nevertheless, distinct from his natural surroundings.

The *Bhagavadgītā*, the Hindu 'Song of the Lord', embraces this paradox of identity and distinctness, claiming for it a cosmic analogy in the relationship of the creator to the created: Brahman, the Lord of this universe, dwells within it as the human soul dwells within its natural body. As their bodies make individual men manifest, so God is manifested through the world. And how does God create the world? Again, the analogy comes from human experience: as our eyes impart form to what we see, so Brahman forms the universe by recognizing it in a creative gesture called *yoga māyā*. Created nature (*prakṛti*) is less real, less absolute, than the spirit (*puruṣa*) which generates it. As a 'construct' (*māyā*) of the creator, the material universe is from his point of view illusory, non-existent.[1]

In the thirteenth chapter of the *Bhagavadgītā* a distinction between matter and spirit, between the Creator and the created, is attempted through a metaphor which will be the intimate concern of this book, the metaphor of the Field and the Knower of the Field. Arjuna the prince, son of Kuntī, addresses his teacher Krishna, a human incarnation of Brahman:

Prakriti and Purusha, the Field and the Knower of the Field, knowledge and that which is to be known—all this, O Keśava, I desire to learn.

The Lord said: This body, O son of Kunti, is called the Field, and he who knows it is called the Knower of the Field by those who describe them.

And know that I am the Knower in all Fields, O Bhārata; and only the knowledge of the Field and its Knower do I regard as true knowledge.

Hear briefly from Me what the Field is, what its nature is, what its modifications are, whence it comes, who its Knower is, and what His powers are.

All this has been sung by sages in many and different ways, in various distinctive hymns, and also in well reasoned and convincing passages indicative of Brahman.[2]

Krishna proceeds to describe the *māyā* which is the Field: it is shown to include not only the natural elements, but also all possible desires, virtues, and attitudes of the mind. The 'Knower of the Field' is Brahman, creator and soul of all. In the twenty-sixth *śloka*, his creation is defined as an interaction between spirit and matter:[3]

Whatever is born—whether animate or inanimate—know, O Bhārata prince, that it is through union of the Field and the Knower of the Field.

Nikhilananda, following the ancient commentaries of Śaṃkara, refers to this creation not as a real physical union, but as a superimposition of spirit upon matter through the power of *yoga māyā*. The world in its variety of forms is 'conjured up' by the Knower; the chaos of becoming, of 'non-being', is fixed in the world of being by his attention:

As the one sun illumines this whole world, so does the Lord of the field illumine this entire field, O Bhārata.[4]

This Hindu version of the creative act, then, differs from that of the Judaeo-Christian tradition. God does not act to bring creatures out of nothingness; instead, he directs his ordering gaze upon a 'non-world' which was there all the time, the world of becoming. By informing it with his spirit, he brings nature into being.

Krishna encourages man to recognize his essential kinship with the Creator, the Knower of the Field, and to strive for oneness with Him who is called elsewhere 'the Seer, the ancient, the ruler, subtler than the subtle, the supporter of all, whose form is beyond conception, who is sun-coloured beyond the darkness'.[5] 'Seer' is Radhakrishnan's translation of the Sanskrit *kavi*; the word is translated 'Poet, Creator' in Mascaró's version of the same *śloka*, and with some justification: *kavi* seems to embrace the range of meaning assigned to *vates*, a Latin word for 'prophetic singer' which, in the Augustan age, came to designate the poet himself.[6]

The author of the *Bhagavadgītā*, then, visualized the act of creation as a juxtaposition of the Field and its Knower. This metaphor does not, on reflection, seem a strange one for a poet to use; we are accustomed to it in a context directly related to the poet's own creativity. Consider, for example, the following poem by Robert Duncan:[7]

OFTEN I AM PERMITTED TO RETURN TO A MEADOW

as if it were a scene made-up by the mind,
that is not mine, but is a made place,

that is mine, it is so near to the heart,
an eternal pasture folded in all thought
so that there is a hall therein

that is a made place, created by light
wherefrom the shadows that are forms fall.

Wherefrom fall all architectures I am
I say are likenesses of the First Beloved
whose flowers are flames lit to the Lady.

She it is Queen Under the Hill
whose hosts are a disturbance of words within words
that is a field folded.

It is only a dream of the grass blowing
east against the source of the sun
in an hour before the sun's going down

whose secret we see in a children's game
of ring a round of roses told.

Often I am permitted to return to a meadow
as if it were a given property of the mind
that certain bounds hold against chaos,

that is a place of first permission,
everlasting omen of what is.

This poem stands first in Duncan's collection entitled *The Opening of the Field*. However we wish to interpret it, its programmatic character is unmistakable: it is a record of the poet's reflection upon his art, upon the work presented in the collection. Poetry is seen as a landscape, a 'meadow' or 'pasture' to which the poet is sometimes 'permitted to return'. The ancients, too, had spoken this way of poetry, sometimes as explicitly as Aper in Tacitus' *Dialogus de oratoribus*, who refers to 'the forest pastures and parks' (*nemora et luci*) into which a poet must be permitted to withdraw. 'Those pastures and parks, the whole hiding-place to which you chidingly refer', rejoins the poet Maternus, 'afford me great pleasure: I count it among the chief joys of poetry that it is *not* composed amid noise either of plaintiffs sitting at the door or of ragged, tearful defendants. The mind retreats into unspoiled, gentle places and has what amounts to a sacred dwelling. These places are the source of eloquence, its inmost shrines. In this guise and aspect did it first become accessible to mortals and flow into breasts pure and untouched by sin. This is how the oracles used to speak.'[8]

There seems to be a place in the mind, 'an eternal pasture', where the poet meets his Muse. Alone amid the living stuff of poetry, he awaits the creative act which will gather from sources wild and cultivated a new offspring of the spirit inspired. The fruit of this Muse's garden is the finished poem. Poets do not always refer to the garden; often, however, the place will be celebrated for its own sake, as it is in Duncan's work. When this happens, we may call the poem self-conscious. It emerges as a natural landscape; the poet feels himself labouring to create as nature creates. Ancient Greek poets who saw an analogy to their own *poiesis* ('producing', 'creating') in the *poiesis* of nature often chose metaphors from the natural world to designate their work.[9] 'Streams' of inspiration are a commonplace at least from the time of Pindar; the metaphor is in keeping with the notion that words 'flow' and the thought that brooks 'babble', and harks back to the spirits of poetry and prophecy who dwell in springs (water-nymphs and Muses are often identical in ancient lore).[10] Sappho called her poems 'roses from Pieria (the Muses' mount)'; the word 'anthology' is Greek, and signifies a gathering of flowers.[11] Poets from the time of Archilochus compared themselves to nature's musicians: the sound of running water, birdsong, and the din of cicadas represent paradigms of melody and rhythm to the ancient poet. The humming of bees occurs among such metaphors, though bees are celebrated not so much for their sound as for their function, the gathering of honey from blossoms of every scent and hue; this activity is nature's perfect analogy to the writing of poetry. Moreover, Homer's literary tradition had compared sweet words to honey, and Hesiod's Muses made 'honeyed words' flow from their poet's lips.[12]

When a Greek poet contemplates and characterizes his own work in a poem, one or more of these natural metaphors will often appear. The more self-conscious the poet becomes, the more he imagines himself united with his Muse in an imitation of natural processes. Around him flourish the works of nature, his first model: a landscape appears in the mind. Inevitably a type of poetry emerged which sustained the landscape and permitted the poet to dwell within it at greater length, to unify and cultivate the 'garden' as he perfected his own art.[13] The conscious recognition of this landscape, however, had to await an era of self-conscious poetry, a literary atmosphere in which the poet, divorced from all civic function, was alone with his Muse, so to speak, and free to look within himself, to reflect on the nature of his art. The cleared space under an open sky which we associate with classical Greek poetry—the hollowed hillside in that spring landscape where a Homer or a Sophocles performed—had, at the moment when poetry lost its wider function in the community, retreated into the poem itself. The 'Muse's garden', in other words, was consciously discovered in bucolic poetry of the Hellenistic age. Theocritus stumbled upon it almost by accident; it was Virgil's clear vision which fully recognized the garden nestled among the rustic landscapes of his Hellenic predecessors. In Virgil (for the first and last time in ancient literature) the pastoral landscape was completely transformed into a garden of poetry.

I

Idylls

Cyclops

The third century B.C. provided conditions necessary for the new internalization of poetry. A crisis in patronage had developed during the political turmoil following Alexander's death. The old *polis*, the traditional Greek community, had lost its integrity. No longer capable of self-determination, it had gone limp in the grip of Macedonian generals and their successors. Bureaucratized and cosmopolitan, it ceased to seek self-expression in the voice of its poets. These, in desperation, looked to the great rulers for patronage; but for the most part, the rulers were Philistines. One of Theocritus' earliest poems—the sixteenth in our collection of *Idylls*—is dedicated, half-heartedly, to one of them (Hieron of Syracuse), and seems to foretell the ruler's rejection of the poet:[1]

> For the daughters of Zeus and for poets the task is ever this,
> to hymn the immortals, to hymn the glories of noble men.
> Muses are goddesses; goddesses sing the praises of gods.
> But mortal are we; of mortals let us mortals sing.
>
> Who, then, of all who dwell beneath the gleam of dawn
> will open his house to our Graces? Who will welcome them in
> and bid them farewell—but not, again, without reward?
>
> (Home they come; they've lost their tempers, lost their shoes,
> they mock me over and over again for their fruitless chase,
> cringing, crouching once more in that empty space
> of a bottom drawer, resting their heads on chilly knees,
> the way they sit when they've returned without their price.)
>
> Who in this day and age will cherish the poet's good word?
> I know not. Gone are the heroes who loved old-fashioned praise
> for deeds well done; overwhelmed are they by greed.

(Everyone keeping his hands in his pockets, a sharp eye out
for coin, won't scrape off the tarnish to make a donation;
instead, a ready lecture: 'Charity begins at home.'
'Wish I had some myself.' 'The gods will pay the poets.'
'Homer's enough for all; who wants to hear another now?'
'The best of poets is he who costs me nothing.')

(1–21)

Theocritus was to see better days in Alexandria, settled in
the brilliant metropolis and supported by a benevolent
Ptolemy.

His poetry first flowered amid the rustic landscapes of Sicily
and the Dorian island of Cos. He had begun his career as a
writer of mimes. Like his contemporary, Herondas, he at-
tempted to reproduce in verse the speech of humble folk—
their mundane conversations, their wrangling, their lover's
complaints and serenades. Theocritus might once have earned
his livelihood by composing such pieces for the theatre in
Syracuse, where this form of entertainment was traditional.
Among the *Idylls* there may be a few early mimes which were
actually performed: *Idyll* 5, 'The Way Goatherds and Shep-
herds Behave', and *Idyll* 15, 'Women Going to the Adonis-
Festival', sound very much like scripts or libretti for the
recitation of several voices. In other *Idylls*, the mime-routine
exists only as the sketchy framework for a kind of self-expression
which would probably shun the stage (*Idyll* 7, for example).
Though three of the mimes have little to do with country life
(*Idylls* 2, 14, and 15), most draw upon the rustic songs and
banter of herdsmen in Sicily, Theocritus' birthplace. The
earliest of these country mimes (we would say today 'the
earliest of his pastoral poems', though Theocritus would hardly
have known what we meant) was probably the *Cyclops* (*Idyll* 11),
a lover's lament sung by Theocritus' fellow-countryman, the
one-eyed monster of the *Odyssey*. The poem takes its cue, in fact,
directly from Homer. In *Odyssey* 9 Polyphemus, blinded and
cheated, strikes for a brief moment a pathetic, almost tragic
pose as he sings a plaintive lament to the leader of his flock
(the same ram, incidentally, under whom Odysseus hangs,
remote from the Cyclops' gropings):

Ram, my dear, why bustle through the cave that way, of all my
    flock
the very last? Never before were you left behind the rest,
but first by far were you to crop the tender clover's bloom,
prancing as you went, first to find the rivulets,
first to crave return to the sheepfold in your
evening mood. But now you're last of all. Your master's
eye—can it be you grieve for the eye that scoundrel dashed
    from me,
that Noman? There's no way, I say, for him to flee destruction!
                              (*Odyssey* 9.447-55)

There is a mood in the Cyclops' song which captured
Theocritus' imagination. The monster expects a favourite sheep
to share his grief and misery. The slow movement of this ram
(burdened, actually, with Odysseus) is a sign to Polyphemus
that his pastoral world has been turned upside down. Like a
grieving parent, he reminds the ram of better days, days of
clover and of laughing brooks. Homer, in short, has for a
moment changed the Cyclops from a monster into a loving,
mourning shepherd.

The Cyclops' rôle as 'noble savage', however, had not been
developed before Theocritus. In post-Homeric literature, Poly-
phemus became the incarnation of the bestial, the lawless, the
uncivilized. His monstrous figure lent itself to parody: the
dithyrambist Philoxenus used him to portray the Sicilian
tyrant Dionysius in love with a flute-girl named Galatea.
Philoxenus, with intentions more polemic than poetic, had
given the Cyclops a harp with which to woo his love. The poem
was influential: from about 400 B.C. onward, Polyphemus was
a musician who pined for the love of Galatea.[2]

She appears in Theocritus as a sea-nymph whom the Cyclops
woos in vain from the shore, offering her his boundless wealth
of herds and cheese. As Homer had found in Polyphemus an
object of the poet's sympathy and affection, so Theocritus, for
the first time since Homer, ennobled his Cyclops, idealizing
him as a lonely shepherd, singer, and lover in the bucolic
landscape. The poet seems almost to identify himself with the
Cyclops and to encourage other poets to follow suit. The *Idyll*
is addressed, in fact, to a friend who, like Polyphemus, has been

unlucky in love; he is encouraged to find a remedy in song, as
the Cyclops did: 'No other cure for love exists, Nicias, nor
balm nor plaster, except the Pierian Muses' (*Id.* 11.1–3).

Theocritus' debut as a writer of rustic mime had been suc-
cessful. He went on to compose the seven or eight other poems
which have earned him, for better or for worse, the title
'founder of pastoral'. Many of the country mimes, indeed,
remain merely 'pastoral' in the modern, conventional sense:
they evoke a world of leisure and of amorous dalliance in a
rustic 'plaisance', and can be fruitfully compared with similar,
if less interesting, endeavours on the part of English poets of
the seventeenth and eighteenth centuries.[3] Surprisingly, Theo-
critus continued to compose in heroic verse. The dactylic
hexameter had been used in the *Cyclops* to remind his audience
that the poem harked back to Homer, to the Cyclops of the
Odyssey and to the ancient myths associated with Theocritus'
Sicily. Yet almost *all* the major poems of Theocritus—the
mimes, the myths, the encomia—show the same choice of
rhythmic form, the epic verse of Homer with its stately, un-
interrupted flow of language, a verse form hitherto held
appropriate (as Callimachus might have put it) for heroic
battles and the exploits of kings. The form became, to be sure,
'rusticated' through Theocritus' craftsmanship. His use of
repeated sounds, of refrains, and of breaks within lines (the
'bucolic diaeresis', for example) served to segment the poetry
into small, discrete units of thought which could stand on their
own without dependence upon an overall continuity.[4] Yet the
same form was used in the non-rustic *Idylls*, which far out-
number the pastoral pieces. And why did he go to such pains,
in the first place, to *overcome* an unwieldy form to suit his
content? Why could he not have followed, for instance, the
example of his contemporary, Herondas, who was achieving
natural effects with perfect ease through the conversational
rhythms of iambic verse?

It is not certain that the title was assigned to his collected
poems by Theocritus himself. If it was, it may give some clue
to his preference for the hexameter. *Idylls* (Greek *eidyllia*)
means, in the simplest interpretation it will bear, 'little forms'.
Theocritus saw himself as the creator of miniatures, of diminu-

tive vignettes which portrayed in a charming, sometimes quaint, always humanizing manner the scenes and milieux which classical poets had taken much more seriously.[5] Their charm is enhanced by the hexameter, the poet's playful nod to an old tradition. If ancient poets had sung the labours of mighty Heracles in epic verse, then surely the infant hero's first exploit (the strangling of serpents in *Idyll* 24) deserves the dactyl's grace. Polydeuces' obscure boxing match with Amycus —already a 'discovery' of Hellenistic sculptors—must likewise be celebrated in heroic verse (*Idyll* 22).[6] In hexameters, too, the dead Adonis is mourned—and told 'Goodbye 'til next year, sweet' by giddy housewives (*Idyll* 15).

He found the heroic verse to be 'right' for his rustic miniatures as well. Cadences once suited to kings and vassals now sport with herdsmen and flocks. Beyond the fields and thickets, courts and citadels are implicit in the dactyls. Theocritus' rustic stage, moreover, is peopled with a strange breed of herdsmen. Their names and their behaviour can often be traced to the *thiasos* of Dionysus, to the satyr-band which accompanies the god's epiphany. 'Tityrus' itself is a Doric word for 'satyr', while 'Thyrsis' may be 'short' for *thyrsophoros* (bearer of the mystic staff of Dionysus).[7] T. B. L. Webster has already noticed similarities in the rustic *Idylls* and in their characters to the classical Satyr drama, a little play which customarily followed the performance of three tragedies.[8] It is just possible that Theocritus regarded his country *Idylls* as a kind of pendant to epic poetry, just as the Satyr-drama had provided comic relief to high tragedy without departing from the *form* of tragedy. If so, the title *eidyllia* acquires further significance, for it may also mean 'minor forms' or 'subspecies'. This strictly formal connection with traditional Greek epic may explain why Quintilian, over three centuries later, could assign Theocritus' *Musa rustica et pastoralis* to the epic genre (*Inst. Or.* 10.1.55).

Whatever the real significance of the title, it was clear from the first that epic verse worked well for the *Idylls*. The Cyclops, a mock-hero, had offered in hexameters his mock-kingdom for a kiss from Galatea. Theocritus had found a happy coincidence of Homeric theme and rustic mime. Taking a hint from the ancient bard, he had developed Polyphemus into a full-fledged pastoral hero, a lovestruck shepherd-poet. In a later poem (*Idyll* 7) Theocritus was to imagine himself in the herdsman's rôle, and was to characterize the writing of poetry as a herdsman's work. In the meantime, the thought of a lone shepherd-lover in the bucolic landscape had led him to entertain a grander vision, a vision which became programmatic for the *Idylls*. The hero of the poem placed first in his collection became for the bucolic tradition, and for Virgil above all, the pastoral hero *par excellence*.

Daphnis

Like the Cyclops, Daphnis belonged to Sicilian myth, and was likely to have had a rustic cult on the island. Of the several sources which tell his story, all are at variance in the details, and we have lost any trace of the version which Theocritus followed. Some sources report him to be the mythical founder of 'bucolic song'; in the first *Idyll* he does join in singing his own lament, is called 'beloved of the Muses' (141) and dedicates his pipes to Pan (123–30). Some say he was blinded by a nymph named Thalia for his infidelity; but in Theocritus he dies for *refusing* to love—if the *communis opinio* is correct in interpreting a poem which defies interpretation. Enough are the points which all versions have in common: Daphnis was a herdsman and a musician; his beauty was admired by all; love brought Daphnis to a tragic end; and his lament was sung ever after.[9]

These details are enough to distinguish Daphnis sharply from other characters in the bucolic landscape. He is a serious figure, a paragon devoid of the satyr-like qualities to which we are accustomed in Theocritus. His very name sets him apart from the others: 'Daphnis', which points to Apollo's sacred laurel (*daphne*), removes him from the sphere of Dionysus and associates him with the god who (according to a later tradition, at least) presides over all herdsman-poets—Apollo Nomius, Apollo of the pasture, who first showed how to charm flocks and wilderness with his lyre.[10]

Above all, a religious aura surrounds Thyrsis' 'Lament for Daphnis', an aura created by the refrain 'Muses, take up, take up the herdsman's song', repeated sixteen times. The thrice-repeated refrain, 'Go, leave off, leave off the herdsman's song', closes the lament. It will soon become apparent that this lament and its refrain place Daphnis in a religious and literary setting as old as human memory, that Theocritus had cast him in a rôle which had belonged through the millennia to a herdsman whose death is a symbol for the mystery of life itself. It is sufficient for the present to remark that Daphnis aligns himself with this tradition in *Idyll* 1.105–10, where he reminds Aphrodite of her crimes against the herdsmen Anchises and Adonis.

The song of Daphnis was made the showpiece of Theocritus' collection; the poet had taken him very seriously. This cannot be said of the Cyclops, however much Theocritus empathized with the one-eyed poet's plight. Gilbert Lawall has shown just how seriously the figure of Daphnis is presented: the first *Idyll* should stand as a caution to those who expect no more from Theocritus than an 'idyllic' experience in the country. The poet, in Lawall's words, 'seems to be trying to compress the whole history of archaic and classical Greek poetry into a single creation which, as a combination of all these earlier traditions and as a pastoral poem, is totally unprecedented'.[11] Theocritus casts his Daphnis in the rôle of a pastoral Prometheus, a champion of a lofty ideal who is willing to die for his convictions, proof against the blandishments of compromisers (Priapus) and the threats of those whose selfish pride he has offended (Aphrodite).[12]

How important Daphnis is to Theocritus' pastoral vision is shown by the prelude to the Daphnis-lament, the description of a herdsman's cup which balances and 'pays for' the song of Daphnis. A humble wooden vessel, it is marvellously wrought and carved with the intricate designs of an Alexandrian silversmith. This cup is obviously meant as the poet's *sphragis*, the signature upon his work: it forecasts, for the first poem of the collection, Theocritus' poetic programme. There are three scenes on the cup: a suitors' quarrel, with the beloved impassive between her wrangling lovers; the cast of an old fisherman, his muscles straining to the net's pull; and a careless boy, lost in the plaiting of a cricket cage, whose breakfast, like the vineyard he guards, is foxes' prey (27–58). These static vignettes, these

eidyllia, are the stuff of Theocritean poetry. The reader hovers
peacefully in the herdsman's dream world, admiring and even
enjoying a panorama of human struggle framed forever in ivy
and acanthus.[13] The cup, which foreshadows the nature of the
Idylls, is represented as a fair exchange for Thyrsis' 'Lament for
Daphnis'. The goatherd is willing to stake all of Theocritus'
themes for the theme *par excellence*, that of a herdsman-musician
sacrificed on love's altar. The point was not lost on Theocritus'
successors: in the Greek bucolic and epigrammatic tradition,
Daphnis came to epitomize the herdsman/poet/lover. For Virgil,
Daphnis not only dominated the bucolic landscape; he became
its god. Theocritus' cup, too, was transformed by Virgil to
include rather than to balance the ultimate goal of bucolic
poetry. Within two of Virgil's cups stands not Daphnis, but
Orpheus himself, the archetypal herdsman/poet/lover whose
song transforms all nature (*Ecl.* 3.44–6).

In order to discover the source of the poet's fascination with
the noble shepherd who is wounded by love and who sings his
lament in the wilderness, we must abandon some conventional
ideas about the nature of ancient bucolic poetry. The presence
of such singing herdsmen in the Greek poet's landscape cannot
be explained merely through reference to the isolated circum-
stances or musical abilities of real herdsmen. Critics are fond
of pointing out that Theocritus and Virgil, antiquity's ranking
pastoral poets, spent most of their time in the city anyway, and
could not have known much of country life. This mere fact is
misleading, for it seems to support the conventional view of
ancient pastoral as poetry written by and for city-dwellers as a
pleasant escape from the strain, noise, and complexity of urban
life.[14] Theocritean and Virgilian pastoral is not an escape from
life, but an intensified experience of poetic inspiration, of the
tropes and themes which underlie all poetry. The herdsman's
presence in that pastoral landscape reflects an idea derived
from literary and religious traditions as old as culture itself.
Even in the sophisticated age of Hellenism, Greece had not
forgotten that the shepherd had once been a sacred personage.
The memory of his former rank and function was preserved in
songs of worship and in myths once recited by long forgotten
peoples. From religious texts of the ancient Near East, and

from the earliest works of Greek literature, emerges the figure of the first shepherd-poet, a singer of hymns and oracles. As a personification of the year-god and consort of the love-goddess, he stands, too, as a great symbol for the mysteries of life and death in crops, in animals, and in men. His song is the ultimate theme of all poetry.

The forebears of Daphnis

> Wherefrom fall all architectures I am
> I say are likenesses of the First Beloved
> whose flowers are flames lit to the Lady.
>
> Robert Duncan

The first prophets, theologians, and founders of cult are often represented in Mediterranean lore as nomadic herdsmen. The shepherd Orpheus, priest and prophet of Apollo, who sang of the birth of the cosmos, was reckoned to be the first poet among the Greeks. Even the historical figure Hesiod, who, while pasturing his flocks on Helicon, was consecrated by the Muses 'to celebrate the future and the past, to hymn the race of blessed ones who are forever',[15] reminds us of the religious aura which once clothed the shepherd.

The relationship of this lonely denizen of hillside and woodland to the community was always exceptional. In fertile valleys where stable methods of agriculture had become the rule, and where the pasturing of flocks was not absolutely essential to the economy, nomadic herdsmen were regarded as 'wild men', albeit endowed with uncanny physical and spiritual powers.[16] The Sumerian epic of Gilgamesh, a poem of the third millennium B.C. and a source of inspiration, directly or indirectly, for all subsequent epic poems, including the *Iliad* and the *Odyssey*, is still unsurpassed in the purity of its statement of the human condition. Gilgamesh, king of Uruk, embodies the new civilization with its wealth, its effete luxury, and its abuses of power. The 'wild man' is Enkidu, as untamed as the wilderness which nurtured him; yet the gods have created him to ennoble Gilgamesh through his friendship. Enkidu is lured from his haunts by a woman's wiles:

> And as for him, (for) Enkidu, whose birthplace is the
>   open country,
> (Who) eats grass with the gazelles,
> Drinks with the game at the drinking-place,
> (Whose) heart delights with the animals at the water,
> Him, the wild (?) man, the prostitute saw,
> The savage man from the depths of the steppe.[17]

Sexual initiation results in Enkidu's alienation from the world
of nature:

> Six days and seven nights Enkidu had intercourse with
>   the prostitute.
> After he was sated with her charms,
> He set his face toward his game.
> (But) when the gazelles saw him, Enkidu, they ran away;
> The game of the steppe fled from his presence.
> It caused Enkidu to hesitate, bound was his body.
> His knees failed, because his game ran away.
> Enkidu slackened in his running, no longer (could he run)
>   as before.[18]

The wild man is now tame, and ready to enter the city.
Physical love has unmanned him; already he has lost some of his
physical strength and his rapport with nature. The prostitute
leads him to his fated friendship with Gilgamesh, which will
soon bring about his death.

Before he enters Uruk, Enkidu lives for a time among a
band of shepherds; they are a 'half-way house' to civilization,
and ease the transition by teaching him the use of bread and
wine, of ointment and garments. The wild man rejoices in their
company, for they resemble him; indeed, the prostitute had
mocked this similarity when she summoned him to Uruk:
'Come, arise from the ground, (the bed?) of the shepherd!'[19]

In lands where the soil was too poor and rocky to sustain
large-scale agricultural operations, the driver of flocks, in
addition to his important contributions to the survival of the
community, exerted a profound influence upon its religious and
political life. We need look no further than the Bible for
examples of this influence.[20] The strong pastoral tradition of
Israel culminates in the story of David, a young shepherd-poet
whose rustic innocence triumphs in every confrontation with

military and political power. Like Enkidu, David is undone by sexual love; but even in this detail, his figure remains true to a pastoral type which western literature continues to celebrate.

Near Eastern cuneiform texts make frequent mention of a shepherd-king named Dumuzi by the Sumerians and Tammuz by the Akkadians. He is loved by the love-goddess herself, the lady Ishtar (Sumerian Inanna, Phoenician Astarte). As a punishment for ignoring the travails of Ishtar in the under-world, Tammuz is sent to hell in her place. In the Sumerian text, he calls upon nature to mourn his lot. He sings, in fact, the archetypal 'shepherd's lament':[21]

His heart was filled with tears,
   He went forth to the plain,
The shepherd—his heart was filled with tears,
   He went forth to the plain,
Dumuzi—his heart was filled with tears,
   He went forth to the plain,
He fastened his flute (?) about his neck,
   Gave utterance to a lament:
'Set up a lament, set up a lament,
   O plain, set up a lament!
O plain, set up a lament, set up a wail (?)!
Among the crabs of the river, set up a lament!
Among the frogs of the river, set up a lament!
   Let my mother utter words (of lament),
Let my mother Sirtur utter words (of lament),
Let my mother who has (?) not five breads (?) utter words
   (of lament),
Let my mother who has (?) not ten breads (?) utter words
   (of lament),
On the day I die she will have none to care (?) for her,
On the plain, like my mother, let my eyes shed tears (?),
On the plain, like my little sister, let my eyes shed tears'. . .

Among the buds (?) he lay down, among the buds (?) he lay
   down,
   The shepherd—among the buds (?) he lay down,
As the shepherd lay down among the buds (?), he dreamt a dream,
He arose—it was a dream, he trembled (?)—it was a vision,
He rubbed his eyes with his hands, he was dazed. . .

'My dream, oh my sister, my dream,
 This is the heart of my dream:
Rushes rise up all about me, rushes sprout all about me,
One reed standing all alone, bows its head for me,
Of the reeds standing in pairs, one is removed for me,
In the wooded grove, tall (?) trees rise fearsomely all about me.
Over my holy hearth, water is poured,
Of my holy churn—its stand (?) is removed,
The holy cup hanging from a peg, from the peg has fallen,
My shepherd's crook has vanished,
An owl holds a . . .,
A falcon holds a lamb in its claws,
My young goats drag their lapis beards in the dust,
My sheep of the fold paw the ground, with their bent limbs,
The churn lies (shattered), no milk is poured,
The cup lies (shattered), Dumuzi lives no more,
 The sheepfold is given over to the wind.'

When he is dead, Ishtar causes the world to mourn her shepherd-lover annually; this practice is mentioned by Gilgamesh, who has cause to complain against Ishtar's demand for his own love. Like Daphnis, he reminds the love-goddess of her transgressions:

What lover of thine is there whom thou dost love forever?
What shepherd (?) of thine is there who can please thee for all
 time?
Come, and I will unfold thee the tale of thy lovers.
. . .
For Tammuz, thy youthful husband,
Thou hast decreed wailing year after year.[22]

The story of Tammuz and Ishtar is, of course, an aetiological myth. It represents an attempt to justify ritual mourning for the dying year which took place in Near Eastern lands during the midsummer harvest. The 'year god' Tammuz was mourned to propitiate the generative principle (Ishtar), and thereby to insure the return of fruitfulness to the earth.[23]

 For at least three millennia, Tammuz was mourned annually. One of his semitic epithets, *adon* ('Lord'), became his name among the Greeks. Adonis, beloved of the Greek love-goddess Aphrodite, was made the object of a cult and the subject of a pretty myth which did little to conceal his identity as a vegetation spirit. Born miraculously from a tree, he grew to be so handsome that Aphrodite herself fell in love with him. Persephone, appointed to protect Adonis, betrayed Aphrodite's trust and kept him in the underworld for a third of the year, thereby forcing him to share her own fate and function. All versions of the story tell of his death in the upper world: mortally wounded by a boar, he is mourned by Aphrodite, who repeats her mourning annually.[24] The lament for Adonis was already a ritual in Greece in the seventh century B.C.; four centuries later, he had become a theme for the pastoral poets.[25]

In Anatolia, Adonis' place in myth and ritual was taken by Attis, a shepherd loved by the Great Mother, Cybele. Also born miraculously, he is driven mad when Cybele discovers his infidelity. Attis castrates himself and dies, mourned by a repentant mother-goddess (the castration has been introduced for aetiological reasons: priests of Cybele were eunuchs).[26]

Nearly the same circumstances befall Anchises, whose place in cult has been obscured by his rôle in literature as father of Aeneas. He, too, is wooed by Aphrodite while pasturing his herds; after satisfying her own desire, the love-goddess destroys his manhood. The Homeric *Hymn to Aphrodite* is our earliest description of the seduction of Anchises. In the company of wild beasts, who respond to her approach with joyful copulation, she comes to the Idaean pastures (76–80):

> Him she found alone, apart from the others, left to the stables,
> Anchises the hero, who had his beauty from the gods.
> The others were tending the herds in the grassy pastures,
> All of them; but he, alone, apart from the others, left to the
> stables,
> Was wandering here and there, playing his resonant lyre.

For the Greek poet of the *Hymn to Aphrodite*, Anchises is not the subject of a song of lament; the herdsman-consort of the love-goddess is himself a musician, alone in the landscape with his lyre.

'The very gods have dwelt in wilds—Dardanian Paris, too.' So sings Virgil's Corydon, an avatar of the Cyclops, in a vain attempt to induce his love Alexis to live with him in the

pastoral landscape (*Ecl.* 2.6of.). He reminds us that Anchises'
fellow-countryman, the great seducer, had also been a herds-
man and a musician before his life, too, was disrupted by the
interference of Aphrodite. Greek poets like Euripides enjoyed
the vision of Paris, alone in the landscape, playing his Pan-
pipes:

> You went your way, O Paris, where you,
> a neatherd, had been raised among
> the snowy heifers of Ida,
> piping strange notes on the reeds
> as you played the patterns
> of Olympos' Phrygian flutes.
> With udders full your cows were growing up
> when a Judgment of Goddesses made you mad . . .
> (Euripides, *Iphigeneia in Aulis* 573–80)

This list of mythical shepherds through the ages would not
be complete without mention of Orpheus, whose songs and
whose love have been a favourite theme of art, of literature, of
music, and of religion down to our own times. Like the others,
his life was destroyed by love, a love which, however humanized
by the poets, still bears the vestiges of a great religious arche-
type. 'Eurydice' is more than a name; it is an epithet signifying
'wide dominion', and may originally have belonged to Perse-
phone, queen of the underworld, the Greek goddess of fruitful
renewal.[27]

Enkidu, David, Tammuz, Adonis, Attis, Anchises, Paris,
and Orpheus: these are the forebears of Daphnis, of the
pastoral hero.[28] Alone like him in the wilderness, they had been
destroyed by love, and their stories were told by generations
after. For Tammuz, Adonis, and Attis, a lament was sung
which became the core of a ritual meant to insure the rebirth
of nature. Like Daphnis, Tammuz could sing his own lament.
Like Daphnis, David and Orpheus were themselves great
poets. Above all, they share in common the torments of love;
love comes to all, with the exception of Enkidu and David, in
the form of a goddess who is herself the principle of birth in all
living things. Alone with nature in the wilderness, these shep-
herds combine the facts of life and death into one great mystery,
the mystery of love.

The presence of a lone herdsman in the poet's landscape can now be appreciated; the loving herdsman, living and dying among the works of nature, is a perfect symbol for the poet himself. This is why Daphnis meant so much to Theocritus and to poets like him who reflected seriously on the nature of their art. And this is why bucolic poetry, a happy discovery of Theocritus, became more and more the medium which poets chose to express their poetic selves. The love theme became an integral part of the pastoral landscape, whose very existence is often made to depend upon it:

> Here the sheep, and here the goats who bear twin kids; here
>   the bees
>   fill honeycombs, oaks are higher,
> where the comely Milon strides; but if he slip off
>   the shepherd there is parched, and so the pastures.
> Spring everywhere, and everywhere green pastures, everywhere
>   with milk
>   the udders flow, and young ones grow,
> where the comely Naiad visits; but if she slip off
>   the one who herds the cows is withered, so the cows.
>   (*Idyll* 8.41–8)

As the bucolic tradition grew, the love theme grew and acquired higher significance for the poet. Wherever the poets followed their Muse, they seemed to find an erotic subject determined as the *Leitmotiv*. A century after Theocritus, the bucolic poet Bion could declare that the beloved of the Muses must himself be capable of great loves and must have wide experience with Eros (6):

> Of Eros, the wild, the Muses have no fear,
> they love him with their heart and track him with their step.
> And if, therefore, one sing with soul not touched by Love,
> him the Muses avoid and refuse to instruct.
> But if he sweetly sing, with mind distraught by Love,
> for him they all arise, to him they all rush forth.
> I bear you witness that my words are true for all.
> For if I hymn another mortal or immortal god,
> my tongue is tied, no longer sings as once before;
> but if, again, to Eros and to Lycidas I sing,
> rejoicing flows the sound, then, from my lips.

Without love, then, the bucolic poet lost his creative powers.
As time went on, the poet's involvement with love became more
refined and even more self-conscious. In Virgil, the place of
Eros and of Aphrodite was eventually usurped by the Muse
herself, the rightful mistress of the poet's garden. This develop-
ment had been foreshadowed in Hesiod (*Theogony* 96f.: 'Happy
is he whom the Muses love; a sweet sound flows from his lips.')
and is reflected in the last line of Bion's poem quoted above.
The sentiment found its most frequent expression in the
Hellenistic period. Callimachus made rejuvenation in poetic
activity a corollary to the Muses' love. Theocritus stresses this
love-relationship more than once; Daphnis is called 'beloved
of the Muses' (1.141), and in the seventh *Idyll*, verse 95, Lycidas
is invited to hear a song with the words 'Yet listen, for you are
dear to the Muses'.[29]

Theocritus' harvest of poetry

The seventh *Idyll* (called *Thalysia*, 'first-fruits', after Demeter's
harvest festival) is a poem about poetry. The setting of his
rustic mimes remains, and is immeasurably enriched by the
poet's use of the landscape as a metaphor to designate what is
closest to his heart, the creation of poems. *Idyll* 7 is the first
conscious evocation of the pastoral landscape as a garden of the
poet's mind.

Theocritus represents himself and two friends on their way
from town to the Thalysia, a harvest festival sponsored by
noblemen (Phrasidamus and Antigenes) who counted among
their ancestors the hero Chalcon himself,

> . . . who started from under his foot the spring Burina
> by pushing hard his knee against a rock; up to its edge, those
> poplars and pines began to weave a shaded grove,
> having spread their tresses in green foliage.

                                                              (6–9)

This spring, the symbolic source of Theocritus' inspiration on
Cos, is the true destination of the poem. Its miraculous creation
evokes the memory of Hippocrene, produced by a kick from
Pegasus, the spring from which the Heliconian Muses brought

inspiration to Hesiod, their initiated poet; in the *Thalysia*, Theocritus' 'poem of initiation', Burina will have the same function.[30]

Halfway along the road, in the magic of midday, a goatherd appears to Theocritus and greets him with smiles. The apparition is called 'Lycidas'; he addresses our poet as 'Simichidas'. Theocritus' companions seem to vanish from the scene as the two voices of Theocritean verse invite each other to sing. 'Simichidas' professes a lowly poetry which vies with the popular verse of his day 'as a frog vies with crickets' (41). 'Lycidas' praises this originality, for he despises all efforts to 'outdo Homer' (45-8). He presents 'Simichidas' with his staff and with a herdsman's lay (*boukolika aoida* 49), a song of love extolling the joys of country life and promising, as an enticement to the lover's return, other songs of shepherds' love (the tales of the shepherd-poets Daphnis and Comatas). 'Simichidas', the city-poet, answers with verses which 'the Nymphs taught me, too, as I drove herds through the hills' (92). His poem, a brief, witty didactic piece addressed to the poet Aratus, prays that his friend be spared the pangs of love; it is more urbane than pastoral, though it contains elements of both sorts of poetry. 'Lycidas' laughs, realizing that the poem is meant to balance his own too earnest treatment of the love theme.[31] He passes his stick on to 'Simichidas', and departs. Theocritus, once more in the company of his friends, rests and drinks wine by the shaded spring, Burina. He leaves us with an opulent vision of the surrounding sights and sounds of nature, the symbols of his art:

> From up above our heads came the rustle of many
> poplars and pines; nearby, that sacred water
> from the Nymphs' cave went babbling in its downward course.
> There, dusky against the shaded boughs,
> cicadas kept up their prattling task; and the tree-frog,
> far off amid dense brambles, was murmuring in the briar.
> Throughout sang larks and finches, moaned the dove,
> and buzzing bees flew 'round about the springs.
> All smelled of summer's fruitfulness, of harvest time.
> Wild pears at our feet, and by our sides the apples
> in plenty were rolling, the saplings hung,

burdened down to the ground with plums;
and the pitch, now four years old, was pried from the wine-
  jars' top.

(135–47)

At the poem's end, the wine is drunk with a prayer to the
Nymphs for another harvest: no longer the humble nymphs of
Burina, they are addressed as 'Castalian Nymphs who hold the
gorge of Parnassus' (148). Theocritus invokes thereby the
companions of Apollo, the Muses themselves.

The *Thalysia*, like the first *Idyll*, is a 'programmatic' poem,
a conscious attempt on the part of Theocritus to establish his
'poetics', to define and illustrate his art. It exhibits a self-
consciousness typical of Hellenistic poetry, and reminds us of
Callimachus' prologue to the *Aitia*, a programmatic piece full
of similar metaphors for poetic activity (e.g. water and the
cicada). Lawall and others, abandoning the misguided search
for a '*masquerade bucolique*' (the device of a much later age),
have shown that 'Lycidas' and 'Simichidas' are but two aspects
of one and the same poet, two ingredients of Theocritean
poetry.[32] The conferral of Lycidas' staff upon Simichidas is an
old symbol for poetic initiation, and goes back to the laurel
branch which the Muses gave to Hesiod. The celebration of
Theocritus' career as a poet on Cos is symbolized in the
harvest festival itself; at the end of the poem, he imagines
himself surrounded by the 'fruits' of his own harvest. The
'sacred' water and the wine are allegories of inspiration, the
cave of the 'Castalian Nymphs' is its source. The method and
the music of cicadas and bees had for centuries been the
Greek poet's model. The sound of the frog had already been
used in this poem to characterize 'Simichidas' ' poetry (41).
And Theocritus, as his work bears fruit, has seen its analogue
in a fruitful nature. The *Thalysia* is no country picnic; it
celebrates the consecration of a poet, the 'harvesting' of his
poems in a poet's grove, beside the source of inspiration, the
Coan spring Burina.[33] Theocritus' achievement in poetic
allegory is best described by Gilbert Lawall:[34]

All the details in this final scene at Phrasidamus' farm—the grove
and spring, the grotto of the nymphs, the pastoral symphony of

birds and insects, the fruit gathered in, and the strong drink of wine and water—suggest an elaborate rhetoric of poetic imagination and creation which was beginning to develop in the Hellenistic Age. Groves, springs, and grottos are the places where poets imagine themselves as writing their poetry, and the wine and water symbolize respectively the intoxication and artifice prerequisite to poetic creation. The harvest of fruits stands metaphorically for a harvest of poetry and, more specifically, for a harvest collection of Theocritus' Coan poetry.

The allegory of the poet in the Muse's garden was brought to its fullest expression by Virgil. It appears seldom after him, and is not to be found among writers of pastoral in the Middle Ages. But it crops up now and then in the nineteenth and twentieth centuries,[35] and is clearly present in the poem by Robert Duncan, quoted on pp. 3–4 of this book. Can Duncan's piece be called 'pastoral'? Perhaps not, if we take into account conventional views of pastoral poetry. It lacks the frivolity of the *masquerade bucolique* which we have associated with pastoral since the seventeenth century, and have projected all too often upon the ancients. Absent are the Greek names which Milton and others believed essential to the pastoral landscape. There is none of the idealization of peasants, of subordinate classes, which Empson ascribes to pastoral.[36] There is not even a *pastor* in Duncan's piece—no flocks, no shepherd (unless *pasture* in the second stanza be understood to imply both). The twentieth century has little use for herdsmen as personifications of the poet. But love is present; and the 'Lady' is there, the object of his devotion, the mistress of his 'words' and of his 'field'. The lone singer and lover, the Knower of the Field, is there in the 'I', in Duncan's direct reference to himself.

If Theocritus and Virgil were asked to tell us whether or not Duncan's poem is pastoral, they would respond differently. Theocritus, we might imagine, while appreciating the poem's symbolism, would not understand our question—he had never heard of 'pastoral poetry'. Virgil, on the other hand, would surely agree that Duncan had been visited by his *silvestris Musa*.

II

Vergili Bucolica

ECLOGA I

Meliboeus   Tityrus

M. Tityre tu patulae recubans sub tegmine fagi
silvestrem tenui Musam meditaris avena.
nos patriae finis et dulcia linquimus arva,
nos patriam fugimus. tu Tityre lentus in umbra
formosam resonare doces Amaryllida silvas.

T. O Meliboee, deus nobis haec otia fecit.
namque erit ille mihi semper deus, illius aram
saepe tener nostris ab ovilibus imbuet agnus.
ille meas errare boves, ut cernis, et ipsum
ludere quae vellem calamo permisit agresti.   10
M. Non equidem invideo, miror magis. undique totis
usque adeo turbatur agris. en ipse capellas
protenus aeger ago, hanc etiam vix Tityre duco.
hic inter densas corylos modo namque gemellos
spem gregis, a, silice in nuda conixa reliquit.   15
saepe malum hoc nobis si mens non laeva fuisset
de caelo tactas memini praedicere quercus.
sed tamen iste deus qui sit da Tityre nobis.
T. Urbem quam dicunt Romam Meliboee putavi
stultus ego huic nostrae similem quo saepe solemus   20
pastores ovium teneros depellere fetus.
sic canibus catulos similes, sic matribus haedos
noram, sic parvis componere magna solebam.
verum haec tantum alias inter caput extulit urbes
quantum lenta solent inter viburna cupressi.   25

Virgil's Bucolics

ECLOGUE I

Meliboeus   Tityrus

M.   Tityrus, you at ease 'neath cover of spreading beech
rehearse the woodland Muse with slender pipe.
We leave our native boundaries, our fertile fields.
We flee our native land. You, Tityrus, stretched in shade,
teach forests to echo the beauteous Amaryllis.   5

T.   O Meliboeus, for us a god ordained this leisure.
God indeed will he be to me forever—his altar
oft a lamb, new from our fold, will sprinkle red.
He allowed my cows to wander, as you see,
and me to play with rustic reed my heart's desire.   10

M.   I envy not, I wonder more. In all the fields
there's so much chaos. Look at me, I drive my nannies
forth in pain—and this one, Tityrus, barely moves.
She dropped her twins (the hope of the flock!) on
   barren rock
to leave them in the hazel thicket there, just now.   15
I missed the omen at the time, but I recall the oaks,
how often struck by heaven they foretold this woe.
Enough. This god of yours, O Tityrus—give his name.

T.   The town named Rome, Meliboeus, (foolish me) I imagined
like that town of ours, where we as herdsmen often tend   20
to drive and market tender offspring of our ewes.
Pups look like dogs, kids like their mothers. This I knew,
and so I used to liken, side by side, the great and small.
Yet does this city raise her head as high among the rest
as cypress grows above the pliant alder.   25

м.   Et quae tanta fuit Romam tibi causa videndi?

т.   Libertas quae sera tamen respexit inertem,
candidior postquam tondenti barba cadebat,
respexit tamen et longo post tempore venit
postquam nos Amaryllis habet, Galatea reliquit.   30
namque fatebor enim dum me Galatea tenebat
nec spes libertatis erat nec cura peculi.
quamvis multa meis exiret victima saeptis,
pinguis et ingratae premeretur caseus urbi,
non umquam gravis aere domum mihi dextra redibat.   35

м.   Mirabar quid maesta deos Amarylli vocares,
cui pendere sua patereris in arbore poma.
Tityrus hinc aberat. ipsae te Tityre pinus
ipsi te fontes ipsa haec arbusta vocabant.

т.   Quid facerem? neque servitio me exire licebat   40
nec tam praesentis alibi cognoscere divos.
hic illum vidi iuvenem Meliboee, quotannis
bis senos cui nostra dies altaria fumant,
hic mihi responsum primus dedit ille petenti
PASCITE UT ANTE BOVES PUERI, SUMMITTITE TAUROS. 45

м.   Fortunate senex, ergo tua rura manebunt.
et tibi magna satis quamvis lapis omnia nudus
limosoque palus obducat pascua iunco.
non insueta gravis temptabunt pabula fetas
nec mala vicini pecoris contagia laedent.   50
Fortunate senex, hic inter flumina nota
et fontis sacros frigus captabis opacum.
hinc tibi quae semper vicino ab limite saepes
Hyblaeis apibus florem depasta salicti
saepe levi somnum suadebit inire susurro.   55
hinc alta sub rupe canet frondator ad auras

M.   What so prompted you to see the city Rome?

T.   Freedom, which looked, albeit late, upon my idle years,
     after my beard was falling whiter to the shears—
     yet freedom found me, came at length, and only now
     when Galatea's left, and I'm possessed by Amaryllis.   30
     I'll confess, as long as Galatea held me fast,
     I had no hope of freedom, no impulse to purchase it.
     Though many a victim left my folds and pens,
     though cheese was thickly pressed for a thankless town,
     my hands would never return weighed down with coin.   35
M.   Poor Amaryllis, I wondered why you cried to gods,
     and for whom you let the fruits grow heavy in their trees.
     So Tityrus was away. The very pines, O Tityrus,
     the springs themselves, these orchards here, were calling
         you.

T.   What was I to do? I had no leave to free myself,   40
     to find in other places gods so open to my prayer.
     Here I beheld that youth, Meliboeus, the youth for whom
     our altars smoke for twice six days in every year.
     Here he gave me, was the first to give, an answer to my
         plea:
     'Pasture, my children, your cows as before, and let there
         be bulls.'   45

M.   Lucky old man! And so the land will remain your land,
     and for you it's enough, though barren rocks encroach,
         and all
     the pasture's overgrown with rushes from the marsh.
     Strange fodder will tempt no pregnant mother near
         her time;
     the foul contagion of a neighbour's flock will do no harm.   50
     Lucky old man! So here, among the streams you know,
     among the holy springs, you'll seek the shaded cool.
     From here, beyond the fence, on that near boundary,
     the willow grove whose flowers ever pasture Hybla's bees
     will often beckon you to sleep with gentle hum.   55
     From there, a trimmer 'neath the crag will sing to breezes.

nec tamen interea raucae tua cura palumbes
nec gemere aëria cessabit turtur ab ulmo.

T. Ante leves ergo pascentur in aequore cervi
et freta destituent nudos in litore piscis,   60
ante pererratis amborum finibus exul
aut Ararim Parthus bibet aut Germania Tigrim
quam nostro illius labatur pectore voltus.
M. At nos hinc alii sitientis ibimus Afros,
pars Scythiam et rapidum cretae veniemus Oaxen   65
et penitus toto divisos orbe Britannos.
en umquam patrios longo post tempore finis,
pauperis et tuguri congestum cespite culmen
post aliquot mea regna videns mirabor aristas?
impius haec tam culta novalia miles habebit,   70
barbarus has segetes. en quo discordia civis
produxit miseros. his nos consevimus agros.
insere nunc Meliboee piros, pone ordine vitis.
ite meae felix quondam pecus ite capellae.
non ego vos posthac viridi proiectus in antro   75
dumosa pendere procul de rupe videbo.
carmina nulla canam. non me pascente capellae
florentem cytisum et salices carpetis amaras.

T. Hic tamen hanc mecum poteras requiescere noctem
fronde super viridi. sunt nobis mitia poma   80
castaneae molles et pressi copia lactis
et iam summa procul villarum culmina fumant
maioresque cadunt altis de montibus umbrae.

Clucking ring doves, your concern, and turtle doves
will cease not all the while to mourn from lofty elm.

T.   Swift deer, therefore, will crop the ocean's weed
     while waters leave fish stranded, naked, on the shore,   60
     or Parthians will drink the waters of the Saône, while
        Germans
     drink from Tigris, exiles straying through each other's
        land,
     before the countenance of that youth slips from my heart.
M.   As for me, some will depart for thirsty Africa,
     others will get to Scythia and the Oaxis flowing with
        chalk,   65
     and to Britain, cut off so far from the world we know.
     Lo, will I at last, that distant day, admire
     my native land, my humble cottage with its mossy roof,
     peering at my realms behind some sheaves of grain?
     These best-tilled furrows a soldier, hands defiled, will
        hold,   70
     these crops a foreigner. See the grief to which we're led
     by civil strife: for such as these we've sowed the fields!
     Now, Meliboeus, graft the pear trees, set your vines in
        order!
     Go, once happy herd, get along, my nanny goats.
     No longer will I be the one, stretched out in grotto
        green,   75
     to watch you teeter in the distance on a bushy crag.
     No songs will I sing. Not with me as herdsman, nanny
        goats,
     will you crop the flowering clover and the willow's
        pungency.

T.   Here, none the less, you might but rest this night with me
     on verdant foliage. Here we have ripe fruits,   80
     soft chestnuts, and a fine supply of cottage cheese.
     By now, far off, the villas' rooftops send their smoke
     and from the mountain steeps fall longer shadows.

ECLOGA II

Formosum pastor Corydon ardebat Alexim
delicias domini nec quid speraret habebat.
tantum inter densas umbrosa cacumina fagos
adsidue veniebat, ibi haec incondita solus
montibus et silvis studio iactabat inani: 5

O crudelis Alexi nihil mea carmina curas?
nil nostri miserere? mori me denique coges.
nunc etiam pecudes umbras et frigora captant,
nunc viridis etiam occultant spineta lacertos,
Thestylis et rapido fessis messoribus aestu   10
alia serpullumque herbas contundit olentis,
at mecum raucis tua dum vestigia lustro
sole sub ardenti resonant arbusta cicadis.
nonne fuit satius tristis Amaryllidis iras
atque superba pati fastidia, nonne Menalcan   15
quamvis ille niger quamvis tu candidus esses?
O formose puer nimium ne crede colori.
alba ligustra cadunt, vaccinia nigra leguntur.

Despectus tibi sum nec qui sim quaeris Alexi,
quam dives pecoris, nivei quam lactis abundans.   20
mille meae Siculis errant in montibus agnae.
lac mihi non aestate novom non frigore defit.
canto quae solitus si quando armenta vocabat
Amphion Dircaeus in Actaeo Aracyntho
nec sum adeo informis. nuper me in litore vidi   25
cum placidum ventis staret mare. non ego Daphnim
iudice te metuam si numquam fallit imago.

ECLOGUE II

A herdsman Corydon burned for fair Alexis once,
Alexis, master's love; nor any hope had he.
Yet to the beech grove's shadowy height he came
whenever able. There, alone, these artless words
he used to fling in empty earnest at the woods and
    hills: 5

Cruel Alexis, are my songs of no account to you?
Have you no pity? You will force me, in the end, to die.
Now's the hour for flocks to seek the shade and cool,
now the thornbrakes hide the leaf-green lizards;
Thestylis for the reapers overcome by searing heat   10
pounds out pungent cloves of garlic mixed with thyme.
Yet orchards with cicadas' buzz still echo me
under burning sun as I seek trace of you.
Was it not better to endure the vicious rage
of Amaryllis, all her proud contempt? and then   15
Menalcas, though he's black, though you be white?
O beauteous boy, trust not too much to hue!
Pale privets wilt, dark hyacinths are gathered up.

Alexis, you look down on me, nor ask who I might be,
how rich in flocks, how well supplied with snowy milk!   20
My she-lambs roam the hills a thousand-fold in Sicily;
in summertime I lack no fresh milk, nor in winter's cold.
My songs are as he sang, if ever he called flocks,
Amphion son of Dirce, on Actaean Aracynthus.
Nor am I so plain—myself I saw on the shore of late   25
when sea stood still, no wind. From Daphnis, even, I
    shall fear
no competition—you be judge—if mirrors never cheat.

O tantum libeat mecum tibi sordida rura
atque humilis habitare casas et figere cervos
haedorumque gregem viridi compellere hibisco.   30
me una in silvis imitabere Pana canendo.
(Pan primum calamos cera coniungere pluris
instituit, Pan curat ovis oviumque magistros.)
nec te poeniteat calamo trivisse labellum.
haec eadem ut sciret, quid non faciebat Amyntas?   35

Est mihi disparibus septem compacta cicutis
fistula, Damoetas dono mihi quam dedit olim
et dixit moriens: Te nunc habet ista secundum.
dixit Damoetas, invidit stultus Amyntas.
praeterea duo nec tuta mihi valle reperti   40
capreoli sparsis etiam nunc pellibus albo
bina die siccant ovis ubera quos tibi servo.
iam pridem a me illos abducere Thestylis orat
et faciet quoniam sordent tibi munera nostra.

Huc ades o formose puer. tibi lilia plenis   45
ecce ferunt Nymphae calathis, tibi candida Nais
pallentis violas et summa papavera carpens
narcissum et florem iungit bene olentis anethi,
tum casia atque aliis intexens suavibus herbis
mollia luteola pingit vaccinia caltha.   50
ipse ego cana legam tenera lanugine mala
castaneasque nuces, mea quas Amaryllis amabat.
addam cerea pruna (honos erit huic quoque pomo)
et vos o lauri carpam et te proxuma myrte
sic positae quoniam suavis miscetis odores.   55

Rusticus es Corydon nec munera curat Alexis
nec si muneribus certes concedat Iollas.
heu heu quid volui misero mihi? floribus austrum
perditus et liquidis immisi fontibus apros.

If only you would dwell with me in lowly countryside
and live in humble huts and shoot the deer with me
and drive a flock of kids with green marsh reed!   30
Together with me in the woods you'd follow Pan in song
(Pan first taught to join the several reeds with wax,
Pan cares for sheep and for the masters of the flock)
nor let it shame you to have rubbed your lip with reed.
To know this art, what wouldn't that Amyntas do?   35

I have pipes, too, set close in seven stalks
unevenly, a gift Damoetas gave me once
when, dying, he said 'Now they hold you second after me'.
So spoke Damoetas, and that fool Amyntas envied me.
There are besides (I found them in a dangerous vale)   40
two roebucks, hides besprinkled even now with white.
Two udders each of sheep they dry each day. For you
I keep them. Long has Thestylis begged to take them
    from me;
so she will, because my gifts are vile to you.

Be here with me, my beauteous boy. Look, lilies for you   45
the Nymphs do bring in baskets full; for you a snow white
Naiad gathers sombre violets, poppy tops,
joins narcissus, flower of finely smelling dill;
then, weaving in the cinnamon and more sweet herbs,
she dapples the hyacinth soft with yellow marigold.   50
I'll for my part gather quinces grey with subtle down
and the chestnuts that my Amaryllis used to love.
The wax-plums, too, I'll add (this fruit will share the
    honour).
Laurels, you I'll pick, and you, O next best myrtle,
thus arranging mixture of your pleasant scents.   55

A rustic you are, Corydon. Alexis cares not for your gifts,
nor, if you strive with gifts, would Iollas yield the day.
No, wait! This makes no sense—for me, poor fool, to cast
the southwind on my blossoms, let the swine fill crystal
    springs!

quem fugis a demens? habitarunt di quoque silvas　　　60
Dardaniusque Paris. Pallas quas condidit arces
ipsa colat. nobis placeant ante omnia silvae.
torva leaena lupum sequitur, lupus ipse capellam,
florentem cytisum sequitur lasciva capella,
te Corydon o Alexi. trahit sua quemque voluptas.　　　65
aspice, aratra iugo referunt suspensa iuvenci
et sol crescentis decedens duplicat umbras,
me tamen urit amor. quis enim modus adsit amori?

　A Corydon Corydon quae te dementia cepit?
　semiputata tibi frondosa vitis in ulmo est.　　　70
　quin tu aliquid saltem potius quorum indiget usus
　viminibus mollique paras detexere iunco?
　invenies alium, si te hic fastidit, Alexim.

Blind youth, you know not whom you flee. The very
   gods have dwelt   60
in wilds—Dardanian Paris, too. Let Pallas tend
her founded citadels. We love forests best of all.
The raging lioness hunts a wolf, the wolf himself a kid,
who, wantonly frolicking, follows her clover's
   flowering tip
as Corydon you, Alexis. One's passion drags each on.   65
Look up. The ploughs return, from bullock's yoke
   suspended,
and yielding sun spreads shadows' lengths twofold.
And me—love burns me still. What rules apply to love?

    Ah, Corydon, Corydon, what senselessness possessed
      you?
    A vine, half-pruned, awaits you on the leafy elm—   70
    rather, why not find at least a thing to mend
    with wicker (crying to be used) and pliant rush?
    You'll find, if this one spurns you, a new Alexis.

ECLOGA III

Menalcas   Damoetas   Palaemon

M. Dic mihi Damoeta, cuium pecus? an Meliboei?
D. Non, verum Aegonis. nuper mihi tradidit Aegon.
M. Infelix o semper, oves, pecus. ipse Neaeram
    dum fovet ac ne me sibi praeferat illa veretur
    hic alienus ovis custos bis mulget in hora   5
    et sucus pecori et lac subducitur agnis.
D. Parcius ista viris tamen obicienda memento.
    novimus et qui te transversa tuentibus hirquis
    et quo, set faciles Nymphae risere, sacello
M. tum credo cum me arbustum videre Miconis   10
    atque mala vitis incidere falce novellas
D. aut hic ad veteres fagos cum Daphnidis arcum
    fregisti et calamos quae tu perverse Menalca
    et cum vidisti puero donata dolebas
    et si non aliqua nocuisses mortuus esses.   15
M. Quid domini faciant, audent cum talia fures?
    non ego te vidi Damonis pessime caprum
    excipere insidiis multum latrante Lycisca?
    et cum clamarem: Quo nunc se proripit ille?
    Tityre coge pecus: tu post carecta latebas.   20

D. An mihi cantando victus non redderet ille
    quem mea carminibus meruisset fistula caprum?
    si nescis meus ille caper fuit et mihi Damon
    ipse fatebatur sed reddere posse negabat.

ECLOGUE III

Menalcas   Damoetas   Palaemon

M. Answer me, Damoetas! Whose the flock—Meliboeus'?
D. No, it's Aegon's. Aegon gave it me to tend just now.
M. They suffer all the time, the ewes, the flock! Himself,
    he courts Neaera (fears she likes me more than him),
    while this strange shepherd twice an hour milks the ewes   5
    and cheats the thirsty herd and steals the milk from
        lambs.
D. Take care with those complaints—you're talking to a man.
    We know with whom you—goats beheld with sidelong
        glance—
    and in what shrine—its Nymphs, of course, found cause
        to laugh—
M. —the day they saw *me*, I suppose, with spiteful scythe   10
    cut into Micon's saplings and his new-grown vines—
D. —or, here by old beech trees, when Daphnis' bow you
        broke,
    his arrows, too. Perverse resentment grew in you,
    Menalcas, when you saw them given to the boy,
    and if you hadn't done some harm, you would have died.   15
M. What else can masters do when thieves become so
        daring?
    Didn't I see you, rascal, taking Damon's goat
    by stealth, Lycisca barking loudly all the while?
    And while I shouted 'Where's that fellow off to now?
    Tityrus, hold the flock!', behind tall grass you hid.   20

D. Beaten in a singing match, should he not yield
    to me the goat my pipes had won for songs they'd played?
    In case you didn't know, the goat was mine. To me
        Damon
    himself admitted that, but said he couldn't give it up.

M. Cantando tu illum? aut umquam tibi fistula cera   2
iuncta fuit? non tu in triviis indocte solebas
stridenti miserum stipula disperdere carmen?
D. Vis ergo inter nos quid possit uterque vicissim
experiamur? ego hanc vitulam (ne forte recuses
bis venit ad mulctram, binos alit ubere fetus)   3‹
depono, tu dic mecum quo pignore certes.

M. De grege non ausim quicquam deponere tecum.
est mihi namque domi pater, est iniusta noverca,
bisque die numerant ambo pecus, alter et haedos.
verum id quod multo tute ipse fatebere maius,   3:
insanire libet quoniam tibi, pocula ponam
fagina caelatum divini opus Alcimedontis
lenta quibus torno facili super addita vitis
diffusos hedera vestit pallente corymbos.
in medio duo signa, Conon et—quis fuit alter,   4‹
descripsit radio totum qui gentibus orbem,
tempora quae messor, quae curvos arator haberet?
necdum illis labra admovi set condita servo.
D. Et nobis idem Alcimedon duo pocula fecit
et molli circum est ansas amplexus acantho   4:
Orpheaque in medio posuit silvasque sequentis
necdum illis labra admovi set condita servo.
si ad vitulam spectas nihil est quod pocula laudes.

M. Numquam hodie effugies. veniam quocumque vocaris,
audiat haec tantum—vel qui venit ecce Palaemon.   5‹
efficiam posthac ne quemquam voce lacessas.
D. Quin age si quid habes. in me mora non erit ulla

M.   Beat *him* in singing? When have you held Pan-pipes
        joined   25
     with wax? You lack the skill. Was it not you at
        crossroads
     used to spoil a wretched song with screeching reed?
D.   Do you want a contest, then, to see what each of us
     can do by turns? This heifer I (don't back out now,
     she comes to milking twice, she nurses twins each year)   30
     will stake. You, name the pledge by which you vie with
        me.

M.   An animal I dare not stake with you as pledge.
     At home, you see, my father and cruel stepma wait for
        me.
     Both count the herd twice daily, one of them the goats.
     But (what you will yourself agree is much the better)   35
     since you're mad enough to bet, some cups I'll stake
     of beech, carved work of that divine Alcimedon,
     on which a rambling vine, imposed above with chisel's
        skill,
     clothes scattered clusters with the pale green ivy leaf.
     Two figures in the middle: Conon and—who was the
        other   40
     who with measure mapped the sky for men, to show
     which seasons rule the reaper, which the bent ploughman?
     Nor yet to them my lips I've touched, but keep them
        hid.
D.   For us the same Alcimedon has made a pair of cups,
     encircling soft acanthus 'round about the handles.   45
     Orpheus in the middle he set, and woods that follow him.
     Nor yet to them my lips I've touched, but keep them
        hid.
     Look to the heifer: cups you'll find not worth such praise.

M.   No escape for you today. I'll come wherever you call.
     Just let one hear the songs—why, yes! Palaemon's come!   50
     Henceforth your tongue won't be so sharp—I'll see to
        that.
D.   Lead on, if song you have. I won't be slow to answer,

nec quemquam fugio, tantum vicine Palaemon
sensibus haec imis, res est non parva, reponas.

P.　　　Dicite quandoquidem in molli consedimus herba　　　55
　　　　et nunc omnis ager nunc omnis parturit arbor,
　　　　nunc frondent silvae, nunc formosissimus annus.
　　　　incipe Damoeta, tu deinde sequere Menalca.
　　　　alternis dicetis. amant alterna Camenae.

D.　Ab Iove principium Musae, Iovis omnia plena.　　　60
　　ille colit terras, illi mea carmina curae.
M.　Et me Phoebus amat, Phoebo sua semper apud me
　　munera sunt lauri et suave rubens hyacinthus.

D.　Malo me Galatea petit lasciva puella
　　et fugit ad salices et se cupit ante videri.　　　65
M.　At mihi sese offert ultro meus ignis Amyntas
　　notior ut iam sit canibus non Delia nostris.
D.　Parta meae veneri sunt munera namque notavi
　　ipse locum aëriae quo congessere palumbes.
M.　Quod potui puero silvestri ex arbore lecta　　　70
　　aurea mala decem misi, cras altera mittam.

D.　O quotiens et quae nobis Galatea locuta est.
　　partem aliquam venti divom referatis ad auris.
M.　Quid prodest quod me ipse animo non spernis Amynta
　　si dum tu sectaris apros ego retia servo?　　　75
D.　Phyllida mitte mihi, meus est natalis Iolla.
　　cum faciam vitula pro frugibus ipse venito.
M.　Phyllida amo ante alias nam me discedere flevit
　　et longum, Formose vale vale, inquit Iolla.
D.　Triste lupus stabulis, maturis frugibus imbres,　　　80
　　arboribus venti, nobis Amaryllidis irae.
M.　Dulce satis umor, depulsis arbutus haedis,
　　lenta salix feto pecori, mihi solus Amyntas.

nor do I seek escape. Palaemon, neighbour, only
pay our songs the closest heed; it's no small thing.

P.   Sing on, as long as we recline on meadow soft,   55
for every field now, every tree now bears its fruit,
now leafs the forest, now's the season full of grace.
Begin, Damoetas; then, Menalcas, follow him.
You'll speak by turns. These turns the Nymphs
    Camenae love.

D.   From Jupiter the Muse begins, all's full of him,   60
he tends the land, my songs are Jupiter's concern.
M.   And me does Phoebus love, for Phoebus I forever keep
his gifts, the laurels and soft blush of hyacinth.

D.   Galatea throws an apple at me, wanton girl,
then runs into the willows, hopes first to be seen.   65
M.   Unasked, my flame Amyntas gives himself to me;
Diana's known no better to my dogs than he.
D.   For my love, my Venus, gifts are found; I marked the
    place
myself where soaring ring-doves build their lofty nests.
M.   I've done my best, I sent the boy, from sylvan tree
    selected,   70
ten golden apples, and I'll send another ten next day.

D.   How oft she spoke, the things she said, Galatea, to me!
Some words, O winds, may you report to ears of gods!
M.   Although you like me well enough, Amyntas, what's the
    use
if, while you're busy chasing boars, I'm holding nets?   75
D.   Send my Phyllis to me—today's my birthday, Iollas—
and when I sacrifice a cow for harvest, come yourself.
M.   Phyllis is my favourite. When I left, she wept
'Fair one, goodbye, goodbye', and kept it up, Iollas.
D.   Wolf bodes ill for sheepfolds, rains for ripened fruits,   80
winds for trees, for me the wrath of Amaryllis.
M.   Sweet for crops is dew, for kids, when weaned, arbutus,
willow soft for fruitful herds, Amyntas alone for me.

D.   Pollio amat nostram, quamvis est rustica, Musam.
Pierides vitulam lectori pascite vestro.   85
M.   Pollio et ipse facit nova carmina. pascite taurum,
iam cornu petat et pedibus qui spargat harenam.
D.   Qui te Pollio amat veniat quo te quoque gaudet.
mella fluant illi, ferat et rubus asper amomum.
M.   Qui Bavium non odit amet tua carmina Maevi   90
atque idem iungat volpes et mulgeat hircos.

D.   Qui legitis flores et humi nascentia fraga
frigidus, o pueri fugite hinc, latet anguis in herba.
M.   Parcite oves nimium procedere. non bene ripae
creditur. ipse aries etiam nunc vellera siccat.   95
D.   Tityre pascentes a flumine reice capellas.
ipse ubi tempus erit omnis in fonte lavabo.
M.   Cogite oves pueri. si lac praeceperit aestus
ut nuper frustra pressabimus ubera palmis.
D.   Heu heu quam pingui macer est mihi taurus in ervo.   100
idem amor exitium pecori pecorisque magistro.
M.   His certe, neque amor causa est, vix ossibus haerent.
nescio quis teneros oculus mihi fascinat agnos.

D.   Dic quibus in terris et eris mihi magnus Apollo
tris pateat caeli spatium non amplius ulnas.   105
M.   Dic quibus in terris inscripti nomina regum
nascantur flores et Phyllida solus habeto.

P.   Non nostrum inter vos tantas componere lites.
et vitula tu dignus et hic et quisquis amores
aut metuet dulcis aut experietur amaros.   110
claudite iam rivos pueri. sat prata biberunt.

D.   Pollio loves our Muse, although our Muse is rustic.
     O Pierians, feed a heifer for your reader!   85

M.   Pollio makes new songs himself. Feed a bull
     who aims his horn already, scatters sand with hooves.

D.   Who loves you, Pollio, may he come where you too make
       him glad,
     may honey flow for him, harsh brambles bear amomum's
       spice.

M.   Who hates not Bavius, may he love your songs, O
       Maevius,   90
     and may he harness foxes, may he milk he-goats.

D.   O, gathering buds and strawberries that grow so low,
     be off, my boys, a chill snake lurks there in the grass.

M.   Careful, ewes, don't go too far, don't trust too well
     the bank, for now the ram himself still dries his fleece.   95

D.   Tityrus, drive back the feeding nannies from the stream.
     Myself, when time is ripe, I'll wash all in the spring.

M.   Boys, herd the ewes. If heat of day dries up their milk,
     as recently it did, we'll squeeze in vain their udders.

D.   Oh me! How thin my bull, and yet how thick the
       vetch!   100
     His love will be the end of herd and herdsman too!

M.   And these are skin and bone; love's surely not to blame.
     Some evil eye's bewitched my tender lambs.

D.   Tell me in which lands—you'll be my great Apollo—
     sky's expanse extends no more than three elbows.   105

M.   Tell me in which regions flowers grow inscribed
     with names of kings, and keep our Phyllis for yourself.

P.   It's not for me to settle this great match between
       you both.
       You're worthy of the heifer, so is he, and so are all
       who either dread a love that's sweet, or suffer bitter
         loves.   110
       Now close the streams, my boys. The meadow's
       drunk enough.

ECLOGA IV

Sicelides Musae paulo maiora canamus.
non omnis arbusta iuvant humilesque myricae.
si canimus silvas, silvae sint consule dignae.

Ultima Cumaei venit iam carminis aetas.
magnus ab integro saeclorum nascitur ordo.   5
iam redit et Virgo, redeunt Saturnia regna,
iam nova progenies caelo demittitur alto.
tu modo nascenti puero, quo ferrea primum
desinet ac toto surget gens aurea mundo,
casta fave Lucina. tuus iam regnat Apollo.   10

Teque adeo decus hoc aevi te consule inibit,
Pollio, et incipient magni procedere menses.
te duce si qua manent sceleris vestigia nostri
inrita perpetua solvent formidine terras.
ille deum vitam accipiet divisque videbit   15
permixtos heroas et ipse videbitur illis
pacatumque reget patriis virtutibus orbem.

   At tibi prima, puer, nullo munuscula cultu
   errantis hederas passim cum baccare tellus
   mixtaque ridenti colocasia fundet acantho,   20
   ipsa tibi blandos fundet cunabula flores.[1]   23
   ipsae lacte domum referent distenta capellae   21
   ubera nec magnos metuent armenta leones.   22

[1] See Chapter VI note 53.

ECLOGUE IV

Muses of Sicily, let our song have somewhat grander
   strains.
Not all do orchards please and lowly tamarisks;
if woods we sing, let woods have consul's dignity.

Of Cumaean song the final era now has come,
the mighty march of centuries is born anew.   5
Now returns the Maid, returns Saturnian reign,
now new offspring down from heaven on high is sent.
Do you but favour, pure Lucina, his nativity,
the boy whose coming marks the first retreat of race of
   iron,
the rise, world-wide, of golden race. Your own Apollo
   reigns.   10

With you as consul, this adornment of the age will come,
Pollio, yes, the great months' forward movement will begin.
With you as leader, if some traces of our guilt remain
their dissolution will release the earth from endless fear.
And he will lead the life of gods, and he will see   15
heroes mix with gods, and will appear to them himself.
By ancestral virtues he will rule a world at peace.

   And with no cultivation, boy, as her first gifts for
      you
   the earth will cover all with errant ivy, cyclamen,
   and water lilies mingled with acanthus' laugh,   20
   and will herself your cradle spread with floral charms.
   The nannies will themselves bring home their
      udders full
   of milk, nor will the herds have fear of lions' might.

occidet et serpens et fallax herba veneni
occidet. Assyrium volgo nascetur amomum.

At simul heroum laudes et facta parentum[2]
iam legere et quae sit poteris cognoscere virtus
molli paulatim flavescet campus arista
incultisque rubens pendebit sentibus uva
et durae quercus sudabunt roscida mella.

Pauca tamen suberunt priscae vestigia fraudis
quae temptare Thetin ratibus, quae cingere muris
oppida, quae iubeant telluri infindere sulcos.
alter erit tum Tiphys et altera quae vehat Argo
delectos heroas, erunt etiam altera bella
atque iterum ad Troiam magnus mittetur Achilles.

Hinc ubi iam firmata virum te fecerit aetas
cedet et ipse mari vector nec nautica pinus
mutabit merces. omnis feret omnia tellus.
non rastros patietur humus, non vinea falcem,
robustus quoque iam tauris iuga solvet arator
nec varios discet mentiri lana colores,
ipse sed in pratis aries iam suave rubenti
murice, iam croceo mutabit vellera luto.
sponte sua sandyx pascentis vestiet agnos.

TALIA SAECLA suis dixerunt CURRITE fusis
concordes stabili fatorum numine Parcae.
adgredere o magnos, aderit iam tempus, honores
cara deum suboles, magnum Iovis incrementum.
aspice convexo nutantem pondere mundum

2
2

3

3

4

4

5

---

[2] See Chapter VI note 57.

Destroyed will be the snake, the treachery of
    poison plant
destroyed, and wild will grow amomum, Syrian
    spice.   25

When you can read the praise of heroes, read the
    fathers' deeds,
and can understand by then what virtue is,
with soft spikes of grain the Field will yellow, bit
    by bit,
and grapes will redden, hanging from untended
    thorns,
while hard oaks ooze their honey like the dew.   30

Yet ancient fraud's few vestiges will lurk within
to bid a trial of Thetis with the sail, a girding up
of towns with walls, a furrowed scoring of the earth.
Tiphys then will rise anew, an Argo new conveying
chosen heroes. There will be new wars as well   35
and great Achilles will be sent once more to Troy.

Then, when tempered age has made a man of you
the sailor will avoid the sea, the nautical pine
will trade no barter, every land will bear it all.
Hoes the ground will not endure, the vine no scythe; 40
the hardy ploughman, too, will loose the oxen's yoke.
Nor will wool imbibe deceit in different hues,
but in his pasturage the ram himself with soft blush
    now
of purple, now with saffron dye, will change his
    fleece.
On its own, red gold will clothe the feeding
    lambs.   45

'Hurry' to their spindles 'times like these' have said
the Parcae, of one mind by destiny's firm law.
Advance to your great rank, the time will soon be here,
dear offspring of the gods, great seed of Jupiter!
See the cosmos tremble with its vaulted mass   50

terrasque tractusque maris caelumque profundum,
aspice venturo laetentur ut omnia saeclo.

O mihi tum longae maneat pars ultima vitae,
spiritus et quantum sat erit tua dicere facta.
non me carminibus vincet nec Thracius Orpheus   55
nec Linus, huic mater quamvis atque huic pater adsit
Orphei Calliopea, Lino formosus Apollo.
Pan etiam Arcadia mecum si iudice certet
Pan etiam Arcadia dicet se iudice victum.

Incipe parve puer risu cognoscere matrem,   60
matri longa decem tulerunt fastidia menses.
incipe parve puer. qui non risere parenti
nec deus hunc mensa, dea nec dignata cubilist.

of lands, of ocean tracts, of heaven's depths!
See how all rejoices in the age to come!

O then may there remain to me a final part
of life long lived, and breath enough to tell your deeds.
In songs will Thracian Orpheus never vanquish me,   55
nor Linus, though one have a mother's, one a father's aid,
Orpheus Calliopea's, Linus fair Apollo's.
Even Pan, if he vie with me, and Arcadia be the judge,
even Pan will say he's lost—and Arcadia be the judge.

Begin, my little boy, to know your mother with a laugh   60
—ten months have brought your mother long-endured
    disdain.
Begin, my little boy; who has not laughed for parent,
him no god deems fit for feast, no goddess for her bed.

ECLOGA V

Menalcas *Mopsus*

м. Cur non Mopse boni quoniam convenimus ambo,
tu calamos inflare levis, ego dicere versus,
hic corylis mixtas inter consedimus ulmos?
M. Tu maior, tibi me est aecum parere Menalca
sive sub incertas Zephyris motantibus umbras   5
sive antro potius succedimus. aspice ut antrum
silvestris raris sparsit labrusca racemis.
м. Montibus in nostris solus tibi certat Amyntas.
M. Quid si idem certet Phoebum superare canendo?

м. Incipe Mopse prior si quos aut Phyllidis ignes   10
aut Alconis habes laudes aut iurgia Codri.
incipe, pascentis servabit Tityrus haedos.

M. Immo haec, in viridi nuper quae cortice fagi
carmina descripsi et modulans alterna notavi,
experiar. tu deinde iubeto certet Amyntas.   15
м. Lenta salix quantum pallenti cedit olivae,
puniceis humilis quantum saliunca rosetis,
iudicio nostro tantum tibi cedit Amyntas.
sed tu desine plura puer. successimus antro.

M.   Exstinctum Nymphae crudeli funere Daphnim   20
flebant, vos coryli testes et flumina Nymphis,
cum complexa sui corpus miserabile nati
atque deos atque astra vocat crudelia mater.
non ulli pastos illis egere diebus
frigida Daphni boves ad flumina, nulla neque
amnem   25

ECLOGUE V

Menalcas *Mopsus*

M. Why not, Mopsus—since we're met and both good men,
   you at sounding slender reeds and I at telling verse
   —sit together 'mid the elms and hazels here?
M. As elder, you, Menalcas, merit deference from me,
   whether 'neath the restless shadows moved by Zephyr's
     wind   5
   or rather to the cave we move. See how the wild vine
   on the cave has scattered clusters here and there.
M. Up in our mountains only Amyntas vies with you—
M. Let him vie to outstrip Phoebus with his song!

M. Lead on, O Mopsus, first, if song you have of Phyllis'   10
   passion, or of Alcon's praises, or of Codrus' blame;
   lead, and as they pasture, Tityrus will guard the goats.

M. No, this song I recently on fresh beech bark
   wrote down and marked the interchange of tone and word
   I'll venture; then you tell Amyntas to compete.   15
M. As the pliant willow yields to pale green olive,
   as the lowly wild nard yields to scarlet rosebush,
   so to you, in our opinion, yields Amyntas.
   But do you leave off, boy; we have reached the cave.

M.   The Nymphs were mourning Daphnis' death, a
         cruel demise   20
      (hazels, rivers, you were witness for the Nymphs),
      while mother clasped the hapless body of her son
      and called upon the gods, upon the cruel stars.
      In those days there were none to drive the bulls
      from pasture to the chill streams, Daphnis; no, nor
         brook   25

libavit quadrupes nec graminis attigit herbam.
Daphni tuum Poenos etiam ingemuisse leones
interitum montesque feri silvaeque locuntur.

Daphnis et Armenias curru subiungere tigris
instituit, Daphnis thiasos inducere Bacchi   30
et foliis lentas intexere mollibus hastas.
vitis ut arboribus decori est, ut vitibus uvae,
ut gregibus tauri, segetes ut pinguibus arvis,
tu decus omne tuis. postquam te fata tulerunt
ipsa Pales agros atque ipse reliquit Apollo.   35
grandia saepe quibus mandavimus hordea sulcis
infelix lolium et steriles nascuntur avenae.
pro molli viola pro purpureo narcisso
carduos et spinis surgit paliurus acutis.

Spargite humum foliis, inducite fontibus umbras 40
pastores, mandat fieri sibi talia Daphnis,
et tumulum facite et tumulo superaddite carmen
DAPHNIS EGO IN SILVIS HINC USQUE AD SIDERA
  NOTUS
FORMOSI PECORIS CUSTOS FORMOSIOR IPSE.

M. Tale tuum carmen nobis divine poeta   45
quale sopor fessis in gramine, quale per aestum
dulcis aquae saliente sitim restinguere rivo.
nec calamis solum aequiperas set voce magistrum.
fortunate puer, tu nunc eris alter ab illo.
nos tamen haec quocumque modo tibi nostra vicissim 50
dicemus Daphnimque tuum tollemus ad astra.
Daphnim ad astra feremus, amavit nos quoque Daphnis.

did any four-foot taste, no blade of grass was
    touched.
Daphnis, Punic lions even mourned your death
—so say the untamed mountains and the wilderness.

Daphnis even taught to yoke to chariots
Armenian tigers, Daphnis introduced the Bacchic
    troupes,   30
showed how to weave the foliage soft 'round pliant
    wands.
As vines adorn the trees, as clustered grapes the vines,
as bulls the herds, as crops of grain the fertile plains,
so you adorned in every way your folk. Fate took
    you off
and Pales herself, Apollo himself, has left the fields. 35
Furrows where oft great grains of barley we
    entrusted—
in them grow now useless darnel, sterile straw.
Where once soft violets, once narcissus crimson grew
now rise the thistle and the thorn with pointed spikes.

Spread the ground with leaves and shade the
    springs,   40
herdsmen (Daphnis bids that this be done for him),
and build a mound, and scribe a song above the
    mound:
'Daphnis am I in the forest, known from here to
    the stars,
guardian of a lovely flock, and lovelier myself.'

M.   Such was your song to us, O poet divine,   45
    as sleep in the grass to the tired, as in the midst of heat
    a quenching of thirst in leaping brook of water sweet.
    Not only with reeds, but also with voice, do you equal
       the master.
    Fortunate boy, you'll now be second after him.
    But we will try our best to tell you in return this song   50
    of ours, and elevate your Daphnis to the stars.
    Daphnis to the stars we'll bear: us too loved Daphnis.

M. An quicquam nobis tali sit munere maius?
et puer ipse fuit cantari dignus et ista
iam pridem Stimichon laudavit carmina nobis.   55

M.   Candidus insuetum miratur limen Olympi
        sub pedibusque videt nubes et sidera Daphnis.
        ergo alacris silvas et cetera rura voluptas
        Panaque pastoresque tenet Dryadasque puellas.
        nec lupus insidias pecori nec retia cervis   60
        ulla dolum meditantur. amat bonus otia Daphnis.
        ipsi laetitia voces ad sidera iactant
        intonsi montes, ipsae iam carmina rupes,
        ipsa sonant arbusta, Deus deus ille Menalca.

        Sis bonus o felixque tuis. en quattuor aras,   65
        ecce duas tibi Daphni, duas altaria Phoebo.
        pocula bina novo spumantia lacte quotannis
        craterasque duo statuam tibi pinguis olivi
        et multo in primis hilarans convivia Baccho
        ante focum si frigus erit, si messis in umbra   70
        vina novom fundam calathis Ariusia nectar.
        cantabunt mihi Damoetas et Lyctius Aegon,
        saltantis Satyros imitabitur Alphesiboeus.
        haec tibi semper erunt et cum sollemnia vota
        reddemus Nymphis et cum lustrabimus agros.   75

        Dum iuga montis aper, fluvios dum piscis amabit,
        dumque thymo pascentur apes, dum rore cicadae,
        semper honos nomenque tuum laudesque manebunt.

M. And could any gift to us be better than yours is?
The boy himself was worthy to be sung, and for those
songs of yours we've long heard praise from Stimichon.   55

M.   Daphnis, shining, wonders at Olympus' strange new
              threshold,
          sees the clouds and constellations at his feet.
          Sudden pleasure seizes wilds and countryside
          and Pan, and herdsmen, too, and Dryad maids.
          The wolf no ambush for the flock, the nets for deer   60
          no wiles do plan. Good Daphnis loves tranquillity.
          Themselves, for joy they hurl their voices to the
              stars,
          do uncropped peaks. The very cliffs resound the
              songs,
          the very orchards: 'God, he is a god, Menalcas'.

          O be good, propitious to your folk! Four hearths   65
          behold: for you, two, Daphnis, two as Phoebus'
              altars.
          Foaming cups of fresh milk, two in every year,
          two bowls of glistening oil I'll dedicate to you.
          I'll lead the toast exulting in the store of Bacchus'
              grape
          before the hearth in winter, in the shade at harvest,   70
          pouring nectar new from cups, Ariusian wines.
          Damoetas, too, will sing for me, and Lyctian Aegon;
          Alphesiboeus will represent the leaping satyrs
          —rites you'll have forever, when we pay each year
          to the nymphs our vows, and when we purify the
              fields.   75

          As long as boar loves mountain ridge, and fish loves
              stream,
          as long as thyme is food for bees, and dew for
              crickets,
          always will your fame, your name, your praises
              flourish.

ut Baccho Cererique tibi sic vota quotannis
agricolae facient. damnabis tu quoque votis. 80

M. Quae tibi quae tali reddam pro carmine dona?
nam neque me tantum venientis sibilus austri
nec percussa iuvant fluctu tam litora nec quae
saxosas inter decurrunt flumina valles.
M. Hac te nos fragili donabimus ante cicuta. 85
haec nos FORMOSUM CORYDON ARDEBAT ALEXIM
haec eadem docuit CUIUM PECUS? AN MELIBOEI?

M. At tu sume pedum quod me cum saepe rogaret
non tulit Antigenes, et erat tunc dignus amari,
formosum paribus nodis atque aere Menalca. 90

As to Bacchus, as to Ceres, so each year to you
the farmers will make vows; you too will see vows
    paid.   80

M. What gifts to you could I return for such a song?
Not even south wind's whisper makes me so rejoice,
nor shores struck by the waves, nor streams that flow
down among the valley's rocky beds.

M. But first you'll have this fragile hemlock flute as gift,   85
the flute which taught us 'Corydon burned for fair
    Alexis'
and the same that taught us 'Whose the flock—
    Meliboeus'?'

M. You take the crook which, often as he asked,
Antigenes, though worthy then of love, did not bear off,
beautiful for its even knots and studs, Menalcas.   90

ECLOGA VI

Prima Syracosio dignata est ludere versu
nostra neque erubuit silvas habitare Thalia.
cum canerem reges et proelia Cynthius aurem
vellit et admonuit, Pastorem Tityre pinguis
pascere oportet ovis, deductum dicere carmen.   5
nunc ego, namque super tibi erunt qui dicere laudes
Vare tuas cupiant et tristia condere bella,
agrestem tenui meditabor harundine Musam.
non iniussa cano. si quis tamen haec quoque si quis
captus amore leget, te nostrae Vare myricae   10
te nemus omne canet nec Phoebo gratior ullast
quam sibi quae Vari praescripsit pagina nomen.

Pergite Pierides. Chromis et Mnasylos in antro
Silenum pueri somno videre iacentem
inflatum hesterno venas ut semper Iaccho   15
serta procul tantum capiti delapsa iacebant
et gravis attrita pendebat cantharus ansa.
adgressi, nam saepe senex spe carminis ambo
luserat, iniciunt ipsis ex vincula sertis.
addit se sociam timidisque supervenit Aegle,   20
Aegle Naiadum pulcherrima iamque videnti
sanguineis frontem moris et tempora pingit.
ille dolum ridens Quo vincula nectitis? inquit,
Solvite me pueri, satis est potuisse videri,
carmina quae voltis cognoscite carmina vobis,   25
huic aliud mercedis erit. simul incipit ipse.
tum vero in numerum Faunosque ferasque videres
ludere tum rigidas motare cacumina quercus.

ECLOGUE VI

First was she to deign to sport in Syracusan
verse; my own Thalia did not blush to dwell in woods.
When I'd sing of kings and battles, Cynthius pulled
my ear and warned: 'A herdsman, Tityrus, ought to
    fatten
sheep, and hold the song he sings to subtle strains'.   5
Today, I shall (you'll have enough and more who long
to tell your praises, Varus, set grim wars to verse)
rehearse the rustic Muse with slender reed.
No verse unasked I sing. If only someone, someone
seized by love, will read this, too, our tamarisks   10
and all the grove will sing you, Varus; Phoebus finds
    no page
more pleasing than the one that starts with Varus' name.

Lead off, Pierian maids. The boys Chromis and Mnasylos
saw Silenus lying in a cave asleep;
as always, yesterday's Iacchus swelled his veins.   15
Hard by, the garlands lay, just slipped down from his
    head,
and heavy hung, from handle worn, the beetle-cup.
They rush: with hope of song the old one oft had teased
both boys; they cast their bonds, from very garlands made.
To trepidation Aegle adds her company;   20
Aegle, of the Naiads fairest, now as he awakes
paints with berries' blood his forehead, paints his temples.
Laughing at the trick, 'Why fasten bonds?', he asks.
'Loose me, boys; enough to think you might have done
    it.
Songs you want I give you—songs for both of you,   25
for her another prize!' This said, he starts his song.
Then you really might have seen the Fauns' and beasts'
measured sport, the moving tops of rigid oaks;

nec tantum Phoebo gaudet Parnasia rupes
nec tantum Rhodope mirantur et Ismarus Orphea.   30

Namque canebat uti magnum per inane coacta
semina terrarumque animaeque marisque fuissent
et liquidi simul ignis ut his ex omnia primis
omnia et ipse tener mundi concreverit orbis,
tum durare solum et discludere Nerea ponto   35
coeperit et rerum paulatim sumere formas,
iamque novom terrae stupeant lucescere solem,
altius atque cadant summotis nubibus imbres,
incipiant silvae cum primum surgere cumque
rara per ignotos errent animalia montis.   40
hinc lapides Pyrrhae iactos, Saturnia regna,
Caucasiasque refert volucres furtumque Promethei.
his adiungit Hylan nautae quo fonte relictum
clamassent ut litus Hyla Hyla omne sonaret.

Et fortunatam si numquam armenta fuissent   45
Pasiphaen nivei solatur amore iuvenci.
a virgo infelix, quae te dementia cepit?
Proetides inplerunt falsis mugitibus agros
at non tam turpis pecudum tamen ulla secuta
concubitus quamvis collo timuisset aratrum   50
et saepe in levi quaesisset cornua fronte.
a virgo infelix tu nunc in montibus erras.
ille latus niveum molli fultus hyacintho
ilice sub nigra pallentis ruminat herbas
aut aliquam in magno sequitur grege. Claudite
    Nymphae,   55
Dictaeae Nymphae nemorum iam claudite saltus
si qua forte ferant oculis sese obvia nostris
errabunda bovis vestigia. forsitan illum
aut herba captum viridi aut armenta secutum
perducant aliquae stabula ad Gortynia vaccae.   60

Tum canit Hesperidum miratam mala puellam,
tum Phaëthontiadas musco circumdat amarae
corticis atque solo proceras erigit alnos.

much less does Phoebus please Parnassus' gorging heights,
much less Ismarus and Rhodope thrill to Orpheus.   30

He sang, you see, of how through empty vastness seeds
of earth, of soul, of ocean had been forced together,
seeds of flowing fire in all; how from these first things
all beginnings, even heaven's fragile orb, took form.
Then how the land began to harden and exclude   35
Nereus in the sea, to take in time the shape of things;
now how the earth gapes at a new sun's brilliant beams
and how the rains fall now from clouds removed to sky,
when first the forests start to rise, when first
creatures here and there explore the unknown hills.   40
Next, rocks that Pyrrha threw, Saturnian reign,
Caucasian birds, Prometheus' theft, these he relates.
He adds the spring where sailors called for Hylas left
     behind
so all the shore resounded with 'Hyla Hyla!'

And he consoles Pasiphae, so fortunate   45
—if herds had never been!—in love with snowy bull.
Ah, hapless maid, what senselessness possessed you?
Proetus' daughters filled the fields with lowings false,
but not one sought such lewd relations with the beasts,
though feeling on the neck the threat of plow and yoke,   50
though searching often for the horns on forehead smooth.
Ah, hapless maid, you wander in the mountains now
while he, his snowy flank supported on soft hyacinth,
chews his cud of pale green grass 'neath dark holm-oak
or looks for heifers in the teeming herd. 'Close, Nymphs,   55
Dictaean Nymphs, close now the woodland pasturage,
if by chance our eyes may meet the sight of tracks,
wandering tracks of a bull. Perhaps, beguiled
by verdant grass, or searching for the herds,
some cows may lure him on to stalls at Gortyn.'   60

Then he sings a maiden's wonder at Hesperides' fruits,
then he wraps in moss of bitter bark the sisters of
Phaethon, lifts them from the ground as lofty alders.

Tum canit errantem Permessi ad flumina Gallum
Aonas in montis ut duxerit una sororum　　　　　　65
utque viro Phoebi chorus adsurrexerit omnis,
ut Linus haec illi divino carmine pastor
floribus atque apio crinis ornatus amaro
dixerit, Hos tibi dant calamos en accipe Musae,
Ascraeo quos ante seni quibus ille solebat　　　　70
cantando rigidas deducere montibus ornos.
his tibi Grynei nemoris dicatur origo
ne quis sit lucus quo se plus iactet Apollo.

Quid loquar aut Scyllam Nisi quam fama secutast
candida succinctam latrantibus inguina monstris　　75
Dulichias vexasse rates et gurgite in alto,
a, timidos nautas canibus lacerasse marinis,
aut ut mutatos Terei narraverit artus,
quas illi Philomela dapes, quae dona pararit,
quo cursu deserta petiverit et quibus ante　　　　80
infelix sua tecta super volitaverit alis?
omnia quae Phoebo quondam meditante beatus
audiit Eurotas iussitque ediscere lauros
ille canit, pulsae referunt ad sidera valles
cogere donec ovis stabulis numerumque referre　　85
iussit et invito processit Vesper Olympo.

Then he sings of Gallus wandering by Permessus' stream,
how one among the Sisters brought him to Aonian hills,   65
and how all Phoebus' chorus rose to greet the man;
how herdsman Linus, he of song divine
(his hair adorned with blooms and pungent celery)
addressed him, said: 'These reeds the Muses give you—
    take them, here—
which once they gave the old Ascraean, he who used
    them then   70
to lead in song the rigid ash trees from the hills.
With these you'll tell the legend of Grynean Wood;
there'll be no grove that makes Apollo prouder then.'

Why mention Scylla, child of Nisus? Legend holds
that she, with barking monsters 'round her snowy loins,   75
harassed Dulichian boats, and in a deep whirlpool
—ah!—with her sea-dogs tore to bits the panicked crew.
Why mention how he told of Tereus' limbs transformed,
of feast and gifts prepared for him by Philomel,
the course by which he sought the wilds, the wings with
    which,   80
before, he'd hovered (piteous flight) above his roof?
All themes that once, when Phoebus practised, glad
Eurotas heard and bade the laurels learn by heart,
he sings; the songs rebound from valleys to the stars
'til Vesper's come and bade to pen and count the sheep,   85
and made its upward way against Olympus' wish.

ECLOGA VII

Forte sub arguta consederat ilice Daphnis
compulerantque greges Corydon et Thyrsis in unum,
Thyrsis ovis, Corydon distentas lacte capellas,
ambo florentes aetatibus Arcades ambo
et cantare pares et respondere parati.   5
Huc mihi dum teneras defendo a frigore myrtos
vir gregis ipse caper deerraverat atque ego Daphnim
aspicio. ille ubi me contra videt, Ocius, inquit,
huc ades o Meliboee, caper tibi salvos et haedi
et si quid cessare potes requiesce sub umbra.   10
huc ipsi potum veniunt per prata iuvenci,
hic virides tenera praetexit harundine ripas
Mincius eque sacra resonant examina quercu.

Quid facerem? neque ego Alcippen nec Phyllida
  habebam
depulsos a lacte domi quae clauderet agnos   15
et certamen erat Corydon cum Thyrside magnum.
posthabui tamen illorum mea seria ludo.
alternis igitur contendere versibus ambo
coepere, alternos Musae meminisse volebant.
Hos Corydon, illos referebat in ordine Thyrsis: 20

c. Nymphae, noster amor, Libethrides, aut mihi carmen
    quale meo Codro concedite (proxima Phoebi
    versibus ille facit) aut si non possumus omnes
    hic arguta sacra pendebit fistula pinu.

ECLOGUE VII

'Neath holm-oak's rustle Daphnis chanced to have
    his seat;
one flock from two had Corydon and Thyrsis made
(Thyrsis' ewes and Corydon's goats with udders full),
both in youth's full flower, both Arcadians
well matched for song, and skilled in song's
    exchange.   5
There, as I defended fragile myrtles from the frost,
the he-goat, husband of the flock, had strayed, and
    Daphnis
I behold. He looks on me in turn and says,
'Here quickly, Meliboeus. Goat and kids are safe,
and if you have some time to rest, lie in the shade.   10
Unsummoned through the meadows calves will come
    to drink;
here Mincio's stream with gentle reed its verdant
    banks
fringes, here the swarms resound from sacred oak.'

What to do? I had no Phyllis, no Alcippe
left to keep the weaned lambs penned at home;   15
yet Corydon's match with Thyrsis was a mighty one.
In spite of all, I put off business for their sport.
With alternating verses, then, they both began
to vie: the Muses wished to flex their memories by
    turns.
One stanza Corydon recited, Thyrsis took the next: 20

c.   Libethrid Nymphs, I love you. Give me songs like those
my Codrus sings—he makes them most like Phoebus'
    verse—
or else, if I am not sufficient to the task,
my Pan-pipes here on sacred rustling pine will hang.

T.   Pastores hedera nascentem ornate poetam   25
     Arcades, invidia rumpantur ut ilia Codro
     aut si ultra placitum laudarit baccare frontem
     cingite ne vati noceat mala lingua futuro.

C.   Saetosi caput hoc apri tibi Delia parvos
     et ramosa Micon vivacis cornua cervi.   30
     si proprium hoc fuerit levi de marmore tota
     puniceo stabis suras evincta coturno.
T.   Sinum lactis et haec te liba Priape quotannis
     exspectare sat est. custos es pauperis horti.
     nunc te marmoreum pro tempore fecimus at tu   35
     si fetura gregem suppleverit aureus esto.

C.   Nerine Galatea thymo mihi dulcior Hyblae,
     candidior cycnis, hedera formosior alba,
     cum primum pasti repetent praesaepia tauri
     si qua tui Corydonis habet te cura venito.   40
T.   Immo ego Sardoniis videar tibi amarior herbis,
     horridior rusco, proiecta vilior alga
     si mihi non haec lux toto iam longior annost.
     ite domum pasti si quis pudor ite iuvenci.

C.   Muscosi fontes et somno mollior herba   45
     et quae vos rara viridis tegit arbutus umbra
     solstitium pecori defendite. iam venit aestas
     torrida, iam lento turgent in palmite gemmae.
T.   Hic focus et taedae pingues hic plurimus ignis
     semper et adsidua postes fuligine nigri,   50
     hic tantum boreae curamus frigora quantum
     aut numerum lupus aut torrentia flumina ripas.

C.   Stant et iuniperi et castaneae hirsutae,
     strata iacent passim sua quaeque sub arbore poma,
     omnia nunc rident. at si formosus Alexis   55
     montibus his abeat videas et flumina sicca.

T. With ivy-leaf the budding poet, herdsmen, crown,   25
  Arcadians, so that Codrus' belly bursts with envy.
  If he praises me beyond what's just, with cyclamen
  bind my brow, that evil tongue not harm the bard-to-be.

C. For you, this bristling boar's head, Delian maid, from
   little
  Micon—branching horns, too, of a long-lived stag.   30
  And if this luck stays with me, all in marble bright
  you will stand with crimson buskins 'round your calves.
T. A pail of milk, this cake, Priapus, once a year
  are all you can expect. You guard a meagre plot.
  Just for now, we've made you marble, but if you   35
  cause the herd's increase, then shine in gold.

C. Nereus' child Galatea, sweeter than Hybla's thyme,
  whiter than swans and comelier than pale ivy leaf,
  when from pasture to their pens the bulls return,
  Corydon's yours. If you've a care for him, please come. 40
T. May I seem to you more tart than wormwood, bristled
  more than mousethorn, viler than the outcast seaweed,
  if this day's not longer than a year's full span.
  Go home, my calves (have you no shame?), you've
   eaten, go!

C. Mossy springs and grass that's softer still than sleep, 45
  and green arbutus, too, which shades you now and then,
  hold the solstice from our flock; now comes the summer's
  broil, already swell the buds on pliant grapevines.
T. Here the hearth and torches' oil, here the warmest fire
  burns always, and the posts are black with constant soot. 50
  Here we care as much for north wind's chill as wolves
  care to count sheep, or as torrents care for banks.

C. There the stands of juniper and chestnuts rough,
  the fruits of each tree everywhere lie spread beneath.
  Nature laughs now; if the fair Alexis, though,   55
  should leave these hills, you'd see the very rivers dry.

т. Aret ager, vitio moriens sitit aëris herba,
    Liber pampineas invidit collibus umbras.
    Phyllidis adventu nostrae nemus omne virebit,
    Iuppiter et laeto descendet plurimus imbri.   60

c. Populus Alcidae gratissima, vitis Iaccho,
    formosae myrtus Veneri, sua laurea Phoebo.
    Phyllis amat corylos, illas dum Phyllis amabit
    nec myrtus vincet corylos nec laurea Phoebi.
т. Fraxinus in silvis pulcherrima, pinus in hortis,   65
    populus in fluviis, abies in montibus altis.
    saepius at si me Lycida formose revisas
    fraxinus in silvis cedat tibi, pinus in hortis.

        Haec memini et victum frustra contendere Thyrsim.
        ex illo Corydon Corydon est tempore nobis.   70

T.   Dry are the fields, foul weather kills the thirsty grass,
Liber grudges to the hills the shade of grapevine.
Green will all the grove be when our Phyllis comes;
abundant Jove in cheerful showers will descend.   60

C.   To Hercules is poplar most dear, vines to Iacchus,
myrtles to our Venus fair, to Phoebus his own laurel.
Phyllis loves the hazels, and while Phyllis loves those
    trees,
myrtle and Phoebus' laurel will yield to hazels.
T.   Fairest is the ash in woods, the pine in gardens,   65
poplar on the rivers, fir in mountain heights.
If you'd visit me more often, comely Lycidas,
the ash in woods would yield to you, the pine in gardens.

      I recall these songs, and beaten Thyrsis' strife in
         vain.
      From that time it's Corydon, it's Corydon for us.

ECLOGA VIII

Pastorum Musam Damonis et Alphesiboei,
immemor herbarum quos est mirata iuvenca
certantis, quorum stupefactae carmine lynces
et mutata suos requierunt flumina cursus,
Damonis Musam dicemus et Alphesiboei.   5

Tu mihi seu magni superas iam saxa Timavi
sive oram Illyrici legis aequoris—en erit umquam
ille dies mihi cum liceat tua dicere facta?
en erit ut liceat totum mihi ferre per orbem
sola Sophocleo tua carmina digna coturno?   10
A te principium, tibi desinam. accipe iussis
carmina coepta tuis atque hanc sine tempora circum
inter victrices hederam tibi serpere lauros.

Frigida vix caelo noctis decesserat umbra
cum ros in tenera pecori gratissimus herba.   15
incumbens tereti Damon sic coepit olivae:

Nascere praeque diem veniens age Lucifer almum,
coniugis indigno Nisae deceptus amore
dum queror et divos quamquam nil testibus illis
profeci extrema moriens tamen adloquor hora.   20

Incipe Maenalios mecum mea tibia versus.

ECLOGUE VIII

The Muse of Damon and Alphesiboeus, herdsmen
    twain,
whose contest caused the heifer to forget her grass
and marvel; lynxes stood astounded at their song
while rivers changed their currents and stayed their
    course
—our tale will be the Muse of Damon and
    Alphesiboeus.   5

You, who cross already great Timavus' rocks
or skirt the rim of Illyrian sea: will it ever come
for me, that day when I'm allowed to tell your
    deeds?
Will it come, that I'm allowed to carry through the
    world
your poetry, the only match for Sophoclean boot?   10
From you I start, for you I'll cease. Receive the songs
I've undertaken at your bidding, let this ivy
'round your temples intertwine with victor's laurel.

Chilly shades of night had scarcely left the sky
(the time found dew on tender grass most pleasing
    to the flock);   15
leaning on smooth staff of olive, Damon so began:

Morning star, arise, precede the gentle day
while I lament a bride's deceit, my love for Nisa
wasted, and address the gods—although no good
their witness brought me—at the hour of my death.   20

    Take up and sing with me, my flute, Maenalian
    verses.

Maenalus argutumque nemus pinosque loquentis
semper habet, semper pastorum ille audit amores
Panaque qui primus calamos non passus inertis.

    Incipe Maenalios mecum mea tibia versus.   25

Mopso Nisa datur. quid non speremus amantes?
iungentur iam grypes equis aevoque sequenti
cum canibus timidi venient ad pocula dammae.
Mopse novas incide faces, tibi ducitur uxor.
sparge marite nuces, tibi deserit Hesperus Oetan.   30

    Incipe Maenalios mecum mea tibia versus.

O digno coniuncta viro dum despicis omnis
dumque tibi est odio mea fistula dumque capellae
hirsutumque supercilium promissaque barba
nec curare deum credis mortalia quemquam.   35

    Incipe Maenalios mecum mea tibia versus.

Saepibus in nostris parvam te roscida mala
(dux ego vester eram) vidi cum matre legentem.
alter ab undecimo tum me iam acceperat annus,
iam fragilis poteram ab terra contingere ramos.   40
ut vidi ut perii ut me malus abstulit error.

    Incipe Maenalios mecum mea tibia versus.

Nunc scio quid sit Amor. duris in cotibus illum
aut Tmaros aut Rhodope aut extremi Garamantes
nec generis nostri puerum nec sanguinis edunt.   45

    Incipe Maenalios mecum mea tibia versus.

Maenalus holds the rustling grove, the voice of pines
forever, ever hears the loves of herdsmen, hears
Pan, the first to set a task for stalks of reed.

> Take up and sing with me, my flute, Maenalian
> verses.   25

Nisa's given to Mopsus; what may lovers not expect?
With horses now will griffins mate, and in the age to come
the timid docs will come to water-troughs with dogs.
Mopsus, fashion torches new, a wife is brought to you.
Strew almonds, groom; for you the Evening Star leaves
Oeta's mount.   30

> Take up and sing with me, my flute, Maenalian
> verses.

O, how well matched to your man, who sneer at all
and hate my Pan-pipes, hate my nanny-goats as well
as bushy eyebrows, hate the beard I've grown so full
and think that mortals' troubles are no god's concern.   35

> Take up and sing with me, my flute, Maenalian
> verses.

You were little when I saw you in our yard
picking dewy apples with your mother (both I led).
I'd gained a year from my eleventh birthday then,
and from the ground could barely reach the fragile
branches.   40
How I gazed and perished! Madness bore me off!

> Take up and sing with me, my flute, Maenalian
> verses.

Now I know what Love is: him on naked rocks
did Tmaros or Rhodope or the Garamants far-flung
produce, a Boy not of our race, not of our blood.   45

Saevos Amor docuit natorum sanguine matrem
commaculare manus. crudelis tu quoque mater.
crudelis mater magis an puer improbus ille?
improbus ille puer, crudelis tu quoque mater. 50

Incipe Maenalios mecum mea tibia versus.

Nunc et ovis ultro fugiat lupus, aurea durae
mala ferant quercus, narcisso floreat alnus,
pinguia corticibus sudent electra myricae,
certent et cycnis ululae, sit Tityrus Orpheus, 55
Orpheus in silvis, inter delphinas Arion.

Incipe Maenalios mecum mea tibia versus.

Omnia vel medium fiat mare. vivite silvae,
praeceps aerii specula de montis in undas
deferar. extremum hoc munus morientis habeto. 60

Desine Maenalios iam desine tibia versus.

Haec Damon. vos quae responderit Alphesiboeus
dicite Pierides. non omnia possumus omnes.

Effer aquam et molli cinge haec altaria vitta
verbenasque adole pingues et mascula tura, 65
coniugis ut magicis sanos avertere sacris
experiar sensus. nihil hic nisi carmina desunt.

Ducite ab urbe domum mea carmina ducite
  Daphnim.

Take up and sing with me, my flute, Maenalian
    verses.

Love, cruel Love once taught a mother with children's
    blood
to stain her hands. O mother, cruel were you as well!
More cruel was mother, or more shameless was that Boy?
That Boy was shameless; mother, cruel were you as well! 50

    Take up and sing with me, my flute, Maenalian
      verses.

Let the wolf now flee the sheep, hard oaks
bear golden apples, alder show narcissus' bloom;
let tamarisks exude thick amber from their bark,
let owls compete with swans, let Tityrus Orpheus be,   55
Orpheus in the woods, Arion in dolphins' midst.

    Take up and sing with me, my flute, Maenalian
      verses.

If you like, let ocean cover all. Farewell, my woods!
Headlong from lofty mountain crag into the waves
I'll hurl myself, a dying man's last gift for her.   60

    Leave off, leave off now, flute, Maenalian verses.

    This was Damon's; what response had Alphesiboeus,
      you,
Pierians, tell—we're insufficient for the task:

Bring water and surround with fillet soft these altars.
Burn the pitchy boughs and manly frankincense,   65
that I may try by magic rites to steal away
my lover's senses. Nothing lacks here but the songs.

    Lead Daphnis from the town, my songs, lead
      Daphnis home.

Carmina vel caelo possunt deducere lunam,
carminibus Circe socios mutavit Ulixi,   70
frigidus in pratis cantando rumpitur anguis.

    Ducite ab urbe domum mea carmina ducite
    Daphnim.

Terna tibi haec primum triplici diversa colore
licia circumdo terque haec altaria circum
effigiem duco. numero deus impare gaudet.   75
necte tribus nodis ternos Amarylli colores,
necte Amarylli modo et Veneris, dic, vincula necto.

    Ducite ab urbe domum mea carmina ducite
    Daphnim.

Limus ut hic durescit et haec ut cera liquescit   80
uno eodemque igni, sic nostro Daphnis amore.
sparge molam et fragiles incende bitumine lauros.
Daphnis me malus urit, ego hanc in Daphnide laurum.

    Ducite ab urbe domum mea carmina ducite
    Daphnim.

Talis amor Daphnim qualis cum fessa iuvencum   85
per nemora atque altos quaerendo bucula lucos
propter aquae rivom viridi procumbit in ulva,
perdita nec serae meminit decedere nocti,
talis amor teneat nec sit mihi cura mederi.

    Ducite ab urbe domum mea carmina ducite
    Daphnim.   90

Has olim exuvias mihi perfidus ille reliquit
pignora cara sui quae nunc ego limine in ipso
terra tibi mando. debent haec pignora Daphnim.

Songs can even lead the moon down from the sky.
With songs did Circe change Ulysses' fellows.   70
Singing makes the chill snake in the meadow burst.

> Lead Daphnis from the town, my songs, lead
>   Daphnis home.

First of all I bind these loops around you, three
of different colours three, and thrice around these altars
do I lead a doll; the god likes numbers odd.   75
Tie, Amaryllis, colours three in three knots each;   77
just tie and, Amaryllis, say 'It's Venus' bonds I tie'.

> Lead Daphnis from the town, my songs, lead
>   Daphnis home.

As this mud hardens, as the wax here liquefies   80
by one same fire, so Daphnis by our love.
Scatter barley, fire with pitch the tender laurels.
Daphnis burns me hard, this laurel I on Daphnis burn.

> Lead Daphnis from the town, my songs, lead
>   Daphnis home.

Let Daphnis be possessed by love, as when the cow,   85
exhausted by her search for bull through groves and
    wooded heights,
falls prostrate by the water's bank in verdant sedge,
forlorn, nor thinks of yielding to nocturnal darkness—
let such love possess him, let no cure be my concern.

> Lead Daphnis from the town, my songs, lead
>   Daphnis home.   90

These garments once he left me, did that faithless one,
dear pledges of himself: now on the very threshold I
commit them to you, earth. These pledges Daphnis owe.

Ducite ab urbe domum mea carmina ducite
Daphnim.

Has herbas atque haec Ponto mihi lecta venena   95
ipse dedit Moeris. nascuntur plurima Ponto.
his ego saepe lupum fieri et se condere silvis
Moerim, saepe animas imis excire sepulcris
atque satas alio vidi traducere messis.

Ducite ab urbe domum mea carmina ducite
Daphnim.   100

Fer cineres Amarylli foras rivoque fluenti
transque caput iace nec respexeris. his ego Daphnim
adgrediar. nihil ille deos, nil carmina curat.

Ducite ab urbe domum mea carmina ducite
Daphnim.

Aspice corripuit tremulis altaria flammis   105
sponte sua dum ferre moror cinis ipse. bonum sit.
nescio quid certest et Hylax in limine latrat.
credimus an qui amant ipsi sibi somnia fingunt?

Parcite, ab urbe venit, iam parcite carmina,
Daphnis.

Lead Daphnis from the town, my songs, lead
    Daphnis home.

Gathered from the Black Sea, Moeris gave to me himself   95
these herbs and drugs (they grow in plenty by that Sea).
Moeris oft by means of them I've seen become a wolf
and hide in woods, oft raise the dead from graves so deep,
and transfer planted crops to other fields.

    Lead Daphnis from the town, my songs, lead
        Daphnis home.   100

Throw out the ashes, Amaryllis, to the flowing stream,
over your head, and don't look back. With them I attack
Daphnis. Naught cares he for gods, and naught for songs.

    Lead Daphnis from the town, my songs, lead
        Daphnis home.

Look! The ash itself ignites the altars with faint flames   105
on its own, while I delay removal. Bless the sign!
Something's happened. On the threshold Hylax barks.
Can it be? or do we lovers forge our own conceits?

    Cease, you songs, my Daphnis comes from town,
        now cease.

ECLOGA IX

Lycidas Moeris

L. Quo te Moeri pedes? an quo via ducit in urbem?
M. O Lycida vivi pervenimus, advena nostri
    (quod numquam veriti sumus) ut possessor agelli
    diceret: Haec mea sunt, veteres migrate coloni.
    nunc victi tristes quoniam fors omnia versat   5
    hos illi, quod nec vertat bene, mittimus haedos.
L. Certe equidem audieram, qua se subducere colles
    incipiunt mollique iugum demittere clivo
    usque ad aquam et veteres iam fracta cacumina fagos
    omnia carminibus vestrum servasse Menalcan.   10
M. Audieras et fama fuit sed carmina tantum
    nostra valent Lycida tela inter Martia quantum
    Chaonias dicunt aquila veniente columbas.
    quod nisi me quacumque novas incidere lites
    ante sinistra cava monuisset ab ilice cornix   15
    nec tuus hic Moeris nec viveret ipse Menalcas.

L. Heu cadit in quemquam tantum scelus, heu tua nobis
    paene simul tecum solacia rapta Menalca.
    quis caneret Nymphas, quis humum florentibus herbis
    spargeret aut viridi fontes induceret umbra?   20
    vel quae sublegi tacitus tibi carmina nuper
    cum te ad delicias ferres Amaryllida nostras:
        Tityre dum redeo (brevis est via) pasce capellas
        et potum pastas age Tityre et inter agendum
        occursare capro (cornu ferit ille) caveto.   25

ECLOGUE IX

Lycidas Moeris

L. Whither, Moeris, go your feet? along the road to town?
M. O Lycidas, we've lived to see the day we'd never feared.
    An immigrant, new landlord of our little plot,
    said, 'This is mine; go elsewhere, old inhabitants.'
    We're beaten, broken. Luck reverses all: 5
    we drive these kids for him. May evil come of it.
L. I thought I'd heard, at least, that where the hills begin
    to level off and drop a softly sloping ridge
    —up to water's edge, to broken tops of aged beech,
    all this your man Menalcas saved with poetry.   10
M. So you'd heard, and so the story went, but poems,
    Lycidas, of ours prevail among the shafts of Mars
    as Chaonian doves, they say, withstand the eagle's swoop.
    Why, unless, from hollow holm-oak on the left, a crow
    had warned me to end somehow the quarrel just begun,   15
    your Moeris here would not be living, nor Menalcas' self.

L. No! Does such a crime occur to any man? From us
    your consolation and yourself, Menalcas, almost torn . . .
    Who would sing the Nymphs, who 'spread the ground
        with clover',
    who would 'shade the springs' with greenery?   20
    —or the song I held my breath to hear from you of late
    as you took yourself to our love, Amaryllis:
        Tityrus, 'til I'm home (the way is short) do feed my
            nannies;
        drive them, when they're fed, to drink, and while
            you drive
        don't cross the he-goat's path, his horn is sharp,
            beware!   25

M. Immo haec quae Varo necdum perfecta canebat:
      Vare tuum nomen, superet modo Mantua nobis
      —Mantua vae miserae nimium vicina Cremonae—
      cantantes sublime ferent ad sidera cycni.

L. Sic tua Cyrneas fugiant examina taxos,   30
    sic cytiso pastae distendant ubera vaccae.
    incipe si quid habes. et me fecere poetam
    Pierides, sunt et mihi carmina, me quoque dicunt
    vatem pastores sed non ego credulus illis.
    nam neque adhuc Vario videor nec dicere Cinna   35
    digna sed argutos inter strepere anser olores.

M. Id quidem ago et tacitus Lycida mecum ipse voluto
    si valeam meminisse, neque est ignobile carmen:
      Huc ades O Galatea, quis est nam ludus in undis?
      hic ver purpureum, varios hic flumina circum   40
      fundit humus flores, hic candida populus antro
      imminet et lentae texunt umbracula vites.
      huc ades. insani feriant sine litora fluctus.
L. Quid, quae te pura solum sub nocte canentem
    audieram? numeros memini si verba tenerem: 45
      Daphni quid antiquos signorum suspicis ortus?
      ecce Dionaei processit Caesaris astrum,
      astrum quo segetes gauderent frugibus et quo
      duceret apricis in collibus uva colorem.
      insere Daphni piros, carpent tua poma nepotes.   50

M. Omnia fert aetas, animum quoque. saepe ego longos
    cantando puerum memini me condere soles.
    nunc oblita mihi tot carmina, vox quoque Moerim
    iam fugit ipsa, lupi Moerim videre priores.
    sed tamen ista satis referet tibi saepe Menalcas.   55

M. Or rather what he sang for Varus, not yet finished:
      Varus, your name—let only Mantua survive,
      Mantua, woe! too close to poor Cremona—
      swans in song will bear to starry heights.

L. And let your swarms avoid the yews of Corsica   30
      and let your heifers swell their udders, clover-fed.
      Lead on, if song you have. Pierian Muses made
      of me a poet too, I too have songs, the herdsmen
      call me bard as well; I can't believe them, though.
      So far, songs worthy of a Varius or Cinna   35
      I seem not to sing; I screech, a goose amid shrill swans.

M. Of course, Lycidas, I'm just deciding silently
      whether I can recall; it's not a song without renown:
        Come, O Galatea! What's the sport in waves?
        Here Spring wears purple garb, here 'round the
          streams the ground   40
        sprays blossoms varicoloured, here a poplar looms
        bright against the cave, and pliant vines weave
          shadows.
        Come. Let waves in madness dash against the shore.
L. What of the song I'd heard you sing alone, the night
      was clear
      —the measures I recall, just let me hold the words: 45
        Daphnis, why gaze upon old constellations' risings?
        Behold, Dionaean Caesar's star has marked its way,
        a star through which crops might exult in fruitful-
          ness,
        through which the grape might draw its blush on
          sunny hills.
        Graft the pear trees, Daphnis. Descendants will
          pick your fruits.   50

M. Age takes all away, the mind as well: oft, I recall,
      I laid long days to rest with song when but a boy.
      Now, I've forgotten just as many songs, and Moeris' voice
      itself is going—the wolves saw Moeris first.
      Yet oft enough Menalcas will recall these songs for you.   55

L.   Causando nostros in longum ducis amores.
et nunc omne tibi stratum silet aequor et omnes
aspice ventosi ceciderunt murmuris aurae,
hinc adeo mediast nobis via, namque sepulcrum
incipit apparere Bianoris. hic ubi densas   60
agricolae stringunt frondes hic Moeri canamus,
hic haedos depone, tamen veniemus in urbem,
aut si nox pluviam ne colligat ante veremur
cantantes licet usque (minus via laedet) eamus.
cantantes ut eamus ego hoc te fasce levabo.   65

M.   Desine plura puer et quod nunc instat agamus.
carmina tum melius cum venerit ipse canemus.

L. Your excuses heighten my desire to hear.
Now all the sea lies still for you, regard,
and all the howling gusts of wind have ceased.
Our journey's reached its midpoint, for the tomb
of Bianor just appeared. Here, where farmers   60
strip the leaves, here, Moeris, let us sing;
let the kids rest here, we'll still get to the town.
But if we fear that night may first bring on a storm,
we can sing while we proceed—the road's less tedious.
So we may sing while we proceed, I'll help you with this
    load.   65

M. No more, boy. Let us do what stands before us now.
We'll sing songs better then when he himself has come.

ECLOGA X

Extremum hunc Arethusa mihi concede laborem.
pauca meo Gallo sed quae legat ipsa Lycoris
carmina sunt dicenda. neget quis carmina Gallo?
sic tibi cum fluctus supterlabere Sicanos
Doris amara suam non intermisceat undam,   5
incipe. sollicitos Galli dicamus amores
dum tenera attondent simae virgulta capellae.
non canimus surdis, respondent omnia silvae.

Quae nemora aut qui vos saltus habuere puellae
Naides, indigno cum Gallus amore peribat?   10
nam neque Parnasi vobis iuga, nam neque Pindi
ulla moram fecere neque Aonie Aganippe.
illum etiam lauri, etiam flevere myricae,
pinifer illum etiam sola sub rupe iacentem
Maenalus et gelidi fleverunt saxa Lycaei.   15

Stant et oves circum, nostri nec paenitet illas
nec te paeniteat pecoris divine poeta.
et formosus ovis ad flumina pavit Adonis.

Venit et upilio, tardi venere subulci,
uvidus hiberna venit de glande Menalcas.   20
omnes, Unde amor iste, rogant, tibi? venit Apollo:
Galle quid insanis? inquit, tua cura Lycoris
perque nives alium perque horrida castra secutast.

Venit et agresti capitis Silvanus honore
florentis ferulas et grandia lilia quassans.   25
Pan deus Arcadiae venit quem vidimus ipsi
sanguineis ebuli bacis minioque rubentem:

ECLOGUE X

Grudge me not, Arethusa, this last effort.
Gallus wants a poem or two, but poems meant
for Lycoris herself to read. What poet could refuse?
Grant, and may that Dorian sea, as you flow beneath
Sicilian tides, not mix its bitter wave with yours. 5
Lead on: let's tell the troubled loves of Gallus
while our snub-nosed nannies crop the tender shrubs.
No deaf ears here for poetry: the forest answers all.

What groves, what leas detained you, Naiad girls,
when Gallus pined away for unrequited love? 10
No ridges of Parnassus, none of Pindus held you
back, nor yet Aonian Aganippe's spring.
Even laurels mourned him, even tamarisks;
as Gallus lay 'neath lonely cliff, with crest of pine
even Maenalus did weep, and rocks of cold Lycaeon. 15

Sheep stand 'round, they aren't annoyed to be with us,
nor should their flock annoy you, poet divine.
Fair Adonis also pastured sheep by streams.

A shepherd, too, has come, and swineherds moving slow;
Menalcas, soaked with winter's acorn, has arrived. 20
All inquire, 'How came you by this love?', and here's
     Apollo
saying, 'Gallus, why rave on? Lycoris, your concern,
went off with someone else through snows and bristling
     forts'.

Silvanus came, his head enshrined with rustic crown,
brandishing reeds and lilies in full bloom. 25
Pan, Arcadia's god, arrived. We saw him ourselves
painted with vermilion and with elderberry's blood.

Ecquis erit modus? inquit, Amor non talia curat
nec lacrimis crudelis Amor nec gramina rivis
nec cytiso saturantur apes nec fronde capellae.   30

Tristis at ille: Tamen cantabitis Arcades, inquit,
montibus haec vostris soli cantare periti
Arcades. o mihi tum quam molliter ossa quiescant,
vestra meos olim si fistula dicat amores.
atque utinam ex vobis unus vestrique fuissem   35
aut custos gregis aut maturae vinitor uvae.
certe sive mihi Phyllis sive esset Amyntas
seu quicumque furor (quid tum si fuscus Amyntas?
et nigrae violae sunt et vaccinia nigra)
mecum inter salices lenta sub vite iaceres.   40
serta mihi Phyllis legeret, cantaret Amyntas.

Hic gelidi fontes hic mollia prata Lycori
hic nemus, hic ipso tecum consumerer aevo.
nunc insanus amor duri me Martis in armis
tela inter media atque adversos detinet hostis.   45
tu procul a patria, nec sit mihi credere tantum,
Alpinas, a, dura nives et frigora Rheni
me sine sola vides. a, te ne frigora laedant,
a, tibi ne teneras glacies secet aspera plantas.

Ibo et Chalcidico quae sunt mihi condita versu   50
carmina pastoris Siculi modulabor avena.
certum est in silvis inter spelaea ferarum
malle pati tenerisque meos incidere amores
arboribus. crescent illae, crescetis amores.
interea mixtis lustrabo Maenala Nymphis   55
aut acris venabor apros. non me ulla vetabunt
frigora Parthenios canibus circumdare saltus.

He says, 'Such moans must have their limit: Love cares
   not!
Of tears hard-hearted Love ne'er gets his fill, nor grass
   of brooks,
nor bees of clover's bloom, nor nanny-goats of leaves'.   30

His wan response: 'You'll sing, Arcadians, none the less,
these verses to your mountains, you alone are skilled in
   song,
Arcadians. How softly then these bones of mine would
   rest
if sometime pipe of yours could tell my loves!
Would that I'd been one of you, a guardian   35
of your flock, a harvester of ripened grapes!
If, Phyllis or Amyntas, you were mine, or any
cherished frenzy (what of Amyntas' duskiness?
Dark are violets, hyacinthus dark as well),
you'd lie with me in willow groves 'neath pliant vine   40
and Phyllis would gather wreaths for me, Amyntas sing.

Here are icy springs, here meadows soft, Lycoris,
here the forest, here with you I'd live out all my life!
Now passion keeps me under arms of cruel Mars
amid the flying weapons and the looming foe.   45
You, far from home (too much for my belief),
hard-hearted one, behold the Alpine snows, the frozen
Rhine—alone, without me. Let the frost not hurt thee!
Let the jagged ice not cut thy tender soles!

I'll go, and songs, Chalcidian verses formed by me,   50
on pastoral pipe of Sicily I shall arrange.
I vow to like a life of danger 'mid the woodland
caves of beasts, to carve my Loves upon those
tender trees: they'll grow, you'll grow, my Loves.
Maenalus' heights, meanwhile, I'll track among the
   nymphs,   55
or hunt fierce boars; no cold will hinder me
from closing in on forests of Parthenius with dogs.

iam mihi per rupes videor lucosque sonantis
ire, libet Partho torquere Cydonia cornu
spicula tamquam haec sit nostri medicina furoris   60
aut deus ille malis hominum mitescere discat.

Iam neque Hamadryades rursus nec carmina nobis
ipsa placent, ipsae rursus concedite silvae.
non illum nostri possunt mutare labores
nec si frigoribus mediis Hebrumque bibamus   65
Sithoniasque nives hiemis subeamus aquosae
nec si cum moriens alta liber aret in ulmo
Aethiopum versemus ovis sub sidere Cancri.
omnia vincit Amor et nos cedamus Amori.

Haec sat erit divae vestrum cecinisse poetam   70
dum sedet et gracili fiscellam texit hibisco
Pierides. vos haec facietis maxima Gallo,
Gallo cuius amor tantum mihi crescit in horas
quantum vere novo viridis se subicit alnus.
surgamus. solet esse gravis cantantibus umbra,   75
iuniperi gravis umbra, nocent et frugibus umbrae.
ite domum saturae, venit Hesperus, ite capellae.

I see myself now through the canyons, through
   resounding groves,
moving, happy to fire from a Parthian bow Cydonian
darts, as if this could cure my passion, as if that god   60
could learn some mildness from the misery of men!

No pleasure, now, in calling Hamadryads back
or even songs. Retreat once more, you very woods.
Our efforts all are impotent to change that god,
not even if, when Thrace is coldest, Hebrus' stream we
   drink   65
and undergo Sithonian snows and winter's wet;
not even if, when bookbark dies and dries on lofty elm,
Ethiopians' sheep we verse 'neath Cancer's sign.
Love conquers all, let us too yield to Love'.

      This will be enough, divine ones, for your poet   70
      to have sung while resting, weaving mallow basket,
      daughters of Pieria. For Gallus you will make
      my song magnificent, for Gallus grows my love each
         hour
      much as verdant alder lifts its spire in early Spring.
      Let us arise. Shade tends to be the singer's burden,   75
      heavy shade of juniper; shades harm the grain as
         well.
      Go home, you've fed, the evening star is out, my
         nannies, go.

Virgil's Pastoral Muse

The poetry of earth is never dead:
   When all the birds are faint with the hot sun,
   And hide in cooling trees, a voice will run
From hedge to hedge about the new-mown mead;
That is the Grasshopper's—he takes the lead
   In summer luxury,—he has never done
   With his delights; for when tired out with fun
He rests at ease beneath some pleasant weed.
The poetry of earth is ceasing never:
   On a lone winter evening, when the frost
   Has wrought a silence, from the stove there shrills
The Cricket's song, in warmth increasing ever,
And seems to one in drowsiness half lost,
The Grasshopper's among some grassy hills.
Keats, 'On the Grasshopper and Cricket'

Thalia and the Gnat

First was she to deign to sport in Syracusan
verse; my own Thalia did not blush to dwell in woods.

The first two lines of Virgil's sixth *Eclogue* refer to a figure whom the poet had adopted as his pastoral Muse *par excellence*. There is some evidence that Thalia's name refers to the 'flourishing' of crops, and that she was worshipped in the Greek countryside as a deity of vegetation; as such, she would fit well into Virgil's rustic landscape. But Hesiod had taken her name to mean 'Festivity', and she became a Muse of festive song.[1] According to some sources, she is also the nymph whom Daphnis loved; if such a tradition was known to Virgil, it was all the more appropriate that he name his Muse after her.[2] Most important for Virgil's conception of Thalia, however, is the fact that in the Hesiodic tradition she was associated not only with the Muses, but with the three Graces as well (*Theogony*

907). Theocritus, in a poem discussed above (p. 7f.), had used the term 'Graces' to signify his own poetry. Like the Muses, they were associated with Apollo; the early Greek sculptors Angelion and Tectaeus had represented all three in the god's hand on his Delian statue, each with her proper musical instrument: a lyre, a flute, and, on the lips of the Grace in the middle who must be Thalia, a shepherd's pipe.[3]

When the poet calls her the 'first to sport' in his 'Syracusan verse', we are probably meant to take the statement literally: Thalia was the Muse of Virgil's earliest major work, a mock epic called *The Gnat* (*Culex*), which begins

> Lusimus Octavi gracili modulante Thalia
> atque ut araneoli tenuem formavimus orsum.
>
> (Octavius, we've sported to slender Thalia's measure,
> and shaped, like baby spiders, wispy first attempts.)

Like the *Bucolics*, the *Culex* was a pastoral *ludus*, a 'sporting'. Its plot is simple, even trivial. A gnat's bite awakens a goatherd in time to save him from the attack of a deadly serpent; the gnat, swatted by the herdsman, receives a grave monument as a token of gratitude. This hardly seems material enough for an epic, but Virgil, by seizing every conceivable opportunity to digress, expanded the poem to a grand total of 414 verses. Above all, he showed a striking predilection for endowing his landscape with feeling, thus laying groundwork for the pastoral world of the *Bucolics*. Naiads and Dryads (nymphs of water and wood) become his Muses (*Culex* 19, 94–7, 116), and the *bona pastoris*, the blessings of a herdsman's life, are rhapsodized through over forty lines. Like Damon's song of *Eclogue* 8, the action of the *Culex* begins with daybreak (42ff.). Like Tityrus of *Eclogue* 1, *The Gnat's* anonymous *pastor* stretches out on the grass at leisure (*otia*) and plays a flute (or rather—and this *is* Virgilian—hears 'a reed sing back' to him, 69–73, 100). Woodland Satyrs, meadows, grottoes, and Orpheus himself are already present in Virgil's earliest poetic landscape (e.g. 23, 116f.). The loss of Eurydice, a subject which Virgil developed in the fourth *Georgic*, is here given 27 lines (268–95); and the poet's later occupation with Argonautic themes is foreshadowed in v. 137. The gnat's heroic tomb with its inscription reminds us of Daphnis' monument in *Eclogue* 5, while the floral motifs (*Culex* 398–410) are picked up again in *Ecl.* 2.45–55. In Hades the gnat meets not only Greek heroes, but luminaries from the Roman past as well—an uncanny anticipation of *Aeneid* 6.

The *Culex* is a Roman example of consummate Alexandrianism. Though written in the heroic verse of hexameter, the poem is 'light' and 'delicate' (*mollia carmina, tenui versu* 35), professing to be a *ludus* inspired by a playful Muse. Its content adheres to the 'slender' canons (*kata lepton*) of Hellenistic poets who avoided the grand themes of Homer and the tragedians, seeking instead to elevate the commonplace and the prosaic to a realm of elaborate metaphor and pretty conceit. It is poetry calculated to delight the mind. without moving the heart. Its bulky existence is based on the slimmest of pretexts (the death of a gnat); the poet chews far more than he bites off (there are over sixty allusions in the *Culex* to mythological subjects—some of them quite obscure—and over ten to events in Greek and Roman history); and the most elaborate complexity of thought and expression is consciously sought out. For Greek poets of the third and second centuries B.C., these were all virtues of the highest order. For Roman poets of the Augustan age, who were striving for a revolution in Latin poetry which would revive classical or even Homeric standards, they were qualities to be avoided. This may account for the Augustan poets' failure ever to mention the poem; Virgil himself, whose mature art deviated sharply from the canons of the *Culex*, could well have led this conspiracy of silence. The pendulum of taste had swung back, however, by the time of Nero, when the *Culex* achieved its widest circulation.[4]

The poem comes down to us in an irreparably damaged state. The obscurity of its style in terms of grammar and syntax alone, compounded with obscure images and allusions, was evidently too much for the medieval copyists. Restoring such a badly garbled text to its pristine state is virtually impossible, though new attention to the Greek and Latin sources of the poem has borne some fruit.[5] An even greater problem is the refusal on the part of a large number of scholars to accept the poem as a genuine Virgilian work. It must be admitted that the poem's appearance, and above all the company it keeps in the *Appendix Vergiliana* (a medieval collection in which almost no genuine Virgilian work appears), tempt one to write it off as another imitation. It is a hard poem, moreover, to read and to make sense of; the poet we know is not so devoted to obscurity. Many scholars who have dealt with the *Culex* in this century prefer, like Eduard Fraenkel, to see in it not the learned effort of a young Virgil, but the derivative work of a forger in the post-Augustan age.[6] Someone had composed a poem, they claim, in Virgilian language and with Virgilian themes—hence the rustic milieu, for example, and the Roman heroes in Hades—and had foisted it off on a public eager for samples of Virgil's earliest poetry.

It is surprising to find scholars assuming that the *Aeneid*, and the *Aeneid* alone, is the 'appropriate' place for Roman heroes to be found in the Underworld, and insisting that any other poem which finds them there must be an imitation of *Aeneid* 6. We have no direct evidence that Naevius, say, or Ennius envisioned the Elysian Fields with a Roman quarter—but the notion is far from outlandish and would probably have occurred to any patriotic Roman. If the Gnat is the first literary hero to meet Romans as well as Greeks among the Blessed, is the poet not to be commended for this happy invention? *Must* he have stolen the idea from the *Aeneid*? Critics, moreover, ignore the fact that Roman heroes are not really 'at home' in the Underworld of *Aeneid* 6. They are phantoms of a future existence identified by Anchises, whose rôle as a prophet was part of his legend. The traditional Hades had to be expanded to accommodate the prophetic function of a ghost.[7] The Roman heroes of the *Culex*, unlike those of *Aeneid* 6, are at least properly dead.

It is true that the *Culex* is full of striking verbal parallels with the *Bucolics*, the *Georgics*, and the *Aeneid*; but it is also true that there are verbal anticipations of the *Georgics* and the *Aeneid* throughout the *Bucolics*, some of them as long as a verse or more.[8] Conversely, the *Aeneid* and the *Georgics* can be said to contain many echoes of the *Bucolics*. The *Culex*, in other words, is behaving exactly as we would expect a work of Virgil to behave. Arguments based on the supposed appropriateness of a phrase in the major works, as opposed to its inappropriateness in the *Culex*, beg an awkward question. Many other poets imitated and improved on the *Culex*; can Virgil not be allowed the same freedom? Karl Mras illustrates one instance in which Virgil improved on a passage from the *Georgics* by repeating it in a more appropriate context in the *Aeneid*, and suggests that the poet had quarried raw material from his *Culex* in much the same fashion.[9]

One scholar claimed to have found a verse of the *Culex* which clearly derives not from Virgil, but from the poet of a later generation, Ovid. At first sight, his analysis is convincing. The line in question is 181, *manant sanguineae per tractus undique guttae*. It describes the serpent who threatens the sleeping shepherd's life as a monster, down the length of whose body (*tractus*) 'bloody drops' (*sanguineae guttae*) run (*manant*) when he is about to strike. The snake has not been wounded; whence the blood? Is it a 'poetaster's' awkward attempt to heighten the horror of his monster's aspect by making blood instead of venom drip from the mouth? According to Klotz, the unfortunate verse resulted from the poet's fascination with Ovid, *Metamorphoses* 2.360: *sanguineae manant tamquam de vulnere guttae*, where the sisters of Phaethon, transformed into poplars, 'bleed' with sap when their branches are broken: 'bloody drops run as if from a wound'. Ovid has a perfectly 'appropriate' place for 'bloody drops'; the author of the *Culex* 'pilfered' the phrase and applied it ineptly to his serpent.[10] This argument seems to miss the point of verse 181. Nicander's *Theriaca* (a Hellenistic digest of poisonous serpents composed in hexameters) is often cited as a source for the description of the serpent in the *Culex*, and Salvatore draws particular notice to Nicander's account of the way the asp, like our serpent, raises its head over its coiled body.[11] Just as Nicander devotes careful attention to the colour of his reptiles, so our serpent's body is described as 'spotted' (*maculatus*, *Culex* 164), its crest 'spotted with a splash of red' (*purpureo maculatur amictu* 172). The spots explain why, when he moves in for the kill, 'bloody' flecks (*guttae* can mean 'drops' or 'spots') seem to ripple down his body. The poet imagined a visual illusion of movement, and meant not that the spots were of blood, but that they were blood-coloured, red. Just as the serpents who rise from the sea to kill Laocoon are first distinguished by their 'blood-red crests' (*sanguineae iubae*) in *Aeneid* 2.206f., so Virgil, in his earliest poem, enhanced the monster's horror by making spots the colour of blood seem to roll down his body. Half a century later, Ovid saw a new way to transform this lucky phrase from the *Culex*: he made drops flow from the trunks of the hapless Heliades. Again, they were blood-red (*sanguineae*)—but they were not blood.[12]

Ennius had called poets 'sacred' (*sancti*).[13] It is not surprising, then, to find the *Culex* dedicated to a 'sacred boy' (*sancte puer* 26, 37; cf. *venerande* 25) if his literary ventures (*cui meritis oritur fiducia chartis* 24) are indeed poetic.[14] Perhaps because he writes verse, he is accorded the same veneration that Virgil bestows on his fellow poets in the *Bucolics*; like them, he bears the emblem of youthful innocence (*puer*).[15] It is unfortunate for this 'Octavius' that his name was common enough to be confused with that of Augustus before his adoption by Julius Caesar. Those who believe the *Culex* to be a forgery assume an intentional reference to Augustus, in spite of the fact that the author praises Octavius' literary, not political, virtues. As a reasonable alternative, Mras, who takes the poem to be genuine, suggests that Octavius Musa, the son of a public official at Mantua in the region of Virgil's birthplace, is meant; and that he went on to become the epic poet who is praised by Horace and others.[16]

After its heyday during the baroque age of Lucan and Statius, the *Culex* seems to have been neglected. Claudian imitated it in the late fourth century,[17] but his contemporary Donatus (*Life of Virgil*) goes out of his way to summarize the plot and to quote the final verses, as if it were a poem unfamiliar to his readers. Indeed, no early text of the *Culex* survived the end of the ancient world, while among our manuscripts of the *Bucolics*, *Georgics*, and *Aeneid*, no less than seven were transcribed as early as the fourth or fifth century. The authorship of the *Culex*, however, was never once contested in antiquity. Roman poets from at least the first century onward were happy to believe that, for all its quaintness of style, its contorted eloquence, and its effusiveness, the poem contained the *ars* and *ingenium* of Virgil. Lucan, Statius, and Martial may have wanted no better witness to its authorship than their own ears; but if verses of the *Culex* have a flow and ring which are unmistakably Virgilian, the modern student of Latin poetry is hard pressed to substantiate this in objective terms. Plésent, who denied its authenticity, nevertheless gave the 'forger' credit for imitating the metrics of the *Bucolics* even to the point of copying the frequency and amplitude of spondaic modulation. The ratio of spondees (– –) to dactyls (– ∪ ∪) is almost identical in the *Culex* and the *Bucolics*![18] Duckworth's more sophisticated analysis, based on the relative frequency of metrical patterns within sixteen-line units, places the *Culex* securely in the Neoteric period and closer to the Virgilian *Bucolics* than to any other Latin poem.[19] The 'imitator', in other words, had had the almost infinite time and patience to copy what amounted to Virgil's youthful fingerprints.

Once the air is cleared of 'sources' from later Virgilian or post-Virgilian works, the poem emerges as a true child of its times. Adopting the form of a Hellenistic 'short epic' (*epyllion* in scholarly parlance), the poet has turned for aid in expression to authors both Greek and Roman. The Underworld scenes indicate that he was inspired by *Odyssey* 9 and by the Attic tragedians.[20] Nicander's influence has already been discussed; and the floral motifs at the poem's end may derive from Meleager's *Garland*. Among the Latin poets, it is Lucretius who is most frequently imitated; Catullus comes in second with nine clear echoes, seven of them from the great *Epithalamium of Peleus and Thetis*.[21] We expect to find such influences in the poet of the *Bucolics* and the *Georgics*. But what of Theocritus?

When Virgil referred to his *Culex* as 'Syracusan verse' (*Ecl.* 6.1f.), he alluded to the hexameter and pastoral atmosphere of Theocritus. The poem, of course, seems 'Syracusan' in retrospect, especially when we allow the *Bucolics* into the same category. But we cannot identify so much as a trace of direct Theocritean influence in the *Culex*.[22] There is one exception, a notable one—not from the *Idylls*, but from the Greek Anthology. It is a love-epigram describing the shrine of Priapus, and it must have found its way into Meleager's anthology (*The Garland*) which had reached Italy early in the first century B.C.[23] Here is the relevant passage in English translation (Theocritus, *Epigram* IV, = *AP* 9.437.4–12):

A holy shrine encircles, and a spring flows ever
   down the rocky ledge, everywhere flourish
laurels, myrtles, and the fragrant cypresses.
   All around, the vine, mother of the grape,
spreads its tendrils, springtime blackbirds sound with
   shrilling tones their songs' variegated cries.
Warbled trill of nightingales returns the sound,
   ringing from their throats honeyed intonations.

The passage from the *Culex* follows, in Latin and in English:

Ilicis et nigrae species et laeta cupressus   140
umbrosaeque manent fagus hederaeque ligantes
bracchia, fraternos plangat ne populus ictus,
ipsaeque excedunt ad summa cacumina lentae
pinguntque aureolos viridi pallore corymbos.
quis aderat veteris myrtus non nescia fati.   145
at volucres patulis residentes dulcia ramis
carmina per varios edunt resonantia cantus.
his suberat gelidis manans e fontibus unda
quae levibus placidum rivis sonat acta liquorem.
et quaqua geminas avium vox obstrepit auris   150
hac querulae referunt voces quis nantia limo
corpora lympha fovet. sonitus alit aeris echo
argutis et cuncta fremunt ardore cicadis.
at circa passim fessae cubuere capellae
excelsisque super dumis quos leniter adflans   155
aura susurrantis poscit confundere venti.

Beauteous sight of holm-oak's darkness, flourishing cypress,
shadowy beeches abide, and tendrils of ivy binding
poplar's arms lest she strike her breasts for a brother's
   destruction
—ivy, pliantly stretching upward itself toward the treetops,
dapples with verdantly sombre hues the clusters' refulgence;
in the midst was myrtle, teller of ancient fortunes.
Resting then on spreading boughs, the birds give voice to
incantations sweet, through various notes resounding.
Chilly springs give undertones of water descending:
falling droplets run, a gentle flow proclaiming.
There, wherever both ears are struck by clamour of birdsong,
voices complaining re-echo from mud-swimming creatures
   whom water

feeds and fosters; their echo swells the sounds of the breezes;
everything seethes with heated zeal of the shrill cicadas.
Here, meanwhile, lay 'round about the sleepy nannies,
—on the thickets' cover, too, whose noises a lightly
blowing breath of whispered ,wind has sought to commingle.[24]

Inasmuch as the Greek epigram and the *Culex* both describe
a pleasant landscape, they can be said only to share a well-
known tendency in Hellenistic poetry. What is more, the Latin
verses show at first only the influence of Lucretius: there are
verbal echoes of the birdsong and the rustic landscape of *De
rerum natura* 5.1379–98.[25] But a framework emerges in the *Culex*
which the epigram had imposed: trees, vine, song, and echo
appear in the same order in both poems. Water dripping over
rocks came first in Theocritus; in the *Culex* it has been trans-
posed to mediate between song and echo. Virgil, always
fascinated with the intermingling of sounds, has introduced
frogs, cicadas, and wind at the end. He may have been attracted
to the Greek poem precisely because of Theocritus' employ-
ment here of polyphonous imagery. The remarkable *poikilo-
traula melē*, 'variegated cries' (literally 'songs in variegated
twitters') of Theocritus becomes *carmina resonantia per varios
cantus* in *Culex* 147. The voice of the nightingale, echoing that
of the blackbird in Theocritus, is replaced by the frog's com-
plaint in Virgil; the *Bucolics* show an even deeper preoccupation
with echo.[26]

Virgil had not yet seen the landscape of the *Thalysia*; the
absence in the *Culex* of a direct echo from any of the *Idylls*
makes this clear. What he knew of Theocritus he had read in
Meleager's anthology. The *Culex* shows, however, that he liked
what he saw. In the meantime, drawing on native resources,
he created a pastoral atmosphere entirely his own.

Landscape in Latin poetry

The landscape of the *Culex*, with its grassy banks, its noonday
somnolence, its springs and shade, its deities in their sacred
groves, its sympathetic animals, and its music, is something
more lush, more charged with emotion, and more encompassing
than the sketchy countryside of the *Idylls*. Such 'landscape

poetry' was not new with Virgil. Its source is a distinctly western, non-Greek feeling for wilderness, a feeling which may hark back to Etruscan notions of divinity and majesty in nature, notions reflected not only in a dependence upon nature as an index of the divine will, but also in a predilection for painted landscapes which dwarf their human inhabitants.[27] Visible already in tomb paintings of the fifth prechristian century, this tendency is markedly present in the Odyssey landscapes, painted in Rome not long before Virgil had begun to compose his *Bucolics*.[28] One scholar has actually characterized them as 'Virgilian' by virtue of 'the love for nature expressed in them, the smallness of men and of Man in relation to the encompassing unity of the myth'.[29]

Italian nature-painting culminated in the 'sacro-idyllic' landscapes of the third Pompeiian style, while nature found her fullest *poetic* expression as the panoramic backdrop for Ovid's *Metamorphoses*.[30] But this peculiarly Italian exaltation of nature had already made itself clearly felt in the poetry of Lucretius; Virgil's 'sylvan' or 'rustic' Muse, in fact, derives from two 'scientific' passages in Lucretius' work *On Nature*. The first (4.570–94) explains echoes as natural phenomena, as sounds bouncing from solid objects. The poet concludes with an allusion to the naïve notion that mythical creatures (Satyrs and Nymphs) produce the echoed sounds: though he pretends to mock this belief, the passage is one of the most pastoral, most lyrical pieces in Lucretius, and culminates in a 'criticism' of the notion that Pan pours from his pipes an incessant *silvestris Musa* (589). The second passage (5.1379–98) gives an account of the origins of human music; it is worth quoting in full:[31]

> At liquidas avium voces imitarier ore
> ante fuit multo quam levia carmina cantu   1380
> concelebrare homines possent aurisque iuvare.
> at zephyri, cava per calamorum, sibila primum
> agrestis docuere cavas inflare cicutas.
> inde minutatim dulcis didicere querelas,
> tibia quas fundit digitis pulsata canentum,   1385
> avia per nemora ac silvas saltusque reperta,
> per loca pastorum deserta atque otia dia.
> haec animos ollis mulcebant atque iuvabant   1390

cum satiate cibi, nam tum sunt omnia cordi.
saepe itaque inter se prostrati in gramine molli
propter aquae rivum sub ramis arboris altae
non magnis opibus iucunde corpora habebant
praesertim cum tempestas ridebat et anni   1395
tempora pingebant viridantis floribus herbas.
tum ioca tum sermo tum dulces esse cachinni
consuerant. agrestis enim tum Musa vigebat.

(Yet the liquid notes of birds were mimicked with the mouth
long before in chorus men could hymn their polished
incantations and so gratify their ears.
West winds through whistling hollow reeds were first
to teach the rustics how to blow their hollow stalks.
Next, they learned in gradual steps the sweet complaints
the flute poured forth when blocked by songsters' fingers,
found in trackless groves, in woods, in meadows,
found in herdsmen's lonely haunts, in leisure's open sky,
songs that used to soften spirits and delight
at dinner's end, the time when moods are best.
And so, stretched out in company upon soft grass
near water's flow, beneath a tall tree's boughs,
they used to warm their hearts at no great cost,
especially when weather smiled and season
dappled a ground of verdant grass with flowers.
Then the jokes, the gossip, bursts of laughter sweet
had their day: for then the rustic Muse held sway.)

Virgil's debt to the sporting of Lucretius' rustic Muse is
evident throughout the *Bucolics*. Not only does she herself
appear in *Eclogue* 6.8 to inspire a poem which is partially
Lucretian in content (6.31–40); the situation of Lucretius'
original singers has also been reproduced in the world of
Tityrus, the herdsman who introduces us to Virgil's pastoral
landscape in the first *Eclogue*. Like them, he is concerned with
bird song (*Ecl.* 1.57f.); a herdsman himself, he inhabits *silvae*
and has the leisure (*otia* 1.6) to stretch out near water (1.52) or
beneath a shady tree (1.1), and gets along with few resources
(1.47). The seventh *Eclogue*, too, pays tribute to the Lucretian
passage as 'the season laughs' (7.55) and work becomes play
(7.17).
Virgil's pastoral art does exhibit a primaeval quality, a

departure from contemporary reality which could not be more antithetical to the mimetic aspirations of his Hellenistic 'model'. He makes the contrast between himself and Theocritus as clear as possible in the first lines of the first *Eclogue*: whereas Thyrsis in *Idyll* 1.1f. follows nature's lead, finds inspiration in the natural environment ('Sweet the whisper, goatherd, and the singing of that pine by the springs—and you play sweetly on your pipe'), Virgil turns the tables on nature to give Tityrus the lead: 'You, Tityrus, stretched in shade, teach forests to echo the beauteous Amaryllis.' The Roman poet's aim is not to characterize the human personality as it reacts to a rustic milieu, but to find in nature an 'image' of his own voice, to employ a natural landscape to 'sing back' the state of his own mind.[32]

Neoteric poetry

Though the germ of Virgilian pastoral is to be found in the *Culex*, the poem remains in essence a Hellenistic *epyllion*, the sort of *jeu d'ésprit* which might have found favour with Greek poets like Antipater of Sidon, Archias, and Parthenius, the popular tutors of Virgil's school days. These figures (the last in particular) may have been in large measure responsible for the revolution which Roman poetry underwent in the first half of the first century B.C. Archias or Antipater introduced the 'Garland' of Meleager at Rome around 100. This was an early form of what we know as the Greek Anthology, a copious collection of epigrams by poets from every age, with preference given to post-'classical' authors, and to poems composed in elegiac couplets, verses shaped for the concise expression of grief, passion, and wit in brief bursts of sentiment. The anthology found special favour with the consul Lutatius Catulus; his literary circle was the first to make amateurish attempts at reproducing the *Garland*'s content in Latin verse.

The new impact of the Greek epigram upon Roman literature was enhanced by the appearance at Rome of Parthenius of Nicaea in around 70 B.C. A prisoner of war at first, he was freed by a relative of the poet Cinna, and remained in Italy to instruct a new generation of poets in the principles of

Callimachus, the learned librarian at Alexandria in the third
century B.C., whose poetic activity in all genres was guided by
the canons of a variegated 'slender' style. Parthenius also in-
troduced the young Latin poets to a new concept in erotic
epic, the verse of Euphorion of Chalcis (who had flourished in
the late third century). Parthenius' friends and pupils became
the leading poets of their day: Cinna and Calvus produced
epyllia, Catullus expanded his talent for love poetry through
unfamiliar verse forms, Gallus gave lasting shape to Roman
love elegy, and Virgil, while concentrating on pastoral possi-
bilities, maintained a vivid interest in all these genres.[33]

Innovation was the fashion among the poets just mentioned.
A conservative like Cicero, who coined the term *neoteroi* ('young
moderns') to refer to these 'Euphorionic minstrels', was upset
without justification; from its earliest beginnings, Latin poetry
had been strongly innovative, had always managed to trans-
form and transcend its Hellenic models. 'Father Ennius' him-
self, over a century before, had shown a non-Greek versatility
in the use of his Greek sources. In tragedy, comedy, and epic
early Roman authors had shaped Greek metrical schemes into
manageable vehicles for the heavier consonant clusters and
stress accent of Latin. Lucilius, while travelling a 'Calli-
machean' route, had created a genre (satire) which Quintilian
would call 'completely ours' (*tota nostra*). And Plautus, with
an almost perfunctory nod toward his Greek dramatic sources,
had produced an elegant but throughly Latin medium for
native Italian wit.[34]

Classical Greek poets, from Homer through the tragedians,
had no way of escaping the functionalism of their art. They
produced for the polis, for their community, and were respon-
sible for catering to its cultural needs. 'Neoteric' poets of the
first century B.C. had no share in such a tradition. Roman
society needed no bards, no myths for its spiritual sustenance;
the Latin poet had always been self-sufficient, and if self-support
were impossible, he gladly accepted the system of patronage
which had so depressed Theocritus. In effect, the poets had
always been left alone with, and were responsible only to, the
Muses of Latium. This separateness from societal obligations
especially favoured the sort of modernity through which young

poets often seek to assert their novelty and individuality. Such poetry is, in the words of J. V. Cunningham, 'obscure, and its obscurities are largely calculated; it is intended to be impenetrable to the vulgar. More than this, it is intended to exasperate them'.[35]

The Horatian assertion *odi profanum vulgus et arceo* ('I hate the vulgar mob, I fend them off') was superfluous in Virgil's case. His choice of Theocritean verse for a model marked him as a poet of highly eclectic taste who had his finger on the very pulse of literary fashion. It was no Parthenius, no purveyor of Euphorionic passion, who suggested that Virgil imitate Theocritus. The Greek 'Bucolic Muses' had been collected, probably for the first time, in an edition of Theocritus, Moschus, Bion, and others in the first half of Virgil's century by a scholar from Tarsus, Artemidorus.[36] It came somehow to the attention of Catullus, and Catullus, as we shall see, was Virgil's idol— whether he knew him personally or only by report from their mutual friend Pollio.[37] We know that Catullus imitated Theocritus' second *Idyll*, and perhaps other poems.[38] Whether or not Virgil learned of the *Idylls* from this most outrageously original of the Neoterics, we must credit our poet with a kind of one-upmanship for 'discovering' a poet as out-of the-way as Theocritus,[39] while others were imitating their classical Greek authors, their Hesiods, their Callimachuses and Euphorions.

The structure of the Bucolics

> The force that words obey in song
> the rose and artichoke obey
> in their unfolding towards their form.
>   Robert Duncan, 'Yes, As A Look Springs To Its Face'

The ancient tradition gives Virgil a *triennium*, a solid space of three years, in which to compose and 'correct' (*emendasse*) the *Bucolics*.[40] This works out to less than one verse per day on the average; the poems total only 828 lines. When the Muse is upon him, a poet can compose lucidly, prolifically, even swiftly; there is nothing to suggest unusual laziness in Thalia's case. And as each poem was completed, it was probably 'published', i.e. read to a circle of influential poets and patrons. What

might have taken more time than actual composition, how-
ever, was the activity implied in *emendasse*. Virgil's definitive
edition of the *Bucolics* was much more than a mere collection
of poems. It was a unified book, a perfectly balanced master-
piece.

When we think of 'structure' in modern poetry, we envision
simple length of composition, division of parts, and a numerical
rule or two (for sonnets, as an example) which divide the poem
in consonance with an old tradition. Virgil's book of *Eclogues*
was to follow much stricter, more complicated canons of
symmetry. He considered the individual poems mere masonry
in relation to the architectural[41] whole, to the *liber bucolicorum*.
In terms of theme, he arranged the poems reciprocally, so that
Eclogue 1 balances *Eclogue* 9 (poems of lost land), *Eclogue* 2
balances *Eclogue* 8 (poems of love), 3 balances 7 (contests of
song), and 4 balances 6 (poetry itself). These 'recessed panels'
converge upon *Eclogue* 5, the central poem enshrining Daphnis;
5 in its turn reaches through a vertical dimension towards
Eclogue 10, in which Gallus becomes Daphnis.[42]

As striking as such a thematic structure may seem, it is
elementary in comparison with the 'numerical' structure of the
Bucolics. The lines in each poem arrange themselves into
numerically symmetrical verse clusters, some still operating
on a reciprocal (a b c b a) basis, others alternating major with
minor (A a A a), or simply alternating (a b a b). The only
Eclogues which resist symmetrical analysis are 6 and 10, reflect-
ing the influence of catalogue poetry and love elegy respectively,
two genres which, by their very nature, defy the limitations of
balance.[43]

Most astounding is the numerical symmetry within the
Eclogue-book as a whole. The reciprocal pair 2 and 8 contains
verses which add up to 181; so does the pair of *Eclogues* 3 and
7! The pair 4 and 6 comes out to 149 verses, the pair 1 and 9
to 150. Why the lack of symmetry here? Could Virgil not have
added one verse to *Eclogue* 6 (not 4, which develops itself in
multiples of the number 7) or subtracted one from 1 or 9?
Perhaps the very *lack* of symmetry here was meant to call
attention to the central, numerically 'extra' line of *Eclogue* 1,
hic illum vidi iuvenem Meliboee quotannis (42), where the word

iuvenem, 'youth', occurs at the numerical centre of the poem. It is likely to refer to Octavian, the future Augustus Caesar, who had given both Virgil and the world new hope for the future.[44]

Seven, the number sacred to Apollo, the number of Pan-pipes in Virgil's pastoral syrinx (*Ecl.* 2.36f.), is the numerical base of the fourth or 'messianic' *Eclogue*, a fact which holds significance not only for that poem (which foretells a new reign of Apollo and the birth of a child whose praises will rival Pan's music) but for two others as well. Van Sickle notices that *Eclogues* 4, 7, and 10 are the only three which mention Arcadia; that they are equidistant from one another (separated by two poems each); and that their verse-sums are the following multiples of seven: 63, 70, and 77. In other words, the three poems seem to progress, to surge ahead by sevens—towards what goal?[45]

Interpreters have for centuries tried to grasp the meaning of Virgil's 'Arcadia'. The name is that of a region of Greece in the central Peloponnesus, the dwelling of the god Pan, and the home of a people so full of song that in ancient times even their laws were set to music.[46] Arcadia had connections with Rome in the mythical past; her king Evander had migrated to create on the banks of the Tiber an anticipation of Romulus' city (celebrated in the eighth book of the *Aeneid*). Pan, music, and Italian implications: these are enough to make Arcadia the ideal setting for Virgil's pastoral poetry. Yet Arcadia is not, as some have supposed, a 'backdrop' against which the *Bucolics* play themselves out.[47] Virgil's shepherds never dwell in Arcadia; their dreamworld has a western cast, Sicilian or Italian.[48] Some of their number are called 'Arcadians', how-ever, including Corydon and Thyrsis of *Eclogue* 7, whose contest is set paradoxically on the banks of the Mincio, a river flowing through the region of Virgil's birthplace in northern Italy.

Van Sickle contributes the following thought: parallel to the numerical progression by sevens in *Eclogues* 4, 7, and 10 is the growth of the Arcadian 'idea' in these poems. The fourth *Eclogue*, vv. 58–9, promises that Arcadia herself will one day judge a contest between Pan and Virgil, and will decide in

Virgil's favour. The seventh *Eclogue* introduces the first real Arcadians, the master-poets Corydon and Thyrsis. And Gallus, in the tenth and last *Eclogue*, addresses the singers of Virgil's world, presided over by Pan himself (v. 26), as 'Arcadians' (31–3). It is tempting to adopt Van Sickle's suggestion that number and myth co-operate to symbolize a poetic goal, or rather that 'Arcadia' represents the goal of Virgilian poetics, a goal never attained in the *Bucolics* themselves. His notion is in keeping with the theme of this book, with the idea of an evolution of character, situation, and milieu through the pastoral poems towards their final development in the *Aeneid*. We should not, however, forget that the ancient use of number was fraught with mystical opacity, arcane ambiguities.[49] Virgil found more explicit means of indicating to his readership that he regarded the *Bucolics* as a proving ground for ideas which could only come to maturity beyond the pastoral landscape, his 'cradle spread with floral charms'.

The balanced architecture of the *Eclogue*-book as a whole was preserved at the cost, in at least one discoverable instance, of symmetry within the individual poems. The work of Otto Skutsch has revealed that *Eclogue* 2 was originally composed according to a perfectly balanced abcdcba structure: five lines of introduction and five of conclusion, enclosing sections of thirteen, nine, eight, nine, and thirteen lines. Yet it could not stand with its 'partner', *Eclogue* 8, without growing by 11 lines: for some reason, the pair 2 and 8 had to match the 181 lines of the combination 3 and 7. The poet therefore intercalated an 11-line passage after verse 44 which imitated not Theocritus, but the floral motifs of Meleager's epigrams. Though this increment does not spoil the poem, it destroys the symmetry and creates two rather rough transitions; the poem certainly flows more smoothly if v. 56 follows directly upon 44.[50] Why was this overall numerical symmetry of such importance to the *Bucolics*?

Virgil's rationale is now utterly lost to us, though we may conjecture that the positioning of the poems on the *volumen*, the papyrus roll, imposed a physical necessity for such symmetries.[51] This may indeed explain some, but by no means all, mathematical symmetries in the *Bucolics*. The appearance of the poems as they lay spread over the *volumen* (easily scanned when completely unrolled and held at arm's length) must indeed have been pleasing. The *Bucolics* would have appeared to grow and to radiate out from *Eclogue* 5. Perhaps the finer editions were illuminated with simple pastoral motifs; perhaps the 'Daphnis' poem and the 'Gallus' poem had borders of ivy and acanthus to emphasize their relationship. Yet some of the numerical proportions, particularly those which bind *Eclogue*-pairs together, would not have been easy to notice. If we are not expected to see at a glance that *Eclogues* 2 + 8 contain exactly the same number of lines as *Eclogues* 3 + 7, or that the verses of *Eclogues* 4, 7, and 10 add up to multiples of seven, then we must ask if Virgil's notion of symmetry extended somehow *beyond* the visual.

The ancients often referred to the art of poetry as an act of 'weaving'.[52] Though this metaphor may have alluded, now and then, to the weaving of tapestries and other textiles (the purple bedspread, for instance, in Catullus 64), the image usually pertains to construction of garlands and other objects from floral stems and vines. Pindar's use of the metaphor is appropriate to his celebration of athletic prowess: he usually imagines himself 'weaving' a wreath of victory. Virgil, too, finds an appropriate adaptation of the metaphor to his pastoral art; he 'weaves' not garlands, but 'a mallow basket', a useful object created from the marsh reeds of his bucolic landscape (*Ecl.* 10.71). The basket is appropriate, certainly, to the rustic content of Virgilian pastoral, to poetry which banishes the artifice and urbanity of Hellenistic models, poetry meant to echo the voice of nature heard through forest pastures. More important, however, to considerations of structure and symmetry in the *Bucolics* is the *form* which such a basket would actually take. Its sides would spread up from the bottom in woven patterns of increasing complexity, so that the dominant structure would radiate out from a central configuration of crisscrossed reeds. The whole would have a solidity, a stability which dissolves with the removal of any intricately woven part. In other words, while the basket's *material* would be rustic, it would nevertheless exhibit a sophisticated structure based on the weaving of a central area which, through a complex system of interwoven patterns, generates and supports the whole. The *Bucolics* have a close structural analogy in Virgil's 'mallow basket'. The reader of the *Eclogue*-book, like the carrier of the basket, is not always aware of the interrelationship of parts; but Virgil must have felt that complexity of structure was essential to both objects. Without it, they fall to pieces.

Order of composition

It seems therefore certain that the poet altered the individually published poems at will in order to republish them as an organic whole. If this was the case, there would seem little point in attempting to ascertain comparative dates of composition; any or all of the pieces could have been reworked (*emendasse*) up to the last moment before publication of the whole. It is Virgil himself, however, who invites us to perceive in his poems a development through time, a development which is independent of the order of the poems. Menalcas in the fifth *Eclogue* presents Mopsus with 'the flute which taught us "Corydon burned for fair Alexis" and the same that taught us "Whose the flock—Meliboeus'?" ' Virgil does not want this chronological information to be lost: *Eclogues* 2 and 3 preceded 5. Similarly, Lycidas in *Eclogue* 9 cites a line from the fifth *Eclogue* (9.19f., 5.40) to indicate its prior composition. Meliboeus, in the first poem of the collection, makes ironic reference to a broken promise in *Eclogue* 9 (1.73, 9.50). The sixth *Eclogue* asserts its posteriority to 1 by repeating, this time with objective reference to the poet's own work, the name of Tityrus, who continues to 'rehearse the rustic Muse with slender reed' (6.4–8, 1.1f.). The same poem refers to itself as a reaction to the fourth *Eclogue*, if *deductum carmen* (6.5) is meant to contrast with *paulo maiora canamus* (4.1). Finally, *Eclogue* 10 is designated a 'last effort' (10.1).[53]

This leaves us with the following order of composition as specified by the poet himself: 2, 3, 5, 9, 1, 6, 10, with 4 sometime before 6. Since the fourth *Eclogue* commemorates the year of Pollio's consulship (40 B.C.), and since *Eclogues* 9 and 1 refer to the land redistributions of 41 B.C.,[54] 4 must follow 1. The eighth *Eclogue* must be one of the latest, since it refers to

Pollio's command of 39 B.C. and is therefore towards the end of a *triennium* beginning in 41.[55] *Eclogue* 7 is difficult to pin down; its treatment of the love theme fails to show the influence of Gallus exhibited in 6, 8, and 10; as a 'Daphnis' poem, I would place it near 5.[56] A reasonable guess, then, as to dates of composition yields the following order: 2, 3, 5, 7, 9, 1, 4, 6, 8, 10. There is little of the arbitrary in such guesswork; Virgil himself took pains to provide most of the clues.

The second Eclogue

We are meant to see *Eclogue* two, then, as the earliest piece in the collection. It is usually called the most 'Theocritean' of the *Eclogues*; on the surface, it does indeed resemble the eleventh *Idyll*, though Theocritus' *Cyclops* shows nothing of its elaborate structure. Significantly, however, the first five lines of the second *Eclogue* are inspired not by Theocritus, but by Phanocles, a Hellenistic love elegist. A section of his catalogue of 'Boy-Loves' (*Erotes* or *Kaloi*) became Virgil's model:[57]

> . . . Or as the son of Oeagrus, Thracian Orpheus,
>   loved Kalais with all his heart, the son of Boreas,
>   and oft he'd sit in shadowy groves and sing
>   his love's lament, nor did his heart keep still,
>   but always sleepless cares his soul
>   beset, as he beheld the fair Kalais . . .

The mood of *Eclogue* 2, then, is set not by Theocritus, whose *Cyclops* was meant as whimsical 'advice to the lovelorn', but by a serious love-poet. Corydon's model is no one-eyed 'noble savage', no rustic bard, but the first and wisest of singers, Orpheus himself.

While Theocritus shows the coquettish Galatea sporting in the waves before Polyphemus, Virgil substitutes the more serious and more problematic attachment to a boy, Alexis, whom we never actually see. The complaint of Corydon, heard only by the wilderness, to an absent lover is also a tribute to Catullus, who had perfected this lyrical technique for Ariadne's lament in the *Epithalamium of Peleus and Thetis*.[58] Nor is the name 'Alexis' Theocritean or even bucolic; it derives from a

series of love epigrams in Meleager's *Garland*, most of them by
Meleager himself.[59] The plot thickens. Meleager's *Garland* can
also be shown to have contributed the cicadas, the burning
passion at noonday in harvest-time for Alexis, the tracking of a
lover, lovers' colours (16–18), the comparison with Daphnis,
the floral motifs of the eleven 'intercalary' verses, the spurning
of gifts, the 'rules of love' (*modus amori* 68), and evening's
failure to bring relief.[60]

Enough *Quellenforschung*, at least for the moment. The point
is that Virgil, under the pretext of writing a 'Theocritean'
poem in Latin, had used a variety of sources, both Greek and
Latin, to express a series of sentiments and to convey a never-
theless unified mood which turned out to be non-Theocritean,
wholly Virgilian, and anticipatory of his most mature work.
Corydon is unhappy in love, and will remain so; the Muses are
no cure for him, as they are for Polyphemus; not even evening
brings relief. The poet does not stand back from his lonely
creature and mock him, however gently, but takes his part, and
takes it seriously. Corydon is no rustic mime, no character
type. We cannot laugh at his awkwardness, for there is no
distance between him and us. To listen to him is to feel his
pain. Who can miss in him the foreshadowing of love's helpless-
ness in Dido?[61]

The Pastoral Hero:
Daphnis in the Garden

> We bring up as aberrationists, giving way to undirected associa-
> tions and kicking ourselves from one chance suggestion to
> another in all directions as of a hot afternoon in the life of a
> grasshopper.
>
> Robert Frost, 'The Figure a Poem Makes'

The youthful hero

At the age of twenty-eight,[1] Virgil had committed himself to
continuing the Hellenistic tradition of youthful eroticism in
pastoral poetry. In his hands, however, the tradition was to
undergo a transformation in significance; youth and love were
to become not so much the themes of poetry as symbols for
Virgilian poetry itself. What Pöschl has called 'the greatness
of a pure, childlike poet's soul' develops out of the conscious
and careful use of symbols from the Greek literary tradition,
and out of a choice of themes and heroes appropriate for the
genus tenue, the 'slender style'.[2]

Virgil calls almost all of his herdsmen *pueri* ('boys'). Though
identical with a word used to address slaves and menials in
Roman society, *puer* has none of those connotations in the
pastoral world of Virgil, who refuses to specify the social
position of his heroes.[3] The *pueri*, moreover, have nothing in
them of the crudeness, the slapstick-comic banality, or the
lack of easy spontaneity which is seen in so many of Theocritus'
characters.[4] Absent, too, are the brutal invectives and uncon-
trolled emotions of those who people the Greek Anthology.
And in Meleager's epigrammatic tradition, the Greek word
pais ('boy') had acquired erotic overtones related to homo-
sexual love which are irrelevant to Virgil's use of *puer*. The

pueri are part and parcel of the simplicity, purity, and in-
genuousness of Virgil's bucolic world.

The cave of Eclogue 5

The subject of the fifth *Eclogue* is the death and deification of
Daphnis. The songs concerned with this central theme do not,
however, commence until verse 20. Up to that point, a process-
ion has taken place; at the suggestion of Mopsus, the two poets
have moved from the open air into an *antrum*, a cave which
'the wild forest vine has decked with a few grape-clusters' (l. 7).
When the cave is reached, all idle conversation ceases, and the
songs of Daphnis begin.

For the Greeks, grottoes and caverns had always been awe-
inspiring places of worship. Zeus had been born in a cave,
Dionysus had been nurtured in one; the cave was the home of
Pan, of the Nymphs, of gods both rustic and urbane, of healing
divinities and of baneful demons.[5] Such conceptions of the cave
are not, of course, peculiar to the Greek nation; they belong to
a universal regard for the dark, the mysterious, and the
awesome. Distinctly Hellenic, however, is the use of the cave
as a symbol for poetic inspiration. The image seems to occur
first in Pindar, who praises Thrasybulus for 'culling wisdom
in the grottoes of the Pierians' (*Pyth*. 6.49). The poet himself
sometimes replaced the Muse in a cave, deriving oracular
inspiration, as it were, from its dark recesses.

The most famous instance of a cave-dwelling poet is to be
found in the ancient *Lives* of Euripides. Philochorus and
Satyrus report that the tragedian acquired a dark cavern facing
the sea on Salamis;[6] there he was wont to make his retreat
from the crowds and meditate in solitude, working his grander
themes and filling his poetry with nautical imagery. Homer
himself was imagined to have composed poetry in a cave at
the source of the river Meles in Smyrna;[7] in so representing
him, the Smyrnaeans had combined two symbols for poetic
inspiration, the water source and the grotto. The image of a
poet even older than Homer, the mythical shepherd-singer
Linus, had been carved by the Boeotians in a rock on Helicon
worked into the shape of a cave.[8]

The association of poets and caves in the Hellenistic period must have been fairly common, though the extant literature provides little direct evidence. The popularity of the image among Roman poets, who refer it directly to Greek sources, together with their consistent use of the Greek word for 'cave' (*antron*, Latinized as *antrum*), suggest that the image was not unknown among poets like Philetas and Callimachus: Propertius, addressing these two predecessors in the erotic-elegiac tradition, asks 'In what cave did you draw out the thread of song like this?' (3.1.5). In his use of the cave image, Horace stands directly in the Hellenic tradition: in *Odes* 2.1.37–40 he imagines both his Muse and himself composing poetry in an *antrum*; again in 3.4.37–40 the Muses are depicted refreshing Augustus in the Pierian *antrum*; and in 3.25.1–6 Horace feels himself driven by Bacchus, his inspiration, into 'groves' or into a 'hollow', and asks the god in what *antra* he is to glorify Caesar.

The mention of Bacchus recalls the meaningful association of yet another divinity with caves. Dionysus had been nurtured by Nymphs 'in the hollows of Nysa' and had grown up 'in a sweet-smelling cave' (*Homeric Hymn* 26.5f.). As a symbol for Dionysiac inspiration, the cave would in fact fit pastoral poetry better than any other genre. The affinities of Theocritus' characters with Greek Satyr drama have already been mentioned;[9] there is moreover a 'pastoral' milieu which goes with the Satyr-play, and which was dictated by artistic convention. Vitruvius, a master architect of the Augustan period, tells us that this kind of drama, unlike tragedy and comedy, must have a landscape backdrop 'adorned with trees, caves, hills, and the other rustic accoutrements'.[10] The presence of a cavern was evidently *de rigeur* because it symbolized the spirit of Dionysus. Webster points to a painting from the villa in Boscoreale showing an ivy-covered cave enclosing a fountain—a typical background for Satyr drama: the tradition, according to Webster, reaches back into the fifth century B.C. The infant Dionysus himself may be seen within a cave made of terracotta, surrounded by vines and grape clusters, and dating from the early Hellenistic period.[11] A passage in Athenaeus (148 B) leads us to suppose that any cave overgrown with green vegetation was taken to be a *bakchikon antron*, a place of Bacchic worship.[12]

In the poet's cave which Propertius chooses for himself (2.30. 26, 3.3.27–36), Dionysiac elements predominate, though they are mixed with the trappings of a Muses' grotto and show original Propertian touches. The poet has painted the cave of 3.3.27–36 with the clarity of a scene from Pompeian frescoes: from its walls hang the orgiastic tympana, tokens of the Muses, a mask of Silenus (a lusty old companion of Bacchus), and the Pan-pipes. Within the cave are the doves of Venus (symbols of Propertius' own literary genre) and the Muses themselves in the act of gathering ivy for the Bacchic *thyrsi*, tuning the lyre, and weaving wreaths of roses (a symbol for poetic activity since Sappho).

The incorporation of Bacchic elements into the poet's cave by Propertius is an indication of the extent to which Dionysus shared Apollo's role as god of poetry in the Hellenistic and Roman traditions.[13] Were Horace and Propertius the first Roman poets to employ the cave image in speaking of their vocation, and to consecrete the poet's cave not only to the Muses, but to the wine god as well? The singers' cave in Virgil's fifth *Eclogue*, hung with vine and grape-clusters, is filled with the *numen* (divine power) of Bacchus. The shepherds choose the shelter of this *numen* for the composition of their songs; the choice is deliberate, and is marked by a procession. Just as Silenus, past master of poetry and foremost among the Bacchic troupe, emerges from his *antrum* in the following *Eclogue* (6.13–15) to sing a song of wonder and delight, so Menalcas and Mopsus enter the Bacchic *antrum* to put their poetic skill to the ultimate test. Before these new poets lies the task of celebrating the most perfect representative of the pastoral world, a shepherd and poet who is, among his other characteristics, a new type of Dionysus.[14] It was no small task: Virgil meant the fifth and central *Eclogue* to be a masterpiece in which the major part of his literary tradition was summoned to create a symbol for all that was beautiful in the bucolic world.

The cave and Plato's plane tree

A unique feature of pastoral is its apparent fluctuation between prose and poetry. *Daphnis and Chloe*, a Greek novel from the beginning of the Christian era, provides the rustic characters and environment of Theocritus and the Greek Anthology, and is full of the sort of symbolism we are accustomed to in Virgil. An example would be the pronouncements of 'Philetas' (whose name is identical with that of the Hellenistic love-elegist) on Love in Book 2.7: 'All flowers are works of Eros, these plants are his poems/creations (*poiemata*). Through him rivers flow, winds blow.' The novel is so obviously a symbolic representation of the creative process in life, that at least one critic has seen a religious significance in *Daphnis and Chloe* to be associated with the Dionysiac mysteries of late antiquity.[15] Four centuries before, a much more 'mystical' author had planned a dialogue in a pastoral milieu, a milieu full of the very symbols which would be used in a later age by bucolic poets. Murley has shown that Plato's *Phaedrus* is indeed a sort of rustic 'literary contest', with Lysias pitted against Socrates, and Phaedrus as judge. Even the prize—a statue at Delphi or at Olympia—is twice playfully promised (235 D, 236 B). The motifs of pastoral are there: rest in the shade at noon, birds and bees, cicadas, dew as the gift of the Muses, hexameters on wolves and lambs, proverbs, etc. The love theme is sustained throughout, from Socrates' erotic banter with Phaedrus to the mythical rape of Nymphs. It is likely, in fact, that the *Phaedrus*, both for its reflection of the rustic mime of Sicily, and for its rejection of the city as a site for true discourse, heavily influenced the shaping of Theocritus' bucolic poetry.[16]

Virgil, too, in selecting a suitable spot for the Daphnis-songs of *Eclogue* 5, was at least indirectly influenced by the *Phaedrus*. Like the choice of the cave in the *Eclogue*, the choice of the plane tree in the dialogue (229 A–B) is deceptively casual, and is made ostensibly for no more reason than that the place offers shade, grass, and a little breeze. Yet, even before the site is reached, it becomes the occasion for the retelling of a myth (the rape of Orithyia by Boreas) and a discussion of myth in general (229 B–230 B). The plane-tree area, upon closer inspection, turns out to contain a running stream, and to be consecrated to Achelous and the Nymphs (230 B–C). In the magnificent dialogue that follows, in which love, beauty, the soul, poets, rhetoric, and literature in general are among the topics discussed, the site of the conversation has not been forgotten. At the close of the dialogue (278 B–C) Socrates refers the truths which have emerged from the discussion to the *numen* of the plane-tree area:

And you (Phaedrus) go tell Lysias that we two, having descended to the stream of the Nymphs and to the Muses' shrine, have heard words which bade us speak to Lysias and anyone who composes arguments, to Homer and anyone who has composed poetry whether to be sung or not, and thirdly to Solon and anyone who in a political dissertation called his compositions laws . . .

Cicero noticed how the significance of Plato's plane tree became apparent only after the actual discourse had begun. The Roman author used this to good effect in *De oratore* 1.7.28:

The track having been traversed two or three times, Scaevola said: 'Why not, Crassus (*cur non Crasse*) follow the example of Socrates in Plato's *Phaedrus*? So your plane tree advises me: it is no less ample for shading this spot with its spreading branches than was the one whose shade Socrates pursued (*non minus ad opacandum hunc locum patulis est diffusa ramis quam illa cuius umbram secuta est Socrates*), a tree which I think grew not so much out of the rivulet (*ipsa acula*) there described, but out of Plato's discussion; and what Socrates did for his well-toughened feet—threw himself down on the grass to speak what philosophers call "words divinely inspired" (*ut se abiceret in herba atque ita quae philosophi divinitus ferunt esse dicta loqueretur*) —seems more than fairly to be conceded to mine (*certe concedi est aequius*)'.

I have indicated in parentheses some words and phrases which might have been ringing in Virgil's ear as he composed the introduction to *Eclogue* 5. Our impression of Ciceronian and Platonic influence is heightened during the 'break' between Daphnis-songs, where Menalcas compares Mopsus' poetry to 'sleep in the grass to the tired' or 'as in the midst of heat a quenching of thirst in leaping brook of water sweet' (*Ecl.* 5.45–7). Finally, the bees and cicadas from the *Phaedrus* recur in verse 77—cicadas this time with Callimachean dew as their nutriment. The lines were written, after all, in praise of a *magister* of song (*Ecl.* 5.48).[17]

The new Daphnis

The place of honour in Virgil's central *Eclogue*, the fifth, is held by a personage who unites in himself all qualities of the ideal shepherd-poet. From Theocritus and Callimachus through the epigrammatists and Meleager, the name of Daphnis arises again and again to typify the essence of the bucolic hero. For Virgil as for the Greeks, Daphnis was the pastoral poet and lover *par excellence*.[18]

Daphnis' traditional beauty is mentioned in the second and in the fifth *Eclogues*. In the former instance, he appears as the standard of comparison whereby the poet-lover Corydon measures his own good looks (2.26f.);[19] In the latter he is called *formosus*, beautiful shepherd of a beautiful flock (5.44). As the ideal beloved, Daphnis appears in the second song of the eighth *Eclogue*. Here again he plays a rôle which he had often assumed in the Greek erotic-epigrammatic tradition, that of the absent lover. He makes himself desirable precisely by disappearing, by awakening a *pothos*, a heart-breaking longing, in his lover.[20] Ostensibly, Virgil's model for the song of Alphesiboeus in *Eclogue* 8 was Theocritus' second *Idyll*, where the absent lover, a city boy, is called 'Delphis'; by changing the name to 'Daphnis', the Roman poet gives the enchantress the best of herdsmen to love. Simultaneously, he swings his 'model' willy-nilly into a pastoral framework; *Idyll* 2 is no bucolic poem, only a city mime.

Like his less perfect fellows in Virgil's bucolic world, Daphnis is a *puer* (3.14 and 5.54). The erotic implications of this word apply most to him, for Daphnis, in his beauty and desirability, comes very close to being the human incarnation of *Amor* himself (also a *puer* in *Ecl*. 8.45–50), of the winged *pais* whose exploits colour the pages of the Greek Anthology.[21] This association may be reflected in the breaking of Daphnis' bow and arrows in the comic-erotic context of *Eclogue* 3.12–15. Eros is an archer in the Greek Anthology—so much so that Meleager threatens to burn his weapons.[22]

The Daphnis of *Eclogue* 5 not only assimilates the characteristics of the Greek Daphnis; he surpasses and transcends them as well. The novelty of Virgil's conception of Daphnis lies in the harvesting of so many ideas from earlier literary, religious, and mythological traditions into a harmonious whole, the incorporation of several disparate elements into a single symbol which embodies all that is significant in the Virgilian bucolic world. Like Theocritus' Daphnis and other shepherds and loved ones of the pastoral-epigrammatic tradition, the Virgilian herdsman is given the opportunity to die, to be mourned, and to find commemoration in nature.[23] His immortality is assured by Menalcas (*Ecl.* 5.51f.) just as immortality for a poet, a loved one, or a ruler is invoked in song in the Greek Anthology.[24] Menalcas, however, exceeds conventional literary bounds; the song which 'elevates Daphnis to the stars' goes on to assign him the attributes and cult of a genuine rustic god. As a bene-factor of agriculture, Daphnis carries on the tradition not only of such seasonal deities as Dionysus and Demeter, with whom he is actually associated in cult (*Ecl.* 5.79f.); as a bringer of peace to the countryside (60f.) he also shares considerable kinship with the tutelary gods of garden and pasture like Pan, Priapus, and Hermes, who speak so often from Hellenistic epigrams.[25]

Virgil's genius has managed to combine the aforementioned elements from older traditions, both literary and religious, into one great shepherd-poet who presides over the bucolic world in its entirety. The world and its hero exceed in majesty and significance all that had been envisioned by pastoral poets before Virgil. Menalcas designates Daphnis' relationship to his successors in poetic endeavour with the words 'Us too loved Daphnis' (5.52). Through this pronouncement, the erotic motif traditionally associated with the figure of Daphnis acquires a more exalted colouring and is blended with the love connected with the art of poetry—the reciprocal love between Muse and poet, the love that inspires the poet to write, and the love with which the reader is filled when he enjoys a beautiful poem.[26] The idea of love which Daphnis here represents has its origins in the Hellenic notion of the poet's calling. Daphnis, as the singers' source of inspiration, stands in the fifth *Eclogue* in the Muse's stead.

With his apotheosis, however, Daphnis' love for his poets is translated into a beneficent love for the entire bucolic world, whose increase and well-being become his concern (60–80). Nature rejoices and finds peace with herself because 'good Daphnis loves tranquillity'. In the song of Menalcas, Daphnis' love assumes proportions which encompass the cosmos. Theocritus himself had given his Daphnis a 'Promethean' cast: the hero of *Idyll* 1, nobler than his persecutors, suffers in contemptuous silence.[27] Virgil brings his hero into an even closer proximity with Prometheus, for he makes him a *benefactor and saviour* within the scope of pastoral, a blessing for men, for herds, and for crops, an adornment (*decus*) to the bucolic world. To formulate the praises of a hero upon whose presence depend salvation and desolation, Virgil reached back to a classical source, the Prometheus dramas of Aeschylus. Verbal parallels in *Eclogue* 5 and in the *Prometheus Bound* and *Pyrkaeus* confirm this, and reinforce Bruno Snell's observation:[28]

He admired and acknowledged the work of Theocritus, he dwelt lovingly on his scenes; but because he read them with the eyes of the new classicistic age, he slowly came back to the classical Greek poetry, with its earnestness, its deep feeling, its drama.

Daphnis as poet

Several critics have suggested that Daphnis' death and apotheosis in Virgil are primarily those of the ideal *poet*.[29] In fact, it would be difficult to insist that Virgil had meant to lay emphasis exclusively on the poet's rôle. The fifth *Eclogue* seeks to glorify Daphnis as the full embodiment of the bucolic ideal. As in the Hellenic tradition, he is characterized primarily as the beautiful shepherd. A direct reference to his traditional rôle as singer (*aoidos* in *Idyll* 5.80) is suppressed until the intermission between the dirge and the apotheosis-song of *Eclogue* 5, when Menalcas proclaims that Mopsus has equalled the *magister* in both instruments and voice. Both Mopsus and Daphnis are called *puer* (49, 54), and Mopsus receives the title of *divine poeta* (45), which foreshadows the divinization of Daphnis. When Menalcas affirms 'Us too loved Daphnis', he expresses confidence in his own ability to sing because of the tutelage of Daphnis; compare 'And me does Phoebus love'

(3.62), where Menalcas derives his inspiration from the leader of the Muses himself.

It is important to realize that the primary concern of the two poets in *Eclogue* 5 is the emulation of the 'master', the achievement of 'Daphnic' song. This fact is hardly surprising; a shepherd who is not at the same time a poet would have no place in Virgil's bucolic world. Daphnis, as the ideal shepherd, is *ipso facto* the ideal poet. An attempt, therefore, to see reflections of the concern with Daphnis' rôle as poet in the two songs of *Eclogue* 5 is quite valid. Marie Desport has pointed the way to such an investigation through her observation that the response of nature to Daphnis' passing and divinization is precisely that evoked by singers throughout the *Bucolics*, above all by Orpheus. Daphnis' power over the Armenian tigers of verse 29 would, in her view, correspond to the power of Orpheus over tigers in *Georgic* 4.510 and in Horace, *Odes* 3. 11.13f., and to the power of the Muse of Damon and Alphesiboeus in *Eclogue* 8.2f. over lynxes. Desport believes, moreover, that the mourning for Daphnis and the proclamation of his divinity on the part of mountains and forests is only a heightening of the response of those natural elements to the *voice of the poet* elsewhere in the *Bucolics*.[30]

Several comments may be made to supplement Mlle Desport's observations. In the first place, it seems highly significant that the first to mourn Daphnis in the *Eclogue* are the Nymphs, who, for Virgil as for the Hellenistic poets, were interchangeable with the Muses.[31] Again, after his apotheosis, Daphnis is worshipped in common with the Nymphs; this might indicate that his power to inspire poets is shared with them.

Daphnis' rôle as founder of Bacchic rites is presented in 5.29–31:

> Daphnis even taught to yoke to chariots
> Armenian tigers, Daphnis introduced the Bacchic troupes,
> showed how to weave the foliage soft 'round pliant wands.

In Hellenistic literature, Dionysus had begun to function as a god of poetry in general, quite beyond his association with the theatre and with the inspirational effects of wine. Thus it is that Callimachus can pray to Dionysus for success in composing

poetry (*Epigram* 8) and can invoke Dionysus, Apollo, and the
Muses together in the same breath (*Iamb.* 1 fr. 191.7f.).[32] This
view of Dionysus found favour among the Romans. Lucretius
uses the thyrsus as a symbol for poetic enthusiasm (1.922ff.);
the same Bacchic wand is designated 'the learned spear' by
Propertius (2.30b.38). The frequent appearance of Bacchus as
god of poets in Horace is discussed at length by Irene Troxler-
Keller. Boyancé suggests that there were actually 'sodalities' of
Roman poets in the Augustan age who had put their literary
careers under the protection or patronage of Bacchus.[33] The
existence of such a group or groups of poets is, of course, highly
conjectural; it is tempting, however, to see a reflection of such
literary institutions in the 'Bacchic troupes' of *Ecl.* 5.30.

The symbolic importance of the thyrsus for Roman poets
might also be alluded to in verse 31, 'to weave the foliage soft
'round pliant wands'. The temptation to see a literary signifi-
cance in this verse is all the greater because of the verb *intexere*.
From the time of Pindar, 'weaving' had symbolized in Greek
literature the composition of poems, and Virgil himself describes
his poetic activity in *Eclogue* 10.71 as 'weaving a mallow basket'
(*gracili fiscellam texit hibisco*).[34]

A Greek source for vv. 29–31 of the fifth *Eclogue* is to be
found in an epigram of Damagetus in praise of Orpheus:[35]

> . . . Who also introduced the mystic rites of Bacchus once,
> and made a verse for yoking to heroic foot.

Again, the introduction of Bacchic cult is attributed to a poet,
as well as the 'yoking of verse to heroic foot', the invention of
epic poetry. The yoking theme recurs in *Ecl.* 5.29. In the case
of the Greek poet, the verses apply to a particular singer,
Orpheus, who was a model for all poets. In Virgil's lines, the
accomplishments of an ideal shepherd-poet, Daphnis, are
enumerated. Did Virgil's veiled language sum up in Daphnis
the qualities and attributes of such model poets as Orpheus?
The 'chariot' and the 'Armenian tigers' might symbolize a
special type or genre of poetic composition—with meaning,
perhaps, only for the Roman 'initiates' within Virgil's circle—
just as the *thiasi* and the *thyrsi* of 5.30f. might allude to literary
institutions or practices comparable, in the poet's mind, to the

rites of Bacchic initiation. Whatever the case, the mention of the establishment of Bacchic ritual would unavoidably bring thoughts of Orpheus, and ultimately of music and poetry, to the mind of anyone familiar with the Greek literary tradition.

A literary significance may also be seen in Daphnis' association with Apollo in the songs of both shepherds. With his death, Apollo leaves the fields (35); after his apotheosis, Daphnis is given a rustic cult in common with Phoebus (66). If Daphnis in the fifth *Eclogue* embodies the ideal poet as well as the ideal shepherd and lover, his close association with Apollo is to be expected, for this deity, the model of perfection for all shepherd-poets in the *Bucolics*, is mentioned elsewhere almost exclusively with reference to poetic activity.[36] The Apollo with whom Daphnis shares the altars in Menalcas' song, moreover, is specialized to conform with the bucolic realm over which Daphnis presides. In this *Eclogue*, he is Apollo of the Fields, the Apollo Nomius of the Greeks, the Apollo, in short, to whom the bucolic Muse is consecrated. This Apollo was in the Greek tradition not simply a custodian of flocks. He was in the divine sphere what Daphnis is at the human level— a shepherd and a singer. The words of Euripides represent him, in fact, as a perfect embodiment of the sort of poet with 'Orphic' powers whom Virgil represents in the *Bucolics* (*Alcestis* 568–85):

> Master's home, ever full of noble hospitality,
> even Pythian Apollo, lyric god, did deign
> to dwell in you,
> endured to be a herdsman on your estates,
> through sloping hillsides
> playing Pan-pipes to your herds,
> shepherds' hymenaeals.
>
> Spotted lynxes ranged for joy of song beside you,
> while, leaving Othrys' glen, the tawny
> band of lions came.
> Around your cithara there danced,
> Phoebus, a dappled
> fawn beyond the high-tressed
> firs, stepping with an ankle light,
> rejoicing in soothing song.

The chorus of the *Alcestis*, having despatched with a few words Apollo's pastoral duties, becomes carried away with the thought of the god's wondrous song which charmed all beasts, both wild and tame. Under the spell of his lyre, the lynxes mingled peacefully with Admetus' flocks, the lions presented no danger, and the deer moved in delighted rhythm to the music of the god. Such wonders are characteristic of the 'golden age' which Virgil envisions in the fourth *Eclogue*; such are the effects of Daphnis himself, the human shepherd-poet, upon the landscape which he has pacified; such is the spell which the singers of Virgil's bucolic world cast upon their surroundings (6.27f.; 8.2f.; 8.71; 10.16).

The passage from the *Alcestis* shows that the image of a divine musician charming the denizens of an idyllic bucolic world was present in Hellenic literary tradition at least as early as the fifth century before Christ; its roots lie deep within a culture which could represent through this myth the age-old religious aura surrounding herdsman and bard; a culture which remembered, dimly, that the functions of both had once been inseparable; a culture that still called 'pasture', 'rule', and 'melody' by the same name, *nomos*. Surely this passage from Euripides' drama, and others like it, served as guidelines for Virgil as he wove the fabric of his bucolic world. It is eminently appropriate that Apollo Nomius, the divine shepherd-musician to whom bucolic song was sacred, should be paired with the divinized shepherd-poet Daphnis.

Just as appropriate, perhaps, to the content of the fifth *Eclogue* are the literary and mythological associations surrounding the figure of Nomius. His relationship with a shepherd who has overcome the tomb and has found his way to a place among the gods seems to reflect the ultimate victory over Thanatos (Death) in Euripides' drama. The verses in which nature proclaims the apotheosis of Daphnis (*Ecl.* 5.63–5),

> The very cliffs resound the songs,
> the very orchards: 'God, he is a god, Menalcas.'
> O be good, propitious to your realm!

bear a remarkable similarity to the celebration of the dead Alcestis by the Euripidean chorus (*Alcestis* 1003–5):

'Now she is a blessed goddess;
hail, O mistress, be propitious.'
Such praises reach her ears.

It is a lesson in Virgil's handling of his sources that *deus deus ille Menalca* is closer, word for word, to Lucretius' *deus ille fuit deus inclute Memmi* (5.8 'God, he was a god, noble Memmius'), an ejaculation of praise for Epicurus, whose atomic theory and ethical system had freed man (in Lucretius' view at least) from fear of death. Yet the Lucretian passage *contrasts* rather than compares with *Ecl.* 5.64. Virgil has employed Lucretian language to reassert the triumph of an ancient religious idea, a god of death and resurrection; this idea is in direct conflict with the materialism of Epicurean science. Virgil's procedure here is typical of his ambivalent attitude toward the author of *De rerum natura*. On the one hand, he greatly admires Lucretius' poetry, and quotes it often. On the other hand, he finds his own world view antithetical to that of the earlier poet. This impasse was to be given final expression in *Georgic* 2.490–4, where the language of Lucretius is again invoked:

> Felix qui potuit rerum cognoscere causas
> atque metus omnis et inexorabile fatum
> subiecit pedibus strepitumque Acherontis avari.
> fortunatus et ille deos qui novit agrestis
> Panaque Silvanumque senem Nymphasque sorores.

> Happy is he who has been able to know the causes of things,
> who has been able to cast all fears and fate's intransigence
> at his feet, and hollow din of greedy Acheron.
> Fortunate, too, is he who knows his rustic gods,
> Pan and old Silvanus and the sister Nymphs.

One of these 'rustic gods', in a moment of superb Virgilian irony, is made to recite a Lucretian/Epicurean cosmogony in *Eclogue* 6.31–40. The singer is old Silenus, the 'granddaddy' of Satyrs, that breed which once Lucretius himself had banished from his 'rational' landscape.[37]

The seventh Eclogue: Daphnis as the touchstone of poetry

It is generally true that the initial verse of each of Virgil's *Eclogues* determines the tone and often the theme for the entire poem. Yet the fact that ' 'Neath holm-oak's rustle Daphnis chanced to have his seat' (7.1) seems irrelevant to what immediately follows, the introduction of the two youths who will compete for the crown of poetic excellence. Quite apart from the first line, it might be asked how Daphnis functions in this *Eclogue* at all. His presence at first sight seems wholly superfluous; Meliboeus' attention could just as well have been caught by the competing singers themselves, without Daphnis' intervention. Why does Virgil devote a full eight lines to a supernumerary who contributes nothing to the progress or to the outcome of the poetry contest?

We have once more to do with the ideal shepherd-poet Daphnis, the erotic figure of *Eclogues* 2, 3, and 8, and the divine figure of 5. The name of Daphnis occupies the place of honour in the first line of the seventh *Eclogue* for a very good reason: the matter at hand has to do with bucolic poetry, of which Daphnis is the *magister*. He represents the genre itself; it is only natural that he take an interest in its development. Meliboeus is witness to the poetry contest and decides in favour of Corydon. But Daphnis presides over the entire *Eclogue*, lending it as it were a higher, more serious significance—as indeed it has, by comparison with the contest in *Eclogue* 3: for out of this *agon* comes something decisive. A judgment is pronounced upon the quality of two poets staging a 'mighty match' (*certamen magnum* 16) to show forth their best work within the confines of pastoral. The mood is far more earnest, the poetry far more serious than what had been presented by the rustic amateurs of the third *Eclogue*.

This interpretation of Daphnis' function in the seventh *Eclogue* is supported by his character and behaviour during the encounter with Meliboeus in 7.7–13. In his commentary to the first line of the poem, Servius remarks:

(The poet) introduces this divine personage, who is in fact the son of Mercury, as we mentioned above. Hence he can say, a little further on, 'Goat and kids are safe', like a divinity.

Servius' comment is not to be lightly dismissed as stemming from the assumption *a priori* that the name 'Daphnis' will refer to the same person throughout the *Bucolics*. The words *quasi divinus*, 'like a divinity', betray a special reaction on the part of the fourth-century scholar to the words of Daphnis *huc ades o Meliboee caper tibi salvus et haedi*—a reaction perhaps akin to that which one feels on hearing such verses in Matthew as 'Give place: for the damsel is not dead, but sleepeth' (ix 24), or 'Arise, and take up thy bed, and go unto thy house' (ix 6).

It is well to observe exactly what happens in the encounter with Daphnis. Meliboeus' goat, the leader of the flock, has gone astray. The shepherd spies Daphnis: the encounter is unexpected. Meliboeus has no opportunity to greet the other. Daphnis addresses him the instant their gazes meet:

> He looks on me in turn and says,
> 'Here quickly, Meliboeus. Goat and kids are safe.'

Not only is the goat safe, but the entire herd as well—though Meliboeus had not yet begun to worry about the *haedi*. Everything that could possibly prevent him from witnessing the poetry contest is set in order by the almost oracular response of Daphnis.[38]

In setting Meliboeus' flock in order, Daphnis is demonstrating powers assigned to him in *Eclogue* 5, powers which he had inherited from Apollo Nomius and from the tutelary deities of the Greek Anthology. The miracle is a modest one, modest enough for Virgil's bucolic world. As in the first and the ninth *Eclogues*, the safety of a rustic shepherd's possessions is involved. But wonder it is none the less. The appearance and response of Daphnis, together with their effects upon the flock of Meliboeus, constitute the epiphany of a *praesens divus* (to quote *Ecl.* 1.41), the manifestation of a 'propitious deity'.

The very words with which the encounter with Daphnis is expressed have a formulaic quality; they suggest similar epiphany-accounts in Greek literary and religious texts. The rescue of Meliboeus' flocks, besides indicating a known quality of the shepherd Daphnis, also reflects traditional notions of the effects of an epiphany. Pfister cites several instances from Greek literature of a miraculous response in animals and other natural creatures to the appearance of a god.[39]

Daphnis' rôle as 'manifest deity' will later be taken by the Roman heroes developed in *Eclogues* 1 and 4. The *iuvenis* of the first poem, who surely represents Octavian, is encountered by Tityrus as a *praesens divus* (1.41); he delivers a *responsum* (44f.) similar in its oracular quality to Daphnis' words in 7.8–13. The epiphany of the *puer* in *Eclogue* 4 occurs amid gods and heroes: he is *praesens inter praesentes* (4.15f.):

> And he will lead the life of gods, and he will see
> heroes mix with gods, and will appear to them himself.

V

The Roman Hero

In a place where a Stone was, hot in the Sun,
I was once a Mage, dry as a Bone,
And calld to me a Demon of myself alone
Who from my Thirst conjured a green River
And out of my Knowledge I saw Thee run,
A Spring of pure Water.

> *I, late at night, facing the page*
> *writing my fancies in a literal age.*

Robert Duncan, 'The Ballad of the Enamord Mage'

The ninth Eclogue

The famous 'Odyssey Landscapes', the Nilotic frieze from the so-called House of Livia, and the paintings from the villa at Boscoreale are roughly contemporary with the *Bucolics* of Virgil.[1] They are among the earliest representatives of a genre of painting which relied on the repetition of several themes for its effect: the atmosphere is invariably dream-like and misty; the human figures, mostly rustic in appearance and few in number, are dwarfed by their natural surroundings, which inevitably include hills and mountain crags, a few gnarled trees, and a body of water. Pasturing herds are a common motif on the land, a boat or two in the water.[2] Finally—and this gives rise to the designation 'sacro-idyllic landscapes'—the wild countryside is frequently interspersed with small monuments of a largely indeterminate religious character—a diminutive temple, a hero's shrine, a tomb, or a votive pillar.

Jachmann showed long ago that the scene of *Eclogue* 9 cannot be laid anywhere near the region of Virgil's 'ancestral farm' in northern Italy, for the place is near a sea (*aequor* 57).[3] The atmosphere is sombre: night is approaching and clouds have gathered (63). Two shepherds meet on a country road

(1, 59); one is driving a herd of goats (6, 62). Along the road
farmers are at work stripping leaves (60f.). In the vicinity—
perhaps within view, if *aquam* (9) refers to the same body of
water as *aequor* (57)—is that section of the countryside which
the shepherds fear lost to the veteran, a landscape of hills
sloping down to the water (7–9) which is bordered by ancient
beech trees with broken tops (9). Finally, a monument appears
in the distance, the tomb of Bianor (59f.).

Taken as a whole, this description might be compared with
any number of sacro-idyllic landscapes from the extant frescoes
in Pompeii. The dark and sombre atmosphere is common to all
such paintings. A representation of Polyphemus and Galatea
in the 'House of the Priest Amandus' shows goats pasturing by
the sea, an old, broken beech tree, and two (?) votive pillars.
In the background stands a small temple, and behind the
temple slopes a hill.[4]

Another 'dream landscape' in Pompeii shows a diminutive,
rustic figure leaning on a shepherd's crook before a tall marble
herm. Behind the herm are a lone evergreen (?) and a pillar,
and in the distance appears a small circular monument sur-
mounted by a human figure. A few cattle graze among the
rocks and shrubs to the left; the foreground is occupied, again,
by a large body of water.[5]

A 'sacred landscape' preserved in the National Museum in
Naples shows four human figures grouped about a circular
Isiac monument by the water. Near the monument stand two
or three gnarled, broken trees. Again, a hill rises in the dis-
tance.[6] The list needs mention, finally, of the more famous
sacro-idyllic landscape illustrated in the frontispiece of this
book, in which cattle pasture on the right while a tiny herdsman
leads a goat over the bridge spanning a wide brook to the left.
Directly in the centre is the familiar gnarled tree, before which
a roofed, open rectangular monument stands. In the back-
ground a few small houses and lonely trees can be seen, behind
which rise the hills.[7]

The foregoing examples should suffice to show that the same
themes preoccupied both Virgil and the painters, and that the
former had usurped the latter's *schemata* in describing the
landscape of *Eclogue* 9. Shepherds and farmers, herds, water,

hills, ancient trees, the monument, even the atmosphere have been depicted with the painter's brush. The topography of the *Eclogue*, then, is non-specific, and does not relate directly to autobiographical circumstances. By laying the scene not in northern Italy, but in the much wider realm of the Italian artist, Virgil has provided a background for the tragedy of *all* Italian smallholders who suffered during the redistribution of land in 41 B.C. to veterans of the civil war. The complaints of the shepherds do not represent Virgil's private concern for the loss of his personal property; the poet's cry is not for justice in his own regard, but for universal justice.

The short plea to Varus for the safety of Mantua comes as an abrupt and unforewarned shattering of the dusky, wholly imaginary atmosphere in which Lycidas and Moeris dwell. In this second Menalcas-song (27–9), the voice of Virgil himself and the shock of Roman reality break through the illusion and disappear just as abruptly, leaving the dream-landscape shaken but intact.[8] The expression of an exclusively personal interest, if there be any, in the redistribution of land is limited to the three lines of this short poem to Varus. The real concern of the poet in *Eclogue* 9 is not so much the fate of the dispossessed herdsmen as the fate of the singer Menalcas, the instrument through which Virgil expresses his fears for the loss of his vocation as poet. As J. Martin has shown, the discrepancies between the reports of Donatus and Probus as to the dates and personages connected with the 'loss of Virgil's farm' (not to mention the discrepancies occurring *within* each account) indicate that most of the details of the affair were reconstructed by these commentators from the *Bucolics* themselves.[9] The ninth *Eclogue* tells us nothing of a personal loss of property; it does tell a great deal, however, of a crisis in the life of an artist.

The songs of Menalcas in *Ecl.* 9.23–5, 27–9, 39–43, and 46–50 are not mere extracts from earlier, unpublished works. The pattern of their appearance in the *Eclogue* is too meaningful, their themes too complete and concise, and their function too vital, to allow for the suggestion that they could exist in any but their present state and context. Critics are generally agreed that they are meant to be a sort of advertisement for the poet's skill and versatility: Virgil shows himself willing and able to compose not only pastoral poetry of the idyllic or erotic sort (23–5, 39–43), but poems in praise of great men and great deeds as well (27–9, 46–50).[10] They function as more than a mere show of skill, however; the short poems flash vividly against the sombre background of the shepherds' desperation. The voices of the poet and of his creatures constitute an interplay which results in the expression of Virgil's deepest fears and hopes for his own contribution to a society in turmoil.

Menalcas, through whose poetry Virgil speaks more directly in the *Eclogue* than through Lycidas or Moeris, has been exposed to some danger during a conflict involving the redistribution of land. It is not a question of property loss: Menalcas' very life was at stake (16). Had he been lost, his poetry would have ceased; this is the concern of his friends, a concern expressed in words which clearly allude to *Eclogue* 5, probably one of 'Menalcas' ' most recent compositions (9.19f.):[11]

> Who would sing the Nymphs, who 'spread the ground with clover',
> who would 'shade the springs' with greenery?

But the atmosphere of dark foreboding is quickly dispelled with a quotation from Menalcas' poetry, through which Virgil shows how thoughts can be led away from the brutality of real events into a peaceful, idyllic world (23–5; the poem is a close approximation of Theocritus, *Idyll* 3.3–5):[12]

> Tityrus, 'til I'm home (the way is short) do feed my nannies;
> bring them, when they're fed, to drink, and while you drive
> don't cross the he-goat's path, his horn is sharp, beware!

The bucolic veil is torn abruptly away in the verses that follow (26–9):

> Or rather what he sang for Varus, not yet finished:
> Varus, your name—let only Mantua survive,
> Mantua, woe! too close to poor Cremona—
> swans in song will bear to starry heights.

These, too, have their purpose. They attempt to show how much the poet has to offer a world to which, in the last analysis, he is in basic opposition; for upon him depends the enduring

fame of the very warrior who disrupts his peace. The depen-
dence is emphasized in the words 'not yet finished': the loss of
the poem would mean the loss of Varus' glory. But the vision of
imperilled Mantua and the poet's self-assertive boast (32f.)
subside in a helpless gesture of doubt (34–6). Virgil, through
Lycidas, expresses the loss of faith in himself brought about by
his confrontation with the brutal world of political reality, in
which there seems no room for a poet of Virgil's mien. This
dejected mood is eradicated by the third poem, which Moeris
introduces as a not *ignobile carmen* (38ff.):

> Come, O Galatea! What's the sport in waves?
> Here Spring wears purple garb, here 'round the streams the
>   ground
> sprays blossoms varicolored, here a poplar looms
> bright against the cave, and pliant vines weave shadows.
> Come. Let waves in madness dash against the shore.

This poem again makes use of a Theocritean theme (*Idyll* 11),
but has managed to capture in five verses all the yearning that
Theocritus' Cyclops needs three score lines to express. Virgil
represents his poetry in the Galatea-song as an accomplished
voice of man's deepest longings, again showing himself to be a
poet whose loss the world can ill afford.

The final work of Menalcas is another poem of praise,
praise of a sort entirely different from that promised to Varus.
Lycidas introduces it as a song he had heard Menalcas (through
Moeris) 'singing alone, on a clear night' (44). This night
signals a great mystery, the mystery of faith expressed in the
Daphnis-verses (46–50):

> Daphnis, why gaze upon old constellations' risings?
> Behold, Dionaean Caesar's star has marked its way,
> a star through which crops might exult in fruitfulness,
> through which the grape might draw its blush on sunny hills.
> Graft the pear trees, Daphnis. Descendants will pick your fruits.

This mystery involves nothing less than the birth of the new
Virgilian hero, or rather the transformation of the old. 'Menal-
cas' had been characterized earlier in the *Eclogue* as the one
who had 'sung the Nymphs', 'spread the ground with clover',
and 'shaded the springs with greenery' (19f.), as the one who

had composed the fifth *Eclogue*, the great Daphnis-poem. Now, Virgil commands his creature Daphnis, who had had his gaze fixed 'upon old constellations' risings' to behold the new star of Caesar. This is Virgil's announcement that his bucolic hero, hitherto a product of older ideas contemplated in isolation from, and perhaps in opposition to, contemporary reality, has found at last a model in the real world. The Virgilian hero is called upon to occupy a world no longer imaginary, no longer determined by the idyllic dreams derived from Hellenic literary forms. Henceforth he will be a Roman hero, and his milieu will be the concrete reality of the Italian countryside, flourishing under the aegis of the new leader in which Virgil places all his hopes at this moment of desperation and decision.[13]

It is impossible to tell exactly what Virgil expected from Octavian, and how Octavian fulfilled his hopes. That Virgil's crisis, however, was a spiritual one, and that it involved doubts as to his ability to continue functioning as a poet in the face of civil turmoil and hard political reality, is expressed beyond doubt in the ninth *Eclogue*. His hopes for the salvation of his vocation through Caesar, indicated in 9.46–50, are found satisfied in the first *Eclogue*. Between hope and fulfilment remains an aura of fear and uncertainty which stills the aged Moeris' voice (51–5). Virgil's minor bucolic heroes resign themselves to silence for the time, and go about their painful task in a submission to fate as stoic as that of the loneliest of heroes, Aeneas (9.66f.):

> No more, boy. Let us do what stands before us now.
> We'll sing songs better then when he himself has come.

While the ninth *Eclogue* represents a turning-point in Virgil's conception of his literary hero, it also contains hints at a change of emphasis in Virgilian themes. As I have shown above, the scene of the poem is laid in a dream landscape of thoroughly Italian origin. There are fewer of the Greek erotic and fantastic elements as we saw them in *Eclogues* 2, 3, 5, and 7, and more of an atmosphere of the Italian countryside. Daphnis' commission, and the world he now beholds (46–50), are no longer bucolic. He is shown contemplating flourishing fields of grain and grapes reddening on hillsides, and is encouraged to begin an activity wholly agricultural, wholly 'georgic'. His association with agriculture is not unknown, of course, from the fifth *Eclogue*, where flourishing and decay of crops are dependent upon his presence; the *Bucolics* themselves are filled with 'georgic' themes not found in Greek pastoral poetry.[14] But the limitation of landscape details in 9.48f. to the exclusively agricultural would seem to be of considerable significance, especially when the short Daphnis-poem is seen as a crucial statement of Virgil's visions and hopes for his poetic future.

The star of Caesar is described as

> astrum quo segetes gauderent frugibus et quo
> duceret apricis in collibus uva colorem.

> 'A star through which crops might exult in fruitfulness,
> through which the grape might draw its blush on sunny hills.'

Under the influence of this very 'star', Virgil later sought to answer the question (*Georgic* 1.1ff.):

> Quid faciat laetas segetes, quo sidere terram
> vertere, Maecenas, ulmisque adiungere vitis
> conveniat . . .

> 'What makes crops joyful, under which sign the time is ripe
> to plough the soil, Maecenas, join the vines to elms . . .'

Again, the rejoicing of crops, again a star, again the culture of the vine. Virgil had portrayed the future in two senses, both of which held the utmost significance for his poetry. Not only does the pastoral hero look to the star as a new model for his own transformation in Roman reality; Virgil has seen a special relationship between the celestial body and agricultural increase, a relationship meaningful for his poetic activity. *Eclogue* 9.46–50 may allude to the first two books of the *Georgics* (on crops and viticulture), which must have begun to occupy Virgil's attention even before the ten *Eclogues* were completed.[15] Daphnis, in short, looks out of his genre to a new landscape, out of the *bona pastoris* to the more real, more meaningful world of the farmer.

Thalysia in reverse

It will be useful to step back at this point, to seek a perspective which affords a view of the ninth *Eclogue* as it functions within the whole collection. Together with *Eclogue* 1, it constitutes as it were a 'frame' for the *Bucolics*. The two poems share one occasion, one referent in the real world—the loss of land— which rings the *Eclogue*-book in and which echoes ominously as the pastoral landscape darkens out.

No special pleading is necessary to convince the reader that the ninth *Eclogue*, in which the word *carmina* occurs no less than seven times, is about poetry, Virgilian poetry.[16] Its very structure makes this plain: the concentric pattern which dominates the entire collection recurs here, slightly (and deliberately?) askew, in the form a b c b a. The introduction and conclusion contain 16 and 17 lines respectively, and surround two pairs of 'Menalcas-songs', which, together with their preludes, total 13 and 14 verses each. The whole poem is then seen to converge on 30–6, the central verses in which the young and desperate Lycidas attempts to proclaim his poetic worth in Theocritean terms:

> And let your swarms avoid the yews of Corsica
> and let your heifers swell their udders, clover-fed.
> Lead on, if song you have. Pierian Muses made
> of me a poet too, I too have songs, the herdsmen
> call me bard as well; I can't believe them, though.
> So far, songs worthy of a Varius or Cinna
> I seem not to sing; I screech, a goose amid shrill swans.

The allusion is to *Idyll* 7.35–41:

> Lead on, then, since we share the road and share the day,
> let's play the herdsmen's game; sure, each will help the other.
> I am a seasoned Muses' mouthpiece, me they all
> call the finest singer. Not so fast do I believe,
> by heaven; so far, I seem no better, to my mind,
> than the worthy Sicelidas from Samos, than Philetas
> as I sing. I vie, a frog against the locusts.

And yet how differently the action in the two poems ensues! 'Simichidas'' optimistic boast is warmly received by Theocritus' Lycidas; reassurance is coupled with the promise of his own rustic staff. The songs begin, and the event of the *Thalysia* is fruitful.[17] Contrast 'Lycidas'' challenge in *Eclogue* 9: it is

ignored. Moeris has been trying to remember another Menal-
cas-song, and finds Lycidas' words merely distracting (*Ecl.*
9.37). The event of the ninth *Eclogue* is doubtful, even dismal.

The poem is based upon the seventh *Idyll*, but reflects it as
negative film reflects a positive print. Its first line proclaims
Eclogue 9 to be a reverse *Thalysia*: 'Whither, Moeris, go your
feet? along the road to town?' The cue was *Idyll* 7.21, 'Simichi-
das, whither do you draw your feet at noon?' Simichidas is on
his way from the city to enjoy a country harvest-feast; Moeris
is *leaving* the country, leaving a scene of deprivation, driving a
flock to the city. The jolly goatherd of the *Thalysia* is called
'Lycidas': he radiates the confidence of an accomplished
pastoral singer. In *Eclogue* 9, 'Lycidas' is a young and tentative
figure, a bit inept and utterly unsure of himself, of his direction.
Like the Lycidas of *Idyll* 7, he recites two bucolic songs, the one
a translation of *Idyll* 3.3–5, the other a Daphnis-song which
corresponds in length to the Daphnis-passage of *Idyll* 7.73–7.
Moeris responds in one instance with a city song, as did
'Simichidas' in the *Thalysia*—but what a contrast with the
urbane jests of Theocritus is the grisly reference to the destruc-
tion of Cremona!

The *Thalysia* recounts the appearance—one is tempted to say
'the epiphany'[18]—of a 'goatherd', Lycidas. It happens in the
magic of midday, when all is still (*Id.* 7.21–3).[19] The travellers
have not yet accomplished half their journey; the familiar
tomb of Brasilas has not appeared (7.10f.). Suddenly 'Lycidas'
is there, and the songs may begin. Such signals occur in the
ninth *Eclogue*, too, but only towards the end of the poem, when
the evening showers threaten; it is too late for poetry. Yet
Lycidas has read the signs aright, and begs Moeris, forlorn, to
let the miracle happen, to reverse the trend of the poem, to
lay down his burden and sing (57–61):

> Now all the sea lies still for you, regard,
> and all the howling gusts of wind have ceased.
> Our journey's reached its midpoint, for the tomb
> of Bianor just appeared. Here, where farmers
> strip and tie the leaves, here, Moeris, let us sing!

The approach of a bucolic wonder is heralded by the first two

lines of this passage; they echo Theocritus' 'Regard, the sea
lies still, the winds lie still' in a magical context, the invocation
of Hecate in *Idyll* 2 (verse 38). One critic has called the Virgilian
stillness 'a hint at something remote, a more than human
silence that seems to anticipate some of the mysterious and
awesome nightfalls of the *Aeneid*'.[20] More specifically, it is the
silence which precedes an epiphany, a wondrous apparition,
a Daphnis, a Menalcas.[21] The journey's midpoint has been
reached and passed; it is high time.

A tomb comes into view: not Brasilas', but Bianor's. Virgil
has deliberately altered the name, turning away from Theo-
critus and towards a grave-epigram in the *Garland* of Meleager.
Diotimus of Adramyttium, a Greek poet of the third century
B.C., had mourned a mother's labour spent in vain: 'For her
unwed Bianor she raised a tomb'.[22] It is difficult to say why
Virgil turned to Diotimus for a name here. An allusion to the
more real and immediate grief of a bereaved mother may have
seemed more appropriate than the dry repetition of Theocritus'
line. More to the point, perhaps, is the fact that a goodly
number of epigrams in the Greek Anthology are attributed to a
'Bianor'. His symbol, the oak leaf, is woven into a new *Garland*
by Philippus sometime in the first century A.D. One of 'Bianor's'
epigrams seems to refer to an earthquake which occurred in
A.D. 17; this would of course make him far too late for a tomb
in *Eclogue* 9. It is just possible, however, that we are dealing
with two 'Bianors' (or more; the name was not uncommon)—
one from Bithynia, for instance, and another a grammarian—
and that the death of one of them might have been fresh in
Virgil's mind.[23] One Bianor has a sensitive regard for horses
and cattle, which would fit well with Virgil's sympathy for
these animals, especially in the third *Georgic*.[24] Is it the same
Bianor who expresses a 'Virgilian' concern for such 'literary'
creatures as cicadas and the dolphins of Arion, and who is
shocked at the destruction by lightning of the tomb of another
poet, Euripides?[25] Or was Virgil inspired, as he composed
Eclogue 3.92f.,

> O, gathering buds and strawberries that grow so low,
> be off, my boys, a chill snake lurks there in the grass,

by the words of a Bianor, 'O hunter, searching among reeds, be off from the bright-eyed snakes'?[26] If so, the landscape of *Eclogue* 9 would hold the grave not of a vague mythical personage, but of a contemporary poet—a poignant expression of the hopelessness with which Virgil viewed his vocation at that time.

Nothing happens, of course. The stillness, the halfway point, the tomb are there, but no singing match ensues, no laughing epiphany—not, at least, in *Eclogue* 9. It was too late for that.

The poem is a *Thalysia* in reverse, the polar opposite of a 'harvest of poetry'.[27] It constitutes a lesson in *imitatio*, in the manner in which at least one Roman poet felt himself free to imitate a Greek forebear. The poem loses its point without the Theocritean model. The 'point', however, was not to show how well a Roman poet could approximate a Greek master, nor even to go one better than Theocritus. Virgil had indeed *used* a Theocritean framework, Theocritean characters, content, and language; but he did not absorb them into his work, he kept the Theocritean elements intact as points of reference and of contrast. The poem leaves us with the impression that Virgil, on equal terms with his Greek model, has engaged in a dialogue with Theocritus in which the frustration assailing the very core of his existence is compared with the security of Theocritus' Coan harvest. As the Greek poet had portrayed himself and his themes in bucolic guise through the seventh *Idyll*, so Virgil availed himself of the Theocritean precedent, introducing his own circumstances, but a different world of circumstances. Reflect upon the eclectic use of source material in the second *Eclogue*, and upon the direct confrontation with pastoral source in the ninth. Quintilian's *dictum* seems to gain new dimensions of meaning: *Neque enim dubitari potest quin artis pars magna contineatur imitatione* (10.2.1), 'For it cannot be doubted that a great part of art is involved with imitation'.

The first Eclogue

The ninth *Eclogue* was an expression of anguish on the part of a poet who had seen his own career, his poetry itself, rendered meaningless by the brutality of civil war (9.11–13):

> But poems,
> Lycidas, of ours prevail among the shafts of Mars
> as Chaonian doves, they say, withstand the eagle's swoop.

Virgil had been brought to the point of losing faith in himself and in the power of his poetry to offer any solace in the face of a universal turmoil which had extended its destructive influence even to the town of his birth: 'Mantua, woe! too close to poor Cremona!' (9.28).[28]

There glimmered through the mournful tone of the ninth *Eclogue*, however, the hope that his poetry might still survive to celebrate a bringer of peace, that he might yet find favour with one who would elevate him, through inspiration and encouragement, to the rôle of a truly Roman poet (*Ecl.* 9.44–50). What Virgil actually experienced between the composition of the ninth and the first *Eclogues* is specified in neither poem; that an immense change, however, had been wrought upon his poetic resources—upon his themes, his images, the situations which his characters encounter, and upon the very nature of his characters—is the eloquent message of the first *Eclogue*. This poem, as Klingner has shown, is a transformation of *Eclogue* 5: in both works, the central figure is a deified hero upon whom the hope of the bucolic world is made to depend. In the fifth *Eclogue* this hero, the embodiment of the best in the pastoral milieu, is contemplated in isolation, in a dream-world of sentiment created by the poet alone. The hero of *Eclogue* 1, on the other hand, is firmly based in Roman reality, a reality which breaks into the poem in the nineteenth verse and remains throughout the work. The way to *Eclogue* 1 was prepared by the Daphnis-poem of *Eclogue* 9. There, for the first time, the bucolic world had been brought face to face with Rome and with its master. The encounter led to the inseparable union of the two worlds in *Eclogue* 1, and to a representation of the new Daphnis in Octavian himself.[29]

The *Eclogue* is a poem of gratitude: the hopes expressed in *Ecl.* 9.46–50 have been fufilled. Tityrus makes his benefactor a god for whom he establishes a private cult (1.7f.). On twelve days of each year, Tityrus' altars will be fat with victims for this young deity (42f.) whose countenance will never be forgotten (63). The hopes which Virgil placed in Octavian had to do principally with the salvation of his vocation as poet; the first *Eclogue* celebrates the fulfilment of these hopes. More important, it goes beyond a mere expression of gratitude, and becomes a significant milestone in Virgil's conception of his own art and of his poetic mission. A discussion of this aspect of the poem must be preceded, however, by a demonstration of the *Eclogue*'s predominant concern with poetry itself.

On obscurity

When a butterfly has to look like a leaf, not only are all the details of a leaf beautifully rendered but markings mimicking grub-bored holes are generously thrown in. 'Natural selection', in the Darwinian sense, could not explain the miraculous coincidence of imitative aspect and imitative behaviour, nor could one appeal to the theory of 'the struggle for life' when a protective device was carried to a point of mimetic subtlety, exuberance, and luxury far in excess of a predator's power of appreciation. I discovered in nature the non-utilitarian delights that I sought in art. Both were a form of magic, both were a game of intricate enchantment and deception.

Nabokov, *Speak, Memory* 6.2

When Greek poets became conscious of the intricacies of their art to the extent of conceiving it as a true *sophia*, a 'special skill', they began to address their works specifically to those who, in the poets' esteem, would fully understand their meaning; in other words, to those whose intellectual superiority could match that of him to whom the Muses themselves had imparted wisdom.[30] Solon was the first to equate the *sophia* of the poet with that of the politician.[31] Pindar, who calls poets *sophoi*, 'wise', asserts the exclusive nature of this wisdom by pointing out that the mass of men do not understand him as he 'speaks to those who know; as for the crowd, it needs interpreters. Wise is he who knows much by nature.'[32] Bacchylides too, who like Pindar sees himself as a 'divine prophet' of the Muses[33] and a *sophos*,[34] insists, again, that his words will be a riddle to all but the wise: 'I sing what the wise man understands.'[35]

The poet's consciousness of his tendency toward obscurity, of a real need for hermeneutic analysis of his work, seems to indicate little else than an awareness of the nature of poetry itself, the very stuff of which consists in complex images and ambiguous meanings. A conscious exaggeration of these aspects of poetry results occasionally from a need on the part of young poets to make a clean break with what they judge to be out-worn traditions.[36] Obscurity is a symptom of Hellenistic poetry; obscure subjects, words, names, metres, and myths were sought eagerly at the behest of the Muse of Callimachus and Euphorion, to name only two of the more influential poets who rejected all attempts to rival Homer. Lycophron's *Alexandra* is an extreme example of this sort of *sophia*.[37]

Virgil, through the Neoteric movement, is heir to the Hellenistic tradition. Like Catullus, he is not averse to an occasional eccentricity of vocabulary or nomenclature.[38] Nor does he abstain from the more banal manifestations of the obscurantist tendency, as the riddles of *Ecl.* 3.104–7 show. In the realm of myth, he has praise for poets who unearth the most recondite sagas (Gallus' 'Grynean Grove', for example, in *Ecl.* 6.72f.). Conscious ambiguity extends to the major themes of the *Bucolics*, to the identity of the *puer* in 4, of the *iuvenis* in 1, and of the *victor* in 8.6–13. The reason for Corydon's poetic victory in 7 was meant, apparently, to be the subject for eternal speculation. The function of Menalcas in a situation which reflects real historical events is far from being spelled out with clarity in the ninth *Eclogue*.

Virgil avoids, furthermore, a specific reference to his poems and poetic activity in the *Bucolics*. 'I shall write pastoral poetry' is expressed symbolically: 'I shall rehearse the rustic Muse with slender reed' (*Ecl.* 6.8). In the same piece, his own poems are referred to as 'our tamarisks' (10), an expression repeated in *Ecl.* 4.2f., along with *silvae*, another metaphor for poetry. 'Menalcas'' composition of *Eclogues* 2, 3, and 5 is expressed not by naming, but by *citing* those poems (5.86f., 9.19f.).[39] Finally, Virgil characterizes his poetic endeavours at the close of the *Bucolics* as 'weaving a mallow basket' (10.71), which has, at first sight, nothing to do with writing poetry; but he assumed that this image borrowed from the Greek tradition was well known to his circle as a symbol for poetic activity.[40]

Several critics have discussed Virgil's tendency toward obscurity with special reference to the *Bucolics*. Wimmel has designated it in negative terms, calling it an absence of 'the refreshing sharpness of directness', a renunciation of 'the concrete' justified by Virgil's 'Callimachean' stylistic convictions.[41] Klingner has judged it to be a peculiarity of Virgil himself to require the sustenance of ambiguity throughout the *Bucolics*.[42] Jackson Knight borrows Keats' term, 'negative capability', to designate obscurity in Virgil, and pronounces it one of the hallmarks of his 'secret art'.[43] Most satisfying of all, perhaps, is Rohde's praise of obscurity in the *Bucolics*:[44]

But that is in keeping with the character of these compositions, which are the most carefully and tenderly constructed in all of Latin poetry. Such is their quality, that much is only hinted at; in certain passages something that seems to have intelligible meaning will appear, but then disappear again with the next line. A web of relationships and references spreads itself as thin as air over the whole book, but this web is so fragile that it threatens to tear with the first touch of the interpreter's hand. Many a verse undoubtedly has an ambivalence of meaning, but at the very moment when we imagine the ambivalence to be in our grasp, it eludes us again, as if the process of interpretation had bewitched it.

We are invited, then, to embrace rather than to endure obscurity in the *Bucolics*, to appreciate it as an aspect of ancient aesthetics. The Neoteric school did exaggerate the tendency, however, and we admit that we are unable to take the same delight in the obscure while reading the *Bucolics* as Virgil took while writing them. On the other hand, obscurity in poetry is a two-way street; what is dark invites illumination; and every poet wants the reader to interpret his work. Some of the obscurity in *Eclogue* 1, for instance, may be alleviated through attention to its 'mate', *Eclogue* 9, and through an interpretation of its imagery in terms of the literary tradition to which Virgil was a conscious heir.

Tityrus as poet

The contrast between the conditions of Tityrus[45] and of Meliboeus is emphasized in the poem's first lines. The one reclines under a beech, plays his pipe, and sings of 'the beauteous Amaryllis'; the other wanders into exile. Meliboeus is struck, not by Tityrus' retention of his land, but by the pursuit of his artistic inclinations. Tityrus confirms Meliboeus' emphasis on musical pursuits: while his cattle wander, he is permitted to *play what he likes on the rustic pipe* (6–10). This leisure, this freedom in composing pastoral poetry, is what is meant by *libertas* in verse 27, according to Martin, whose interpretation seems fully in keeping with the context: what Meliboeus admires without envy is Tityrus' *otia*, by virtue of which he is free 'to play with rustic reed my heart's desire'; and Tityrus explains his journey to Rome precisely as a quest for *freedom*.[46]

One aspect of Tityrus' *servitium* (40) had to be eliminated before he could think of *libertas*. This was his enslavement to Galatea (31f.):

> I'll confess, as long as Galatea held me fast,
> I had no hope of freedom, no impulse to purchase it.

Galatea is a figure from Theocritean pastoral who plays her traditional coquettish rôle in most of the *Eclogues* composed before the first. She is Damoetas' lover in 3.64 and 3.72; in 7.37 she is Corydon's reluctant beloved; and she reverts to her Theocritean rôle in 9.39, where she plays the scornful Nymph whom the Cyclops loves. Her name is present in none of the *Eclogues* composed after the first. The reason for her frequent appearance in the earlier *Eclogues*, and for her total absence from the later poems, can be found in the sort of subject-matter which she traditionally represents.

For Virgil, as for Theocritus, Galatea typified the erotic motif in pastoral poetry.[47] He had incorporated her into all the earlier *Eclogues* which contain heterosexual love themes (3, 7, and 9) to effect that juxtaposition of erotic and pastoral which had become typical for Greek bucolic poetry. In the fifth *Eclogue*, however, Virgil began to move away from such conventional themes; his shepherd Daphnis stepped out of the pastoral world into the depths of the cosmos. There was no place in this poem for a Galatea. A new note had been sounded within the bucolic genre; it now accommodated themes more elevated and more universal than ever before. The fifth *Eclogue* signals the poet's realization of his own potential and his true interests. Galatea, on the other hand, represents the sort of sentimental, romantic eroticism which Virgil came to find less and less fitting for his artistic temperament. It is the 'bondage', then, of Galatea, of superficially emotional Theocritean love motifs, from which 'Tityrus' had freed himself before seeking the far-reaching *libertas* at Rome.[48]

His absence at Rome is lamented by Amaryllis, and even by his pines, springs, and orchards (36–9). Marie Desport suggests that this is the longing of Virgil's themes for their poet, the bucolic themes which the poet teaches to 'sing'. As with the orchard, the grove, and the 'talking' pines of Arcadian Maenalus which echo the shepherds' *amores* (*Ecl.* 8.22–4), nature is shown again calling for the *poet* who gives her a voice.[49] It is, in fact, the whole pastoral genre which calls Tityrus back. He returns to it, but returns a 'free man', free to pick his themes, free from the 'servitude' of mawkish love motifs.

The words of the oracle (Ecl. 1.45)

The encounter with the *iuvenis* at Rome is represented in the formulaic language of a reported epiphany. He is a *praesens divus* (41) as well as a 'manifest god' whom a mortal beholds face to face: *hic illum vidi* (42).[50] His words, which occupy a complete hexameter verse, have the character of an oracle (*responsum*) and, like all oracles, require interpretation:

PASCITE UT ANTE BOVES PUERI, SUMMITTITE TAUROS

Not a few scholars have recognized the symbolic import of this line. It is, in fact, a convention in Roman literature to allude to a genre through its content.[51] Virgil does it elsewhere in the *Bucolics* in a similarly oracular response, that of Cynthian Apollo (6.4f.):

'A herdsman, Tityrus, ought to fatten
sheep, and hold the song he sings to subtle strains'.

With these words, Apollo bids the poet to observe the standards of the 'slender style' (*genus tenue*) within his own genre, the pastoral. In the seventy-eight lines of his first poem, Tibullus announces the genre in which he intends to compose by portraying himself actually dwelling in a rustic milieu together with his Delia. Propertius refers to Virgil's composition of the *Aeneid* by proclaiming, 'He rouses now the arms of Trojan Aeneas, the ramparts raised on Lavinian shores' (2.34.63f.).

The words of the oracle in *Eclogue* 1 mean 'Continue to compose pastoral poetry'. This is no daring suggestion, and has occurred to many a critic. The symbolic interpretation accords well with the theme of the entire *Eclogue*, a poem of gratitude for the preservation of a poetic vocation. It is well to note that the oracle addresses itself to *pueri*, though Tityrus himself is an old man (28, 46). The word applies, of course, not only to Tityrus, but to all the characters of Virgil's bucolic world, and ultimately to Virgil himself; for the *puer* is part and parcel of Virgilian pastoral poetry.

Thalysia revisited

I confess I do not believe in time. I like to fold my magic carpet, after use, in such a way as to superimpose one part of the pattern upon another. Let visitors trip. And the highest enjoyment of timelessness—in a landscape selected at random—is when I stand among rare butterflies and their food plants. This is ecstasy, and behind the ecstasy is something else, which is hard to explain. It is like a momentary vacuum into which rushes all that I love. A sense of oneness with sun and stone. A thrill of gratitude to whom it may concern—to the contrapuntal genius of human fate or to tender ghosts humoring a lucky mortal.

Nabokov, *Speak, Memory* 6.6

The epiphany promised in *Eclogue* 9 has materialized here. A god appeared to Tityrus: 'Lucky old man! And so the land will remain your land' (46). Meliboeus proceeds to describe the *rura* of Tityrus (46–58), and we find ourselves with the *Thalysia* once more. It is a sparse *Thalysia*: 'Barren rocks encroach, and all the pasture's overgrown with rushes from the marsh'; but the vestigial outlines of Phrasidamus' farm are there—rest in the shade, the sacred water, the bees, and the turtle dove (*Idyll* 7.131–57: see above, p. 23). Lawall and others have interpreted Virgil's Greek model for this passage symbolically; so much the more do the Virgilian lines invite interpretation.

Pöschl, in comparing the two passages, emphasizes formal differences. In Theocritus, an atmosphere of heady opulence prevails; in Virgil, Tityrus' few comforts stand out against the barrenness of his pasturage. The *Eclogue* devotes two lines to coolness, shade, and water (51f.), while the remaining six are occupied with the sounds of *music* both human and natural (53–8). Virgil does not strive for the realism of Theocritus, who includes all sounds, sights, smells, and tastes that delight the senses, who aims at heightening the intoxication of his audience. Virgil allows his landscape-description to culminate in a musical meditation; at the end, only the ear is pleased. Pöschl calls attention to the attempt in 53–8 to imitate through alliteration the actual sounds described, as in the repetition of sibilants for the buzzing of bees in 55, or the predominance of 'u'-vowels for the cooing of doves in 57f. Occupying a central position between the sounds of bees and birds is the striking line in which the voice of man, of the *frondator*, is heard.[52]

This *schema*, the juxtaposition of human and natural music, is far more than a pleasant but basically accidental combination of themes. It represents Virgil's commitment to his own *agrestis Musa*, that Muse of the Italian countryside whose character is so different from that of the Greek *boukolikai Moisai*.[53] The genesis of Virgilian pastoral song through a concord of human and natural voices and resonances is stressed throughout the *Bucolics*. Corydon sings to mountains and woods (2.5), and is accompanied by cicadas (2.13); the woods follow Orpheus' song (3.46); the poet himself 'sings the forests' (4.3); the land of Arcadia becomes a judge of poets (4.58f.); a tamarisk grove is made to sing (6.10f.); a river hears songs from Phoebus and teaches them to laurels, and valleys sing them to the stars (6.82–4); Mount Maenalus and its forest groves hear and repeat the loves of shepherds (8.21–3); and woods reply to Virgil's song (10.8). The sparse countryside of Tityrus, who teaches woods to sing his love (1.5), is naturally a source of pastoral music.

Some features of this countryside lend themselves to a more symbolic interpretation. Martin has already suggested that *insueta pabula* (49), 'strange fodder', refers to poetry which would be alien to Virgilian pastoral; and that *mala contagia*

(50), 'foul contagion', is the envious competition which poets of the 'slender style' ward off by obeying Callimachean canons.[54] It should be understood at the outset that these suggestions, however pleasant, are pure speculation; but it will do no harm to speculate a little further. The interpretation of individual verses stands or falls, ultimately, with the meaning each reader assigns to the entire poem. If the first *Eclogue* is not about poetry, then the search for symbolic references to literary activity in verses 46–58 is a misguided one. *Pergite Pierides*.

An antithesis to the *insueta pabula* may be found in the *flumina nota*, 'the streams you know', in verse 51. Callimachus had used the image of a strange river (the Orontes) to connote the sort of poetry he wished to avoid (*Hymn* 2.108f.):

> Great is the torrent of the Assyrian stream, but most of the
> filth of the earth and much of the refuse it drags on its wave.

The opposite of this 'Assyrian stream' can be understood under *flumina nota*, the streams of inspiration which are familiar, are 'known' to that genre in which Virgil has already shown proficiency.[55]

The Callimachean water image is sustained in *fontis sacros*, 'the holy springs', and continues to parallel Callimachus' sequence of symbols for the 'slender' style in *Hymn* 2 (110–12):

> Not from every place to Deo do the bees bear water—
> just the pure and unspoiled little drop that oozes
> from the sacred spring, the very finest of the fine.

In the *Thalysia*, the rustic setting contains 'sacred water' (*Id.* 7.136), but the water's holiness is explained by the fact that it flows 'from the Nymphs' cave'. In the *Eclogue*, on the other hand, the adjective *sacros* has no apparent explanation. It is an epithet not of *aquas* (as it might have been if Virgil really wanted to echo Theocritus), but of *fontis*. It seems likely that the *sacri fontes*, which are irrelevant if the passage be taken as a mere landscape description, constitute a literary allusion to the 'sacred spring' from which Callimachus, the 'bee-poet', drew his inspiration.[56]

Callimachus is not the only poet whose spring-symbol would

have been evoked by the words *fontis sacros*. Among the Greeks, the association of poets and springs was a literary convention both before and after Callimachus. Pindar had drunk from the spring of Thebe for his inspiration (*Olympian* 6.84–7); the image is to be traced ultimately to the practice of seers who drank from a sacred spring before delivering their prophecy.[57] In the epigrammatic tradition, poets modelled their accounts of Hesiod's calling to the Muses' service upon the Callimachean version, in which Hesiod is made to drink from Hippocrene.[58] The image found its way into pastoral as well, for the poet of the *Epitaph for Bion* represents Homer drinking from the 'springs of Pegasus', while Bion takes a 'draught of Arethusa' (77).

First among the Roman poets to avail himself of Hellenic precedent was Ennius, who imagined himself 're-opening springs' of poetic inspiration.[59] Lucretius 'approached and drank' from *integri fontes*, 'unopened springs' (1.927f. = 4.2f.). Finally, Virgil himself shows exactly what 'sacred springs' meant to him in *Georgic* 2.175, where, in symbolizing his own poetic endeavours, he makes use of the image after Ennius' fashion:

> tibi res antiquae laudis et artis
> ingredior sanctos ausus recludere fontis
>
> 'I embark for you upon the subjects praised of old, upon ancient
>   skill,
> and dare disclose the sacred springs.'

Nor did the use of the symbol cease with Virgil. Horace, probably inspired by Lucretius, addresses his Muse as 'You who rejoice in unopened springs' (*Odes* 1.26.6f.); Propertius imagines himself attempting to drink from Ennius' *fontes* (3.3.5f.), and designates his poetic activity with the words (3.1.3f.):

> primus ego ingredior puro de fonte sacerdos
>   Itala per Graios orgia ferre choros.

Among his *fontes sacri*, then, Tityrus will 'seek the shaded cool'. This *frigus opacum* may be equivalent to the *umbra* which the Roman poets associated with the composition of poetry, and which Virgil uses at least once as a symbol for pastoral poetry itself (*Ecl.* 10.75). It is the shade of the poet's grove, of the cave of inspiration, of the tree which blesses the shepherd's song (1.4f.):

> tu Tityre lentus in umbra
> formosam resonare doces Amaryllida silvas.

A specific allusion to Virgil's literary forebears may be found in verses 53–5:

> From here, beyond the fence, on that near boundary,
> the willow grove whose flowers ever pasture Hybla's bees
> will often beckon you to sleep with gentle hum.

The 'enclosure' does not belong to Tityrus; it is located *vicino ab limite*, and contains a willow grove, which Tityrus' barren pasture land, covered with bedrock and bulrushes, could not support. To Tityrus' lot falls the *benefit* of the grove—the sound, that is, of its bees—but the grove is not part of his *rura*. The bees are 'Hyblaean'—that is, 'Sicilian'; their homeland is Sicily, birthplace of the bucolic Muse.

Sicilian bees are clearly out of place in this *Eclogue*, unless their presence constitutes another symbol. The poem's atmosphere, orientation, and milieu are otherwise Roman. Perhaps Virgil had intended to symbolize in 'Hyblaean bees' the inspirations from Greek bucolic poetry which determine 'Tityrus' ' proper genre. The use of the bee-symbol, long associated with the poet in Greek literary tradition, is the key to this interpretation.[60] If the symbolism is there, Virgil has continued his dependence upon the imagery of Callimachus, *Hymn* 2.105–13, who also saw in the bee an analogy to the poet (110).

Otto Skutsch, who showed that the words *tua cura, palumbes* (57), 'ring doves, your concern', echo one of Cornelius Gallus' love elegies, may have provided another key to interpretation. He compares *Ecl.* 10.22 (designating Gallus' amorous preoccupations as *tua cura, Lycoris*) with a line from Gallus' successor in love elegy, Propertius. This poet, representing symbolically the themes of his poetry in the Muses' cave of 3.3.27–36, designated erotic motifs with the words *Veneris dominae volucres, mea turba, columbae* (31), 'my throng, swift doves of mistress

Venus'. Both Virgil and Propertius, maintains Skutsch, are alluding to a line from Gallus in which he must have represented his amorous commitments as *mea cura, columbae,* 'my concern, the doves (of the love goddess)'. *Cura* makes little sense in *Ecl.* 1.57 except as a reference, through the symbolic language of Gallus, to a specifically *amorous* note amid the pastoral music of Tityrus' landscape. How else could the ring doves be a 'concern' to him?[61]

It is refreshing to retreat from such details (after indicating at least the plausibility of their symbolic function) and to review the relationship of the first *Eclogue* to the *liber bucolicorum.* It introduces the *Bucolics,* it sets the tone for Virgilian pastoral; it incorporates in itself both the dark and the light (the fates of Meliboeus and Tityrus). Together with *Eclogue* 9, it frames the *Eclogue*-book (10 stands apart), it imparts to it its initial structure. These two poems surround the *Bucolics* with a problematic 'web of relationships' whose *nexus* is the *Thalysia,* the 'first-fruits festival' which was programmatic for Theocritus' career as a poet. *Eclogue* 9 was a reverse *Thalysia,* a *Thalysia* that failed. The epiphany was announced, but never came; the festival was never held. The later poem gives us our epiphany (the *iuvenis*) and our farm (1.46–58), though the god has only one line to recite, an ambiguous line ('Pasture, my children, your cows as before, and let there be bulls'), and there are no picnic baskets, no wine jars to cheer us on Tityrus' bleak estate. Yet the later poem stands, optimistically, at the head of the collection. Virgil will continue to write poetry, but a new sort of poetry. The bucolic world has changed its texture. *Eclogue* 1 marks the silence of the Neoteric artist and the emergence of a Roman poet, a poet whose creative activity will from now on be linked with the fate of his people. Beyond all its significance for the poet's own vocation, the first *Eclogue* gives full vent to a complaint which was never uttered in the ninth, a complaint which echoes in the mind long after all thoughts of poetry have subsided (70–3):

> These best-tilled furrows a soldier, hands defiled, will hold,
> these crops a foreigner. See the grief to which we're led
> by civil strife: for such as these we've sowed the fields!
> Now, Meliboeus, graft the pear trees, set your vines in order!

A Hero for the Future

Have you a gold cup
dedicated to thought
that is like clear water
held in a flower?

or sheen of the gold
burnishd on wood
to furnish fire-glow
a burning in sight only?

color of gold, feel of gold
weight of gold? Does the old alchemist
speak in metaphor
of a spiritual splendor?
                            Robert Duncan, 'The Question'

The messianic Eclogue

For almost three decades of this century, academic opinion on
Virgil's fourth *Eclogue* was dominated by a largely German
school of thought inspired by the work of Eduard Norden.[1]
This scholar had suggested that the search for a human child to
identify with Virgil's *puer* be abandoned. Virgil, according to
Norden, had drawn upon a Sibylline oracle to formulate the
essence and attributes of the *puer*. The prophecy had its roots
in the Orient, and ultimately in Egyptian lore concerning
what the Greeks called *Aion*, an anthropomorphic symbol of
astronomical change and renewal in nature. It was not only
Virgil, moreover, who was influenced by this almost pre-
historic doctrine of temporal (yearly or seasonal) renewal. The
entire ancient near eastern world had founded its religious
precepts around the Aion principle; the New Testament itself
shows marked conformity to it in its adjustment of dates,
formulation of events, and so forth. Norden contended that
those like Eusebius and Augustine who saw the fourth *Eclogue*

as a 'pagan prophecy' of the Messiah's coming were closer to the truth than those who tried to link the *puer* with historical personages at Rome; for Virgil had been exposed, through the Sibylline Books, to the same source which inspired the Evangelists to see a fulfilment of their own religious traditions in Jesus.

The complexities of Norden's ingenious construction held the world of classical philology spellbound for years. Until recently, critics tended to accept it as a firm basis for their own observations on the *Eclogue*. The superstructure of Norden's edifice was extensive and dazzling enough to obscure the most serious fault in the foundation, the unproved assumptions that the Sibylline books had contained a world-renowed prophecy which referred specifically to the year 40 B.C., and that the fourth *Eclogue* is a fairly close reproduction of this very oracle. If it had ever existed, the original Sibylline prophecy would have been burned in 12 B.C. by Augustus, along with other oracles which history had proven to be false; but Norden contented himself with the assumption that the original resembled in content an older Sibylline prophecy (still extant today) which predicts, as does the Virgilian poem, the coming of a heavenly saviour who will rule the world.[2] Norden's work leaves one with the impression that the fourth poem of the *Eclogue*-book, unlike its companions, is less Roman than oriental, less Virgilian than Sibylline. The German scholar even managed to pick out what he considered to be rare examples in the *Eclogue* of Virgilian originality—the cradle of flowers, the sheep with coloured wool, the laughing infant, the banquet with gods and wedlock with a goddess; coincidentally, these 'Virgilian touches' are precisely those elements which Norden could not explain in terms of his Aion-hypothesis.[3]

Norden's applecart, already overloaded and heaped with the supplementary fruits of a whole generation of followers, was upset in 1952 by a fresh wind from Pisa. There, in a lecture before the *Scuola normale superiore*, Günther Jachmann took the 'messianic' *Eclogue* away from the *orientalische Vorstellungswelt* and gave it back to Virgil and the Greco-Roman literary tradition. He posed a simple question: if 'the Sibylline oracle for 40 B.C.' were known to the whole world, why is there no mention of it in ancient sources, and why did not a trace of it survive?[4] Jachmann concluded that there is nothing in the poem's content to suggest that the Roman poet went further afield than his own literary tradition for the characteristics of that age which the *puer*'s birth was to herald. Not in Chaldean astrology, nor in Egyptian cult, nor in the Etruscan lore of the 'great year', nor even in the philosophical doctrines of *ekpyrosis*, *palingenesia*, *anakyklosis*, and *apokatastasis*, is the source for Virgil's new age to be found, but rather in the didactic poems of the Greeks, especially those of Hesiod and Aratus. Virgil had not copied a specific Sibylline oracle, but had merely given his poem the general character of a *Cumaeum carmen* in order to cast himself in a prophetic rôle. Norden's belief in the similarities shared by *Orac. Sibyll.* 3 and *Eclogue* 4 rested upon a simple misunderstanding of the Greek.[5]

Turning to the *puer*, Jachmann showed the impossibility of making him a symbol of some eternal principle, of identifying him with Aion or with the *aurea saecla*: the growth and deeds of the *puer* do not take place in the vague timelessness of a divine creature's existence, but in the lifetime of a normal man, of Virgil the poet (*Ecl.* 4.53f.):[6]

> O then may there remain to me a final part
> of life long lived, and breath enough to tell your deeds.

This observation led Jachmann to the conclusion that the *puer* was a human child—the offspring, in fact, of the leading political figure of the time, Octavian, and of his wife Scribonia.[7]

Jachmann's opponents seem particularly disturbed by the audacity of his remark that the fourth *Eclogue* is unsuccessful as a work of art, that the poem has been highly overrated by those who fail to see its lack of consistency and balance. He argues against the view that there is a gradual progression back to the Golden Age which parallels the different stages of the *puer*'s growth in vv. 18–45. How can this be, asks Jachmann, when at the *puer*'s birth the Golden Age exists in full bloom (18–25)? The 'hero passage' (31–6) represents not a development towards, but a regression from the Golden Age.[8] In his eagerness to insert a 'heroic' age for the *puer* (inspired, perhaps, by Hesiod, *Works and Days* 156–73), Virgil has irrevocably destroyed all attempted synchronism in the parallel development of an *aurea aetas* and of the *puer*. The poet should have realized that the Golden Age, which appeared simultaneously with the *puer*, could not be made to develop at all, once it had come.[9]

Another major 'inconsistency' in the fourth *Eclogue* was noticed by E. Pfeiffer: Virgil expresses in 53f. a longing to relate the *puer*'s 'deeds'. What need is there of *facta* on the part of a personage *for whom* the Golden Age flourishes and who never *does* anything of himself? The *puer* is not an efficient cause of the *aurea aetas*; his appearance is merely a visible sign of its coming-to-be. He is himself the presiding regent of a world which has already been pacified for and before him (17). Since 'deeds' are no longer necessary in the Golden Age, the poet seems once more to contradict himself.[10]

Pollio

The fourth *Eclogue* is addressed to C. Asinius Pollio, under whose consulate the miracle of the age was to occur. The poem cannot therefore have been written after 40 B.C., the year of his consulship. It is generally assumed, moreover, that 4.11–14 imply that the *Eclogue* was composed to celebrate some event with which Pollio was connected in his consular capacity, and which afforded Virgil the inspiration for a poem expressing joyful hope.[11] This event is usually supposed to be one of two: either (a) the installation of Pollio himself as consul in January of 40 B C., or (b) the Peace of Brundisium, which Pollio, as intermediary between Antony and Octavian, helped to bring about in the fall of 40.

The first possibility must be eliminated. The triumphant hope with which Virgil announces the approach of a new Golden Age could hardly have been expressed in December of 41, when the clouds of strife were still thick over Italy. The Perusian War was not yet over, and would not end until February of 40, the month *after* Pollio's accession to the consulate.[12] On the other hand, the second possibility is equally unlikely. If Virgil were commemorating the Peace of Brundisium, signed in autumn of 40, the expressions 'with you as consul' and 'with you as leader' in reference to 'the great months' forward movement' would have been not only awkward but downright embarrassing; Pollio, if he had ever actually been at Rome to assume the consular insignia, resigned at any rate immediately after the Peace had been signed. Cornelius Balbus and Canidius Crassus were appointed to finish out the consular year, while Pollio retired to Macedonia.[13] If the *Eclogue* refers neither to Pollio's installation as consul nor to the Peace of Brundisium, then two crucial questions remain to be answered: (1) why does Virgil predict the *puer*'s birth and the coming of a new age for the year of Pollio's consulate, and (2) why does Pollio's name occur in the poem at all? The answers are to be found not in historical documents for the year 40, but in the *Bucolics* themselves, which are the only source for the nature of Virgil's relationship with Pollio.

H. W. Garrod was the first to notice that the third and the fourth *Eclogues*, both of which contain references to Pollio, have many themes in common. In both, attention is called to a ram's wool (3.95, 4.43f.) and to a dreaded serpent (3.93, 4.24); in both there is mention of honey (3.89, 4.30), of the rare and fragrant *amomum* (3.89, 4.25), and of flowers (3.92, 4.20, 23). Garrod concluded that these subjects represented themes which Pollio had included in his own poetry, and which Virgil cited in both *Eclogues* as a compliment to his friend.[14] Hubaux, on the other hand, suggested that they represented literary images or subjects in which Virgil and Pollio had shared considerable interest; writing in the 'Norden era', he decided that these subjects were oriental, perhaps themes from the Jewish scriptures.[15]

It was Marie Desport who pointed out that not only the third and the fourth, but the eighth *Eclogue* as well—*all* the poems, in short, in which the figure of Pollio is recalled—show preoccupations with a theme which finds its culmination in the fourth *Eclogue*, the theme of the Golden Age. As 4 presents the blooming of *amomum* and the flowing of honey as symptoms of the Golden Age (4.25, 30), so the same symptoms appear for Pollio's lover in 3.88f.:

> Who loves you, Pollio, may he come where you too, make him glad,
> may honey flow for him, harsh brambles bear amomum's spice.

As wild lions are tamed and no longer molest flocks in 4.22, so *Ecl.* 8.27f. shows the timid deer drinking in the company of hunting dogs 'in the age to come', and Damon bids the wolf flee the sheep (8.52).[16] Furthermore, the serpent motif from 3.93 and 4.24 recurs in 8.71, where the 'chill snake' is once more destroyed, destroyed by the power of song.

It should also be noticed that references to gold appear only in *Eclogues* 3, 4, and 8. In 4 the reference is of course to the *gens aurea* (4.9); in 3 and 8 we encounter 'golden apples' (3.71 and 8.52f.). The *aurea mala* of *Eclogue* 3 are cited in *Eclogue* 8 in a context which has great significance for the literary interests of Virgil and Pollio (8.52–6):

> On his own accord now let the wolf flee sheep, hard oaks
> bear golden apples, alder show narcissus' bloom;
> let tamarisks exude thick amber from their bark,
> let owls compete with swans, let Tityrus Orpheus be,
> Orpheus in the woods, Arion in dolphins' midst.

The passage contains allusions to themes which had appeared in the two previous 'Pollio-poems'. The phenomena appear in the guise of *adynata* (grand impossibilities meant to lend a pseudo-epic bathos to the herdsman's complaint);[17] but the 'Golden Age' manifestations obviously recall the wonders appearing in the *puer*'s infancy in *Eclogue* 4.18–30. As in the 'messianic' *Eclogue*, predatory beasts lose their wildness and nature produces wondrous fruits and flowers; Virgil has actually cited 4.30 (*et durae quercus sudabunt roscida mella*) by employing the words *durae*, *quercus*, and *sudent* in 8.52–4.[18] *Ecl.* 3.71 has also been cited with the words *aurea mala*. And from 8.55 onward, the passage concerns itself overtly with song: owls are made to contend with swans, and Tityrus, a shepherd-poet from the pastoral world, competes with those paragons of poetry, Orpheus and Arion. This abrupt reference to song is not discordant with the tone of the entire passage. In 52–4, Virgil alluded to his own attempt at lofty poetry within pastoral, to the fourth *Eclogue*; it is no coincidence that he shows a pastoral poet contending with great epic and dithyrambic singers in the succeeding verses. In the fourth *Eclogue* itself he had adopted the very pose which Tityrus now assumes (4.55–7):

In songs will Thracian Orpheus never vanquish me,
nor Linus, though one have a mother's, one a father's aid
Orpheus Calliopea's, Linus fair Apollo's.

Eclogue 8.52–6 undoubtedly prompted a smile from Pollio, to
whom this poem, as well as the fourth *Eclogue*, had been
dedicated.

Poetry, Pollio, gold as a symbol for song, and 'Golden Age'
motifs: these are the themes that recur together in apparently
significant contexts. Together, they offer the key to an under-
standing of Virgil's relationship with Pollio. The interests
common to the two poets were not so much political as literary,
and the commemorated object of their shared literary attention
was the theme of the Golden Age.

The first allusion to this theme occurs in *Eclogue* 3.88f.:

Who loves you, Pollio, may he come where you, too, make
  him glad,
may honey flow for him, harsh brambles bear amomum's spice.

The unspecified personage for whom the Golden Age flourishes
here is no *puer delicatus* with whom Pollio shares an erotic
relationship. *Amat* must be interpreted in the light of Virgil's
use of *amor* throughout the *Bucolics* to signify the mutual love
of Muse and poet, a love which had long played a rôle in Greek
bucolic poetry. Virgil transferred this love to all sources of
poetic inspiration: Menalcas can sing *amavit nos quoque Daphnis*
in 5.52.[19] Perhaps *Ecl.* 3.88f. is a prayer that inspiration come
to Pollio, that his preoccupations with the Age of Gold find
expression in his *nova carmina* (3.86). This section of the *Eclogue*
is, after all, devoted entirely to poetry (84–91); the romantic
themes had already been despatched with verses 64–83. *Qui
te Pollio amat* represents a 'love' of quite a different order.

Whence came Pollio's interest in an *aurea aetas*, and why
did Virgil share it so enthusiastically? The critic's attention
must be diverted away from Pollio the statesman, soldier, and
Caesarian politician, and must be fixed upon Pollio the poet,
for Virgil's relations with him, whether of a patron-protégé
character[20] or simply of a warmly amicable nature, centred
around interests which were most likely to be literary.[21]
Pollio's place in the Roman literary tradition is in fact far from

insignificant. Dramatist, erotic poet, and historian, intimate of Gallus, Virgil, and Horace, he was recognized by his peers and by posterity to be much more than a merely competent author.[22] As an older contemporary of Virgil, Pollio's literary career must have been influenced enormously by the one poet who, up to his time, had given the Latin Muse her most eloquent voice, who had discovered for the first time the boundless possibilities of Latin poetry: C. Valerius Catullus.

Pollio's friendship with Catullus is confirmed by the great Neoteric himself.[23] Cartault was the first to see Pollio as the intermediary between Catullus and Virgil;[24] whether or not the two geniuses ever met, Virgil's spiritual outlook and ideas of literary style must have acquired a marked Catullan character through association with Pollio. What was it that the two friends admired most in Catullus, and what aspect of his poetry did they strive most to emulate?

The Epithalamium of Peleus and Thetis

Friedrich Klingner's study shows why Catullus' great experiment with epic poetry, the *Epithalamium of Peleus and Thetis* (64), is by far his finest achievement.[25] In his longest extant work, Catullus departed from Greek models to create a new medium for self-expression, a blending of the spirit of elegy with epic; shunning the purely descriptive techniques of Hellenistic poets, Catullus had for the first time freed the epic from conventional trappings by projecting his own personality into his characters, assigning them the emotional responses of living and truly present beings.[26]

The plot of 64 is ambiguous; we expect this from Catullus and from the Neoteric school. Floods of colour-bright imagery bring the listener across the waves traversed by Argo to the palace of Peleus, to the gathering of guests for the marriage feast. The poet wanders through crowded halls, through the din of gods and men, and stops in the silence of the wedding chamber; here the connubial couch is spread with a purple tapestry which portrays 'the virtues of heroes' (*heroum virtutes* 51). One scene, Theseus' abandonment of Ariadne, catches the poet's eye and fills his vision, becomes the body of the poem

(52–266). The core of this section, in turn, is the complaint of Ariadne to an absent Theseus, a unique experiment in dramatic monologue[27] sustained for 69 lines; in its midst, Ariadne demands to know why Theseus could not have brought her home as a servant at least, where she might have 'covered his bed with a purple spread' (163). The poem ends with joy and horror: the Parcae prophesy the birth and deeds of Achilles, Thetis' son, and the heroic age is compared favourably with Catullus' own time, a time of 'sin unspeakable' when Justice is banished from the earth and gods no longer deign to visit men (397–408). The work is in many ways a recapitulation and full expression of the themes which preoccupied Catullus in his elegiac love poems. One critic suggests that Ariadne and Theseus actually 'stand in' for Catullus and Lesbia respectively, that the same abuse of love and loyalty is at stake.[28]

Catullus' success in freeing epic from the narrow and exacting principles of objective description followed by Greek poets renders him, in the view of at least one critic who knows him well, superior to his predecessors and contemporaries.[29] As magnificent as his poetry is, even Lucretius allows his chosen theme (the doctrine of Epicurus) to limit free and full expression of subjective attitudes. Subjectivism and the intrusion of the poet's own *persona*, the ultimate in empathetic treatment of a theme, are more exceptional than normal in the Lucretian work. Isolated instances—the newborn infant wailing in anticipation of life's travails in 5.222–7, for instance—are what really make *De rerum natura* worth reading; in such passages the art of Lucretius can be compared favourably even with that of Virgil.

But the themes of Catullus 64—the myths of Peleus and of Ariadne—are continually being subordinated to a higher purpose which is the lyrical, wholly subjective expression of the drama of love. Catullus has discovered that, by blurring the relationship of a poetic account to objective reality, by emancipating the form of his poem from the Greek canons of narrative precision, he is free to strive for a higher unity of theme through the combination of disparate mythical elements. By Hellenic standards, the tragedy of Theseus and Ariadne seems an intrusion into the account of Peleus' marriage. Both myths, however, are forged by Catullus into a lyrical reflection upon the central theme: love between the human and the divine. Ariadne's story is at once a contrast and a complement to the myth of Peleus and Thetis.[30] This achievement of Catullus remained without parallel until Virgil had written the Aristaeus episode of *Georgic* 4, in which the Catullan technique of overlaying seemingly unrelated myths and motifs was again employed to achieve a higher unity under the one exalted theme of death and resurrection.[31]

As Klingner has shown, the central theme of Catullus' monumental milestone in Latin literature, the theme to which all episodes in the poem are subjugated and around which they revolve, is that of the blessed, bygone age when gods and men lived in happy communion, partook of the same festive board, and shared the marriage bed. Then it was when gods deigned not only to be present at all human functions of a religious or festive nature and to assist their favourites in battle, but even to give themselves as mates to human partners (64.384–96). It is no mere coincidence that Catullus refers to the union of the god Dionysus with the human Ariadne immediately before his description of the marriage of another human-divine pair, Peleus and Thetis. The one episode mirrors the theme of the other—the bridal feast of men and gods.[32]

The happy age which Catullus describes and contrasts so poignantly with his own times (382–408) is much more than the traditional 'heroic age' of Greek mythology. It is the most vivid antithesis which Catullus can imagine to the age in which he lives; it is, in short, the best age of all, a 'golden' age; *O nimis optato saeclorum tempore nati heroes* ('You heroes born in a time, of all the ages, longed for all too much!').[33] It seems significant that Peleus, who joined the search for golden fleece (5), should have a house gleaming with gold (44), and that Ariadne should turn the colour of gold in her anxiety for Theseus (100). The heroes live in a time when Nemesis (395 *Rhamnusia virgo*) and *Iustitia* (398) have not yet departed from the earth, when a *scelus nefandum*, an 'unspeakable crime' (397) has not yet been committed. The atmosphere of the poem is so beatific that even wars and sorrows become infused with and resolved in a divine glory.

Is this not the sort of age which Virgil has described in the fourth *Eclogue*? The 'hero-passage' (*Eclogue* 4.31–6), which some scholars have found inconsistent with the other 'Golden Age' phenomena, appears in Virgil in the same spirit in which the heroes function in Catullus: in *Eclogue* 4 as in Catullus 64, heroic virtues, far from detracting from the blessed age, are in fact its great adornment.[34] And like the heroes of Catullus 64, who are *deum genus* (23a), the *puer* of the fourth *Eclogue* is a *deum suboles* (49); like them, he will dwell with gods and heroes (*Ecl.* 4.15f.) and will share the banquet table and nuptial couch of divinities (*Ecl.* 4.63).

Nor are these the only themes which Catullus' *Peleus*-epic and *Eclogue* 4 have in common. The dependence of the Virgilian poem upon Catullus extends to Virgil's choice of words and phrases as well. The correspondences in words and ideas have been investigated most fully by L. Herrmann; according to his calculations, there are over fifteen instances in the *Eclogue* of direct inspiration from the Catullan poem.[35] Even this list may be increased by several examples,[36] so that at least 34 of the *Eclogue*'s 63 lines can be shown with reasonable certainty to have a Catullan colouring, either in content or through direct verbal borrowing (5–8, 10f., 13–18, 26–8, 30–6, 38, 40–2, 44, 46f., 49, 52, 60, 62f.). Small wonder that Herrmann, who found additional sources of inspiration for the *Eclogue* in Theocritus, Moschus, Aratus, Homer, Lucretius, and Cicero, expressed grave doubts that the poem could have been influenced either by a Sibylline oracle or by the sixteenth *Epode* of Horace.[37] Linkomies follows Herrmann's lead in emphasizing the extensive influence of Catullus 64 upon *Eclogue* 4; what others see as oriental influence he attributes to Virgil's Catullan vision.[38] Small wonder, too, that the two poems show an identical verse structure. The 'unity of single lines, the schematization of balanced word order, and the quality of the verse groups' make *Eclogue* 4 the most Catullan of Virgil's poems.[39] Duckworth has made the discovery that certain metrical patterns (arrangement of dactyls and spondees within *cola*-groups) recur in both poems with almost identical frequency. The repetition of these preferred patterns in *Eclogue* 4 with a frequency which is remarkably similar to Catullus' hexameter in 64 makes the fourth *Eclogue* unique among its fellows, all of which show distinctly *non*-Catullan metrical traits.[40]

The literary interest shared by Virgil and Pollio in an age of miracles marked by the mingling of gods and men stems from a mutual admiration of one great figure in their literary heritage, the poet Catullus. Virgil's conversion of Catullus' age of heroes into a real Golden Age is his own contribution to an effort to emulate the master. This contribution was meant to be appreciated by one poet above all, his friend Pollio. Virgil had offered a poem which was largely Catullan in theme, vocabulary, and versification—a poem, in short, whose content and form were to the fullest extent determined by the *Peleus*-epic— to one who had known and admired the dead poet. And this is why Virgil dedicated the fourth *Eclogue* to Pollio.

The nature of Eclogue 4

Many critics would remove the fourth *Eclogue* from the bucolic sphere entirely.[41] This judgment begs the question, of course, as to the application of the term 'bucolic' to Virgilian pastoral as a whole. If 'Theocritean' be understood in the term, then the observation is correct; but how many of the other *Eclogues* can be called 'Theocritean'? *Eclogue* 5, with its deified hero who incorporates in himself elements from classical Greek drama? *Eclogue* 9, with its background of civil disturbance in Italy and its emphasis upon a poet's dilemma? *Eclogue* 1, with its commitment to Rome and to the young Caesar? *Eclogue* 6, modelled almost wholly on Callimachus? or *Eclogue* 10, which honours a Roman elegist?[42] The fourth *Eclogue* has as little to do with Theocritus as do these other poems; but it is nevertheless a 'bucolic' poem, at least as far as it fits our definition of Virgilian pastoral.

The *Sicelides Musae*, Theocritus' Muses of pastoral poetry, are affirmed by Virgil to be his inspiration for the fourth *Eclogue*, even though they are asked to sing 'in loftier strains' (*paulo maiora*). The poet still claims himself to be 'singing the woods' (4.3), those *silvae* which respond elsewhere to his pastoral song (*Eclogues* 1.5 and 10.8), the forests inhabited by his *silvestris Musa*; Virgil has not yet 'emerged from the wilderness' (*egressus silvis, Aen.* 1.1b). The poem does not maintain a solemn tone throughout, and often exhibits the character of a bucolic *ludus*, particularly in the passages describing the sheep who vary their hue (42–5) and the laughing infant (6off.). The word *ridere* is, in fact, in perfect consonance with Virgilian pastoral;[43] it seems significant that the *acanthus* (20) is made to laugh for a *puer* who is himself told to laugh (60). Laughing or not, the gaily coloured flowers which bloom for the infant (20, 23) are reminiscent of the flowers gathered by Corydon and the Naiad for another *puer*, Alexis (*Eclogue* 2.45–55). The child of *Eclogue* 4 is born into a world which is unmistakably bucolic.

If the fourth *Eclogue* be seen as less of a studied politico-religious oracle than as a vision from the dreamworld of poetry, it will be easier to understand why it is that Apollo, of all the gods, ushers in Virgil's *Saturnia regna*. Precisely because it is presided over by the divine patron of pastoral poetry, and not by Saturn, the Virgilian Golden Age is something completely new.[44] Herrmann infers the literary function of Apollo in *Ecl.* 4.10 from his function in 4.56f., where he is plainly a god of poetry.[45] If Apollo did not have this capacity in 4.10, the passage would be exceptional not only for Virgilian pastoral, but for the entire bucolic tradition. Apart from 4.10, the god's name occurs fourteen times elsewhere in the *Bucolics* (including its appearance in this *Eclogue*, verse 57). In every case he is mentioned with reference to poetic activity, for to him the pastoral is consecrated; he is the model of perfection for all shepherd-poets.[46] Theocritus had also referred to Apollo exclusively as god of poetry.[47]

If one of Virgil's concerns in composing *Eclogue* 4 was to offer, for Pollio's delectation, the description in poetry of a blessed age which would rival Catullus' achievement in the *Epithalamium of Peleus and Thetis*, it is not surprising that he would make Apollo, the divine patron of his poetry, preside over the new age. In vying with his great Catullan model, Virgil had launched a new 'age' of his own poetry, a new direction for his art.

The nature of the 'puer'

It has often been remarked that, of the two major themes in the fourth *Eclogue* (the return of the *aurea aetas* and the birth of the *puer*), one is without parallel or precedent, and appears to be entirely a creation of the poet himself. Descriptions of the Golden Age had existed before Virgil, and Sibylline prophecies of a 'turn for the better' in human events were well known to the Roman world. But Virgil had been the first to make a *human child* the focal point around whom and for whom the new age would flourish, to make a *puer* the sign of its arrival.[48]

Though Virgil's literary and religious traditions may offer no solutions to the enigma of the *puer*, there is ample precedent for him in the *Bucolics* themselves: the inhabitants of the pastoral world are almost *all* designated by the term *puer*, a word which captures the essence of the pure and childlike soul of the Virgilian shepherd-poet. Virgil's bucolic heroes are and must be *pueri*: even the paragon Daphnis holds this title in the central *Eclogue* (5.54). The one exception is made in the case of a personage who is not a Virgilian creation, but a hero from the real world, the *iuvenis* of *Eclogue* 1.

The *puer* of *Eclogue* 4 is actually a new and developed aspect of the Virgilian pastoral hero. As Virgil designated the shepherd-poet Daphnis the 'adornment of his world' (*Ecl.* 5.34), so the *puer* is called in 4.11 the 'adornment of the age'. Like Daphnis and the *iuvenis* of *Eclogue* 1, the *puer* appears in the world as a wonder, and imparts wondrous and salutary benefits; in *Eclogue* 4, however, these effects extend beyond the bucolic world to assume universal significance. Like Daphnis and the *iuvenis*, the *puer* is a deified hero: his commerce with gods is, however, foreordained before his birth, and seems to occur without any previous effort of his own (4.15f.). He encounters gods and heroes through his own 'epiphany', and through theirs.

The *puer*, then, is himself divine, though his position as a divinity is not unique in the *Bucolics*. Aside from the various Olympians mentioned throughout the poems, and from the deified heroes themselves (Daphnis and Octavian), there is yet another figure who bears the epithet *divinus*: the poet. For his Daphnis-song, Mopsus is called *divinus* in 5.45, and Virgil addresses Gallus as *divine poeta* in 10.17.

The *puer*'s appearance has effects upon the world similar to those which Virgil's *poets* have upon nature, though to a higher degree. The *puer* is nowhere called a poet; he is far more the *subject* of song (4.53ff.). Yet he evokes, through his presence, the blooming of fruits and flowers, as well as peace among beasts (4.18–30), just as Daphnis' absence means the loss of harvests and flowers (5.36–9), and his apotheosis brings peace among beasts and men (5.60f.). Other poets in the *Bucolics* can charm nature with their song (e.g. Silenus in 6, Damon and Alphesiboeus in 8.1–5); but Daphnis the singer, in whom Virgil found his definitive pastoral hero, creates this effect through his *presence* alone. In *Eclogue* 4, this power to enchant, originally the prerogative of the bucolic poet, is transferred wholly to a hero who is *not* a poet.

Nevertheless, Virgil bestows the poet's insignia upon the *puer* in 4.19 by making *hedera* and *baccar* bloom for him. The significance of ivy and cyclamen for Virgil must be seen in the light of *Eclogue* 7.25–8, where Thyrsis sings of himself

> Pastores, hedera nascentem ornate poetam,[49]
> Arcades, invidia rumpantur ut ilia Codro;
> aut, si ultra placitum laudarit, baccare frontem
> cingite, ne vati noceat mala lingua futuro.

Both the *puer nascens* and the *poeta nascens* receive Bacchic ivy as their attributes; both the child of the future and the *vates futurus* (7.28) receive the apotropaic *baccar*.[50] Why should the *puer* be surrounded with the trappings of poetry?

As I have suggested earlier, the fourth *Eclogue* represents an attempt to show Pollio what could be done with Catullan themes in the pastoral landscape; Virgil seeks to rival in pastoral poetry the vision of a blessed age in the *Peleus*-epic. Could it be that the *puer*, as Virgil's own creation, is incorporated into the Golden Age to show the poet's hopes for his own literary future, and to represent the further possibilities which he envisions for his own poetry? Like Daphnis and the *iuvenis* before him, the *puer* is a literary hero, worthy of celebration in song. Unlike his predecessors, however, he does not assume his title or his realm in 'the here and the now': the fourth *Eclogue* celebrates only the moment of his birth.

Virgil's intimate connection with the career of this *puer* is expressed in 4.53–9. In these verses, Virgil seems to consecrate his life and career as poet to the celebration of the *puer*, and expresses the hope that he may live to complete the praises of his deeds. If this hope is fulfilled, he will become the greatest of poets, and will even rival gods in song.

This great hope was realized when Virgil became the poet of the *Aeneid*. With the composition of this epic poem, the *puer* had achieved his full 'growth'. Born into an enchanted bucolic world, Virgil's literary hero had in *Eclogue* 4 looked out of this world into his own great future, a future which was surprisingly well foreseen by its creator. The *puer* was really and truly born, in Virgil's own lifetime, and in the year of Pollio's consulship. He was born not in Rome, nor in Egypt, nor in some far celestial region, but in the soul of a bucolic poet who was on the verge of creating a Golden Age of poetry. The *puer* is Virgil's literary hero of the future.[51]

As a great poetic hero, the *puer* will be both real and imaginary. His reality will rest upon Virgil's ability to create and develop him in his works. To him will be attributed great *virtutes* and *facta*, but the implementation of his virtue and the accomplishment of his deeds will be the work of Virgil alone. The *facta* of the *puer* will be done *for* him, so to speak, rather than *by* him. Nevertheless, they will be *his facta* when sung by Virgil (4.54). Under this interpretation there exists no inconsistency between the *puer*'s apparent inactivity throughout the *aurea aetas* and the *facta* assigned to him. Pfeiffer's objections have been answered.

'All people like their own works better, just as parents and poets do': Aristotle's remark (*Nicomachean Ethics* 4.1.20) does much to explain the ecstatic tone of the fourth *Eclogue* and the choice of a newborn child to represent Virgil's new hero.

In 41 B.C., during the civil discord produced by the appropriation of land throughout Italy and its redistribution to the victorious veterans of Philippi, a change was wrought in Virgil's life which restored his faith in his own vocation, in spite of the political chaos which had seemed at first to render it meaningless. His rôle as poet was confirmed by Octavian, and he was assured of perpetual freedom to pursue his calling (*Ecl.* 1.10).

The first *Eclogue* celebrates this assurance, and is at the same time a declaration of new allegiance to his benefactor and to the interests of the Roman people. Virgil's outlook had become a Roman outlook, and his hero had become a Roman hero. His view of himself as a *Roman* and no longer a Neoteric poet must have effected a profound change in his plans for future poetry. These new plans were formulated not long after Octavian stepped into his life in 41 or 40 B.C. The adoption of a new programme was symbolized in the birth of a *puer* in 40 B.C., which by happy coincidence was the year of his friend Pollio's consulship. Virgil seized the opportunity to honour him with a poem which both commemorated their mutual interest in Catullus and the Golden Age theme, and at the same time gave Pollio an ecstatic preview of Virgil's future work. The consciousness of his ability to become Rome's poet laureate produced the joyous vision which the fourth *Eclogue* offers.

But since the *puer* had to be a Roman hero, he was to be patterned after some great hero from the real world who would actually bring about universal salvation and pacification. The first *Eclogue* marks Virgil's realization that his literary hero must a basis in the world of Roman reality; his choice for that poem was Octavian. Virgil cannot predict in *Eclogue* 4 that the hero will still be Octavian in that 'final part of life' devoted to celebrating the *puer's facta*. But he is certain that the *puer* will rule *patriis virtutibus*, an expression which della Torre rightly interpreted to mean 'by ancestral virtues', i.e. 'by Roman virtues'.[52] In the end, the *puer* became the Trojan hero Aeneas, though the visage of an idealized Augustus lurks beneath the mythic mask. The words of Anchises introducing Augustus (*Aen.* 6.788ff.) are surely meant to echo the fourth *Eclogue*:

> Huc geminas nunc flecte acies, hanc aspice gentem
> Romanosque tuos, hic Caesar et omnis Iuli
> progenies magnum caeli ventura sub axem,
> hic vir hic est tibi quem promitti saepius audis
> Augustus Caesar, divi genus, aurea condet
> saecula qui rursus Latio regnata per arva
> Saturno quondam, super et Garamantas et Indos
> proferet imperium.

'Here turn the twin sights of your eyes now, here behold this
   race
and your own Romans, here is Caesar and Iulus' whole
offspring under heaven's mighty pole to come,
here the man, here, whom you heard more often promised you:
Augustus Caesar of immortal stock will found again
for Latium Golden Ages through the fields once ruled
by Saturn; past the Garamantians, past the Hindu
he will push his empire forth.'

The world of Roman reality is brought into close connection
with the *puer*'s development in 4.13f., where a compliment is
paid to Pollio, and a charge laid upon him as well:

> With you as leader, if some traces of our guilt remain
> their dissolution will release the earth from endless fear.

Pollio is to take part in preparing the way for the *puer*, in
making possible the Roman hero Virgil envisions. If the world
sinks back into chaos there will be no basis in reality upon which
the poet can create his literary hero. Whatever Virgil expects
of Pollio's consulship and political future, it is clear that the
puer's future is contingent upon the instrumentality of such
forerunners.

A programme for the future

The stages of the *puer*'s growth in 4.18–36 suggest an outline
of Virgil's work in similar stages. The spirit of 18–25 is the
spirit of Virgilian bucolic poetry.[53] Not only are the flowers,
herds, and smiles of traditional Greek pastoral present; motifs
have also been cited from Virgil's previous works: the *hedera*
and *baccar* from *Eclogue* 7.25–8, the *acanthus* from 3.45, and the
amomum from 3.89. The peace among beasts, which had
occurred for Daphnis in 5.60, recurs here.[54]
   Verses 28–30 have a decidedly different flavour:

> With soft spikes of grain the field will yellow, bit by bit,
> and grapes will redden, hanging from untended thorns,
> while hard oaks ooze their honey like the dew.

Here there are no more miracles, only an atmosphere of
agricultural abundance: the field is rich with wheat, grape-

vines climb even the thornbushes, and the oaks are full of
beehives. The passage is exclusively 'georgic', and pertains to
the *bona agricolae*. It contains the themes of the first *Georgic* (on
crops), of the second (on viticulture), and of the fourth (on
beekeeping), in that order. Virgil may have hinted at the first
and second *Georgics* in *Eclogue* 9; the fourth *Eclogue* seems to
confirm those preoccupations.[55]

The two verses which precede the 'georgic' passage may
indicate how Virgil prepared for the composition of his first
thoroughly Roman work, the *Georgics*:

> When you can read the praise of heroes, read the fathers' deeds
> and can understand by then what virtue is . . .

It has long been recognized that *heroum laudes*, 'praise of heroes',
is a translation of Homer's phrase for the content of Achilles'
song at *Iliad* 9.524.[56] The *facta parentum* sound like an echo of
the old adage (*paroimia*) reported in Greek by Polybius, accord-
ing to which Roman *virtus* consists in preserving and perpetuat-
ing 'the fathers' deeds well treasured up'.[57] Ennius repeats
the formula in Latin, inscribing a fanciful gravestone for
himself:[58]

> Aspicite o cives senis Enni imaginis formam.
> hic vestrum panxit maxima facta patrum.

> 'Citizens, behold the beauty of old Ennius' image:
> this man worked up your fathers' greatest deeds!'

These *facta parentum* bear a close relationship to the *patriae
virtutes* (4.17): they are the valiant deeds of Roman ancestors.

Legere (27) can have a number of meanings ('gather',
'choose', 'read', 'read aloud') but is usually, on the basis of the
obvious reference to Homer in *heroum laudes*, taken in a literary
sense. Perhaps Virgil identifies himself so closely with his work,
with the *puer*, that he shows the *puer* reading what he himself
reads. In any event, these readings consist first in Homeric
poetry (*heroum laudes*), then in historical accounts of Roman
facta, and will ultimately lead to an understanding of *virtus*.[59]
Could the theme of *virtus* be reconciled with an agricultural
theme? Yes, if Virgil was already planning the *Georgics* as an
Ascraeum carmen (*Geo.* 2.176), a song modelled on the *Erga*, the

'Works and Days' of Hesiod of Ascra. Under the aspect of a farmers' almanac, the *Erga* gave fundamental expression to the world of Greek experience—a world of competition, of divine rewards and punishments, and of a single god as dispenser of justice. No less an authority than Cicero documents the importance of Hesiod's *Works and Days* even for the education of a Roman youth: 'Tell your sweet Lepta', he writes to his friend Quintus Lepta, 'to learn Hesiod by heart and have on his lips "But sweat in front of excellence" and so forth.' Cicero cited in Greek the key words to the nucleus of the *Erga*, the climactic exhortation to *areté*;[60] the Greek word signifies 'excellence', and is normally expressed in Latin as *virtus* (*Erga* 286–92):

> I give you useful, sage advice, my silly Perses:
> failure can be had in heaps with ease;
> the road is level and lies very near.
> But sweat in front of excellence the gods have set,
> immortal gods; the path to it is long and steep
> and rough at first, but when you reach the top,
> however hard, it turns out easy afterward.

The controversial 'hero passage' (31–6) foreshadows that poem which was to become the *Aeneid*. It seems to contain allusions to the three great epic poets of Greece, to Homer, Hesiod, and Apollonius, who would necessarily stand as models for any Roman poet venturing into the epic genre. At the same time, the verses anticipate themes which were to be incorporated into the Virgilian epic. The *Odyssey*-reference ('a trial of Thetis with the sail') foresees Aeneas' wanderings over the sea; 'a girding up of towns with walls', a motif from the *Iliad*, looks perhaps toward the task of founding the Roman state; 'a furrowed scoring of the earth' sounds Hesiodic, and might also foresee Aeneas' planting the colony in Latium.[61] The Argonautic references (34f.) also fit Aeneas' search for the *Saturnia tellus* over the seas. Finally, the list of themes culminates in verses which capture, far more than the rest, the spirit of the *Aeneid* (35f.). These last two lines are echoed in the only other 'Sibylline' prophecy to appear in Virgil's works (*Aeneid* 6.86–90):

Bella horrida bella
et Thybrim multo spumantem sanguine cerno.
non Simois tibi nec Xanthus nec Dorica castra
defuerint. alius Latio iam partus Achilles,
natus et ipse dea.

'Wars, bristling wars
and Tiber foaming with much blood I see.
No Simois, no Xanthus, nor the Dorian army will you
miss; already born to Latium is a fresh Achilles
also goddess' son himself.'

When the 'hero passage' is understood to be a prophecy of
Virgil's future work, the interpretation of *priscae vestigia fraudis*
(31) becomes easier. 'Ancient fraud's vestiges' refers to the first
sin of man, and is modelled on the *veteris vestigia poenae* ('old
punishment's vestiges') which Prometheus bears in Catullus
64.295.[62] This *fraus* is the theft of Prometheus, the ultimate
cause of the gods' anger. Without it, there would have been no
wars, but there would also have been no epic poets to celebrate
deeds of valour. It is quite different from the *scelus nostrum*,
'our guilt' of 4.13. The *fraus* refers to an ancient deception of
the gods in myth, the *scelus* to actual crime which must be ex-
tirpated from the real world. Both *fraus* and *scelus* are, however,
interrelated; the Roman hero of Virgil's projected epic will
accomplish in a mythical setting what Virgil expects Pollio
and other statesmen to achieve in the world of Roman reality.

If *Ecl.* 4.18–36 be seen not as a description of a Sibylline
Golden Age, but as a prediction of a 'Golden Age' of Roman
poetry, then the 'hero passage' can hardly be considered in-
consistent with the rest of the poem. It does not constitute a
regression from the Golden Age, but represents the culmination
of the *puer*'s career. Virgil has not destroyed all synchronism in
his simultaneous development of the *aurea aetas* and of the *puer*.
The *aetas*, which is Virgilian poetry, and the *puer*, who is its
hero, are aiming towards the fulfilment of a prophecy far
different from that of any Sibylline oracle.

The *risus* of *Ecl.* 4.60, the 'laughing' motif, is, like *ludus*, part
and parcel of the bucolic mode; Virgil's *puer* spends his infancy
in a world of 'laughing acanthus' and other pastoral themes
(4.18–25). With the mention of *Pan* in 58, the poem, together

with the *puer*, re-enters the bucolic world. The *risus* becomes the newborn *puer*'s first duty; in his infancy he is still a bucolic hero, and must behave accordingly. The mother whom he recognizes, the mother who has brought him into the world after long *fastidia*, is likely to be Virgil's Muse, just as the only other mother in the fourth *Eclogue*, the mother of the poet Orpheus, is the Muse Calliope.

Fastidia is a strange word to describe the discomforts of an expectant mother (61). Normally, even elsewhere in the *Bucolics*, it means something like 'aversion' (2.15, 2.73). Why should the *puer*'s mother be susceptible to this unmaternal reaction to her confinement? As I have suggested, the fourth *Eclogue* marks a momentous occasion in Virgil's life, the adoption of his new programme for the future. From this point onward his major involvement will be with themes which would interest a Roman poet. He will continue to compose bucolic poetry, but now 'by appointment only'.[63] There remains little to attract Virgil in the pastoral genre; his Muse has called him elsewhere. If this Muse is the mother of his new hero, it is small wonder that her reaction to a confinement in the bucolic world takes the form of *fastidia*.

The repetition of *incipe parve puer* lends the poem's concluding verses an almost ceremonial beat, as do the other repetitions in the *Eclogue* at the beginning of lines (6,7; 11,13; 23,21; 24,25; 50,52; 58,59). *Incipe*, 'begin', holds a special significance, a significance to be sought in the *puer*'s nature as a poetic hero. It was della Torre who noticed that Virgil uses this form elsewhere in the *Bucolics* only to indicate that someone is about to *sing*.[64] It is eminently appropriate that Virgil should address the hero of his poetry with a formula in keeping with his rôle as poet. The poem ends with the final promise of a Golden Age for the *puer*, if he will only laugh for his mother. Significantly enough, Virgil summed up in the last verse Catullus' vision of the blessed age, the sharing of banquets and bridal beds of the gods.[65] By this means, he indicated the essence of his own poetic ideals, and pointed again to the transformation his poetic hero was to undergo.

The pastoral landscape itself was transformed in *Eclogue* 4 into a wondrous scene of fruitfulness which contrasts sharply with, for instance, Tityrus' bleak pasturage in *Eclogue* 1. Virgil's tradition here was the 'automatic' landscape of the Golden Age upon which western culture had reflected from its very origins. The legend of the friendly terms on which man and nature had once co-existed is a perennial antithesis to the war and technology which have given western culture (including the ancient Near East) its growth and definitive shape.[66] The tradition is reflected not only here in Virgil, but also in an earlier poet, Lucretius (5.925–1010) and after him in Catullus (64, especially 38–42), Horace (*Epode* 16.41–66), and probably Pollio. A few years after the fourth *Eclogue* was published, Virgil transferred the landscape of the *aurea saecla* to the real countryside of the Italian peasant, the new *Saturnia tellus* (*Geo.* 2.173). In the second *Georgic*, it is the farmer's labours which produce a Golden Age in Italy (513–40): 'This life did golden Saturn lead on earth' (538). So firmly had Virgil committed himself to the notion of *Roman* poetry that his fondest fantasy, the world of the *puer* in the fourth *Eclogue*, along with the hopes of a thousand generations, was transplanted, finally, to Italian soil.

The *Georgics* were an attempt to make a Virgilian dream accessible to the Roman people; in the *Aeneid* this dream becomes inseparable from the Augustan political ideal. In the cold marble of the *Ara Pacis*, a monument to the universal imposition of Augustan peace, the flowers of the *puer*'s cradle and the agricultural opulence of the fourth *Eclogue* intertwine with fantastic vegetation symbolizing the miracle of Peace. There *Itala tellus*, the human form of abundance itself, dandles offspring on her knee, coaxing a smile from the infants that seems to echo wistfully the *risus* of a poet's landscape.[67]

VII

The Last Labours

There first I knew
the companions name themselves
        and move
in time of naming upward
        toward outward
forms of desire and enlightenment,

but intoxicated,
        only by longing
belonging to that first company
of named stars that in heaven
call attention to a tension
        in design,
                compel
as the letters by which we spell words compel
        magic refinements;

and sought from tree and sun, from night and sea,
old powers—Dionysus in wrath, Apollo in rapture,
Orpheus in song, and Eros secretly

four that Christ-crossd in one Nature
Plato named the First Beloved

that now I see
in all certain dear contributor
        to my being
has given me house, ghost,
image and color, in whom I dwell
        past Arcady.
                Robert Duncan, 'A poem slow beginning'

The final structure

Octavian's intercession on Virgil's behalf in 41 B.C. had a twofold effect: it restored Virgil's faith in his own poetic vocation, and it made a Roman poet of him. The fourth

Eclogue expresses Virgil's wish to begin work immediately on his fully Roman poetry, and to bring his newborn hero out of the bucolic sphere into the next stage of 'growth'. This impatience led to the idea of 'wrapping up' the *Eclogue*-book in five reciprocal pairs. The last three *Eclogues* to be written by Virgil have several characteristics in common which set them off from the other poems. The most striking of these is the fact that they were all composed at someone's behest. The sixth was written for Varus, though Varus had evidently requested something other than a pastoral poem (6.6f.)—knowing, perhaps, that Virgil intended to abandon the pastoral. The poet puts him off with the information that he is not at the moment disposed to sing *maiora carmina*, at least not for Varus. On the other hand, the contrast of *deductum dicere carmen* (6.5) with *paulo maiora canamus* (4.1) may indicate, as Hubaux suggested, that Varus had expected a poem on the order of the fourth *Eclogue*.[1] Whatever the case, Virgil, in refusing the original request, made use of a literary device, the formal *recusatio* or 'polite refusal' which would serve another generation of Roman poets in their hour of need.[2]

The eighth *Eclogue* was written at Pollio's bidding (11f.)—unlike the fourth, which mentions no 'orders' and seems to have been a voluntary effort to honour the consul (4.3). Here again there is a hint that Virgil is now thinking beyond the pastoral genre (8.7f.): 'Will it ever come for me, that day when I'm allowed to tell your deeds?' The phrase *tua dicere facta* was doubly meaningful for Pollio, who had heard it used once before of Virgil's new poetic hero (4.54).

It was Gallus, finally, who requested the last poem (10.3):

> Gallus wants a poem or two, but poems meant
> for Lycoris herself to read. What poet could refuse?

Yet the poem is designated a *labor* (10.1). The use of this term to describe the pursuit of a genre in which the poet had once been at home can be compared to the *fastidia* which the Muse, pregnant with Virgil's new hero, experienced through her detainment in the bucolic world. In point of fact, the pastoral atmosphere in *Eclogue* 10 is soon replaced by the spirit of another genre, that of love elegy.

It is perhaps significant that Virgil needed a commission as impetus for the further composition of bucolic poems. Apparently, only the call of friendship or obligation could distract him from those loftier preoccupations which would eventually produce the *Georgics* and the *Aeneid*.[3] The time spent on the sixth, eighth, and tenth *Eclogues* was far from wasted, however; Virgil saw in them an opportunity to develop those themes which would play an essential rôle in his later works. The sixth poem is an experiment with the *epyllion*, the eighth an approach to the love theme of unprecedented depth and lyrical intensity, and the tenth a novel introduction of the elegiac motifs of Cornelius Gallus into hexameter verse.

Poetry, love, and Gallus: those themes were to a certain extent predetermined by the themes of *Eclogues* 4, 2, and 5, with which 6, 8, and 10 were 'matched'. It is evident, as Brooks Otis has shown, that the juxtaposition of the two poems on loss of land (9 and 1) suggested a structure for the *Eclogue*-book as a whole—reciprocal pairs converging on a centre occupied by Daphnis, the deified shepherd-poet.[4] Moreover, two other poems had been composed which could conveniently join 9 and 1 in flanking the Daphnis-poem. The third and seventh *Eclogues* are variations on an old Theocritean motif, the singing-contest, which had formed a part of the mime-routine, and was sometimes set off from the rest of the poem by a change in metre (*Idyll* 10); in Virgil, the contests lost their dramatic function, the 'contestants' ' voices presenting instead various modes and aspects of Virgilian poetry.

Those who attribute the central position of 5 to Virgil's devotion to the Julian *gens* misunderstand its real relationship to 10. The great Daphnis-poem commemorates not Julius Caesar, but a beautiful young herdsman who is a *magister* of poetry, and who becomes through his deification the shepherd-poet *par excellence* of Virgil's bucolic world.[5] The hero of *Eclogue* 10 is also a poet cast in the rôle of Daphnis. This poet, too, is divine (10.17) and is the central figure in a world which responds, like the world of *Eclogue* 5, to the hero's plight. But Gallus replaces Daphnis in 10 because the world has become more elegiac than pastoral. Virgil's bucolic world, once the realm of Daphnis, is transformed into the world of love elegy by Gallus. This is why, in the overall structure of the *Bucolics*, *Eclogue* 10 stands apart from the rest: it is more than a pastoral poem.

The sixth Eclogue

The *rationale* behind Virgil's arrangement of the pairs of poems around 5 has long been recognized:[6] in 5 Daphnis becomes a god, in 10 Gallus becomes Daphnis. 1 and 9 have in common a historical background (the dispossessions of 41 B.C.), as well as the crisis in Virgil's life, and its resolution. 2 and 8 are both concerned with love themes. The amoebaean dialogue of 3 and 7 belongs to the form of the pastoral poetry contest.[7] But with 4 and 6, critics find themselves resorting to vague generalizations in order to 'marry' the pair. This is no longer necessary, thanks to a recent re-interpretation of the sixth *Eclogue*. As the Daphnis-*Eclogue* enshrines an archetypal pastoral poet from the world of myth, so the two poems which 'enclose' it pay tribute to the inspiration of real poets.

Since the discovery of the papyrus-fragment containing a large portion of the prologue to Callimachus' *Aitia*, it has become obvious that the poet's encounter with Apollo in *Eclogue* 6.3–8 imitates a similar scene in the *Aitia*.[8] Wimmel has discovered the thematic thread which binds the prologue of *Eclogue* 6 to the song of Silenus, and has shown that these two major elements of the poem are vitally interrelated through their common origin in the *Aitia* of Callimachus.[9] This discovery is of considerable significance for our understanding of Virgil's attitude toward his sources of inspiration.

Callimachus had represented his call to poetry in two phases in the *Aitia* prologue. The first phase involved his encounter with Apollo as a child (fr. 1.21–30), the second his encounter in a dream with the Hesiodic Muses on Helicon as a young man (fr. 2, the so-called *Somnium*). Virgil imitated both phases of the Callimachean *Berufungsgeschichte*, substituting Gallus for himself in the second phase in order to avoid the repetitive quality of Callimachus' 'doublet'. Furthermore, instead of letting the second phase follow directly upon the first (as Callimachus had done), he allowed the song of Silenus to intervene. By

introducing Silenus' collection of myths, Virgil actually trans-
formed the *Eclogue* into a new *Aitia*.[10] The achievement is now
apparent: through an ingenious system of separation and sub-
stitution, the poet managed to compose a piece which imitates
not only the prologue to the *Aitia*, but the entire Callimachean
work as well; he has placed the second phase of the 'call to
poetry' (the striking Gallus-episode) toward the end of Silenus'
song, so that it appears to be only one in a series of myths.

Critics today generally follow Franz Skutsch in his assump-
tion that the major theme of *Eclogue* 6 is poetry. Though
interpretations differ as to the nature of this poetry, it is now
communis opinio that the song of Silenus is a *Kataloggedicht*,
whether a catalogue of Gallus' poems, of Alexandrian themes,
of major literary genres, or of themes worked by Virgil him-
self.[11] His discovery of a Callimachean framework for the
Eclogue as a whole brought Wimmel to a fresh view of the
poem's content. Virgil was primarily concerned with imitating
Callimachus' account of his 'consecration' as a poet; the song
of Silenus therefore holds considerable significance for Virgil's
own call to poetry, and the material it contains must allude in
some way to the models in which the poet found inspiration.
The dependence of *Eclogue* 6.34–40 upon Lucretius, for example,
has been noticed too often to require elaboration.[12] Further,
the celebration of Gallus in 6.64–73 increases the probability
that the remaining myths refer in some way to the works of
other *Roman* poets whom Virgil considered worthy of emula-
tion[13]—the lost poems of Varius and Cinna, for whom Virgil
had already expressed admiration (*Ecl.* 9.35f.), would be likely
candidates. Calvus and Pollio might also figure somewhere in
the list. Catullus would not of course be represented here;
Virgil had erected a monument to him in the 'matching' poem,
Eclogue 4.

As the fourth *Eclogue*, in which Catullus was honoured as the
supreme model for Virgil's literary efforts, had been an ecstatic
preview of the poet's future work, so the sixth *Eclogue* was
meant to pay tribute to those pioneers of new tendencies in
Roman poetry whose works were inspiring Virgil as he de-
veloped and perfected his art. Of these other poets, only Gallus
receives the distinction of being named. His influence upon

Virgil had been expressed once before, in the first *Eclogue*.[14]
At the time Virgil was composing the sixth *Eclogue*, Gallus'
influence must have exceeded that of all contemporary poets.
Virgil's *amor* for Gallus, and for Gallus' poetry, eventually
became so great that, in the end, the poet cast his friend in a
rôle hitherto reserved for the bucolic hero *par excellence*, the
rôle of Daphnis. In making a Daphnis of Gallus, Virgil
acknowledged the conquest of his bucolic world by the spirit of
Roman love-elegy.

The *Leitmotiv* which *Eclogue* 4 and *Eclogue* 6 share, then, is
the acknowledgement of Virgil's debt to Roman poets who
inspired the new direction his own literary style was taking.
It is not only this theme, however, which makes of the two
Eclogues a 'reciprocal pair'. As I have attempted to show, the
fourth *Eclogue* represents an effort to match or to rival within
the pastoral genre the vision of a blessed age presented in
Catullus 64. The sixth *Eclogue* reveals a similar effort with
regard to a series of themes for short epics, for '*epyllia*'. The
successive tales in Silenus' repertoire are told as briefly and
succinctly as possible; at the same time, an attempt has been
made to capture in a very few lines the *dramatic essence* of each
myth.[15] To this end, Virgil has exercised all his talent for
lyrical or 'subjective' representation. The *pièce de résistance* in the
series is the myth of Pasiphaë. While the story of Pasiphaë's
love could well have been extended to full *epyllion*-length,[16]
the kernel of the myth's emotional impact has nevertheless
been captured whole and entire in *Eclogue* 6.45–60. The most
tragic moments of Pasiphaë's experience have been painted
with a vividness and brevity which only Virgil's new 'sym-
pathetic-empathetic' style could have achieved. As Pasiphaë
enacts her own tragedy, we are made to 'see *through* her eyes'.[17]

In *Eclogues* 4 and 6 Virgil has expressed his debt to the great
innovators in Roman poetry—Catullus, Lucretius, Gallus, and
others; at the same time, he has shown what he himself can
contribute to the themes and techniques pioneered by them.
In *Eclogue* 6 he is, as Cartault put it, 'dreaming of his poetic
future';[18] the same is true on a grander scale in *Eclogue* 4. The
latter poem presents a long-range view of his poetic activity,
of the great work which will extend to Virgil's *pars ultima vitae*

(4.53). The sixth *Eclogue*, for its part, concentrates on projects which were to play a rôle in the more immediate future. Lucretius, for instance (alluded to in *Ecl.* 6.31–40), was to exercise tremendous influence upon the composition of the *Georgics*; and the subject of tragic love, worked out within the form of an *epyllion*, was to become a major theme in the fourth *Georgic* (the Aristaeus-Orpheus episode), and would find its fullest expression in the fourth book of the *Aeneid*. The impact of Gallus' love-poetry, in the final analysis, had profound implications for the development of Virgil's art.

The eighth Eclogue

Virgil's preoccupation with the depiction of love in literature increases in *Eclogues* 8 and 10. His poetic hero of the future emerges more and more as a figure who must be made to confront the problem of human love with all its tragic implications, and to find a solution, even though it be a tragic solution, on human terms. The sixth, eighth, and tenth *Eclogues* explore the many facets of this subject; Virgil's diligence here will find its *telos* later in the formulation of that tragic situation which confronts the hero of *Aeneid* 4.

Prior to the composition of the later *Eclogues*, the treatment of heterosexual love in the *Bucolics* had been restricted to the traditionally superficial romances of Theocritean pastoral. This sort of theme was rejected definitively in *Eclogue* 1, where its personification in the coquettish Nymph Galatea was bidden a final 'adieu'. In the same poem, Virgil indicated his new allegiance to another kind of love theme—that represented in the elegies of Gallus, whose treatment of love held greater appeal for Virgil as a serious poet.[19] From Gallus more than from any other contemporary, he seems to have learned how to depict the tragic love of a man for a woman, of a woman for a man.

Otis' study has done much to show how the profundity of emotion expressed in *Ecl.* 8.17–61 (the song of Damon) far exceeds that expressed in the lover's complaints of Theocritus. In Damon's song, the poet elects to portray a single moment in a lover's experience, the moment before his suicide, the moment in which the tragic history of a love, from its tender beginnings to its ultimate end in disillusionment, is dramatically portrayed within the lover's soul. This first-person 'flashback', with a moment of utter despair as its focal point, is the development in a short poem of what Catullus had done with a long series of discontinuous Lesbia-poems.[20]

At the same time a tremendous turbulence is generated between the lover and his world in the song of Damon. 'The familiar bucolic landscape is engulfed in a cataclysmic vision, in which all semblance of order and peace vanish':[21] Fantazzi's words refer primarily to the *adynata* of 8.53–9. It is perhaps an exaggeration to say that all semblance of 'peace' vanishes; the *adynata*, with their Golden Age characteristics, refer if anything to a more peaceful if less natural world. But the fact remains that the lover wishes the order of nature reversed. He finds himself alienated from the tranquil *silvae*, and bids them good-bye forever (59). Though he has invoked the Maenalian Muse repeatedly, he has failed to restore himself to the familiar state of *otium* which the bucolic world has hitherto offered.

The song of Alphesiboeus (8.64–109) is also a psychological drama of frustrated love. The object of the lover's devotion is Daphnis, playing a familiar rôle from the Greek epigrammatic tradition—that of the beloved who awakens yearning by his absence.[22] The formal model is Theocritus' *Sorceress* (*Idyll* 2); like Theocritus, Virgil employs a refrain, an incantation to support the casting of spells: 'Lead Daphnis from the town, my songs, lead Daphnis home' is modelled upon *Idyll* 2.17 etc., 'Iunx, draw thou that man to my home'. Unlike Theocritus' voodoo, however, Virgil's *songs* become the most powerful charm; unlike the *Sorceress*, the eighth *Eclogue* ends on a happy note: the *carmina* have been effective. The song of Alphesiboeus ought to be construed as a real answer to that of Damon. *Eclogue* 8 is, after all, a poetry contest (8.1–3), and Alphesiboeus has won the day in finding a solution to the problem of unhappy love.[23] The solution is a typical one for the poet to find; by affirming the power of song to charm and heal the wounds of love, he has made the 'Song of Alphesiboeus' into a love charm, and has asserted for his own poetry what had been claimed by Pindar for his songs: the character of an *epaoidé*, of a healing incantation.[24]

The idea that *song* has the power to effect a lover's return was to find full expression in the fourth *Georgic*, where Orpheus, the greatest of poets, almost succeeds in charming his beloved back from the house of death (453ff.). And the heroine of *Aeneid* 4 pretends to Anna that she will employ a Massylian priestess whose *carmina* will effect the desired change in Aeneas' purpose. Dido's description of her power is strikingly similar to the claims for the power of song which Virgil makes in the eighth and in other *Eclogues* (*Aen.* 4.487–91):

> She promises to soothe by songs the minds she wants
> to soothe, but others to inflict with cruel cares,
> to halt the flow of streams, turn back the stars;
> she stirs up ghosts at night; you'll see earth rumble
> 'neath her feet, ash trees descend from mountains.

The eighth *Eclogue* deals with the theme of unrequited love. Damon's song presents the dilemma; it is resolved in the song of Alphesiboeus. The lover in Damon finds himself alienated from the landscape, but the lover in Alphesiboeus discovers that *carmina* can draw her beloved back to the landscape from the town, *ab urbe domum*.

The tenth Eclogue

The transformation of the bucolic world and its hero, begun in the sixth and intensified in the eighth, becomes complete in the tenth *Eclogue*. Inevitably, the hero of *Eclogue* 10 is Gallus, the new *magister* of a theme which had captured all of Virgil's attention.

The healing power of song is once more recalled in *Ecl.* 10.31–4, where Gallus is made to invoke the shepherds of Arcadia, and to beseech them to quiet with their songs the pangs of his love:

> His wan response: 'You'll sing, Arcadians, none the less,
> these verses to your mountains, you alone are skilled in song,
> Arcadians. How softly then these bones of mine would rest
> if sometime pipe of yours could tell my loves!'

The tenth *Eclogue* is not so much an invitation to Gallus to find diversion through composing poems in the pastoral genre, as it is a supreme tribute to Gallus for having made Virgil's bucolic poems, through his inspiration, a suitable vehicle for portraying tragic *amores*. Why else should Gallus become the new centre of attention in Virgil's bucolic world? Would the poet really invite Gallus to spend his literary energies on a genre of which Virgil himself was taking final leave?

The tenth *Eclogue* is first and foremost a gift for Gallus (10.2f.) and is meant as a tribute not only to the man, but above all to his poetry.[25] As the curtain rings down upon the pastoral world, the last glimpse of Arcadia presents a paradox: gone is its once idyllic atmosphere, its vague outlines, its heroes from the realm of myth. Instead, it has become a world of 'troubled loves' (6), of martial visions (44f.), of images taken from realms all too real (47 *Alpinas nives, frigora Rheni*; 59 *Partho cornu*). It is a world inspired by its last hero, a hero of flesh and blood; it is the world of the elegiac poet, created as an *extremus labor* for his pleasure and honour (72–4):

> For Gallus you will make
> my song magnificent, for Gallus grows my love each hour
> much as verdant alder lifts its spire in early Spring.

Gallus must have enjoyed the poem immensely. Servius reports that at least some verses in the lover's complaint (10.31–69) are borrowed from Gallus' own elegies;[26] since the poems are lost, this information cannot be checked. But Virgil does allow the lovelorn poet to make the gestures and to strike the poses which belong to the love-elegist's proper *persona*. It is impossible to miss the good-natured humour in all this. Gallus carries on throughout the poem in much the same fashion as Tibullus and Propertius. He never seems to get a grip on his emotions; he indulges in death fantasies and wishful thinking to an extreme found only in his genre.[27]

Kidd has noticed that the *Eclogue* is so infused with symbols for poetry that much of the Theocritean imagery has been deliberately changed to accommodate them. Theocritus had suggested that the Nymphs were detained in Thessalian vales (Peneius or Pindus), and so were not at home in their native Sicily to mourn Daphnis (*Id.* 1.67–9). Virgil has no idea what kept the Nymphs from mourning Gallus; at least, he claims, they were not held on the heights of Parnassus or Pindus, or by the spring Aganippe (10.9–12). Two of these places have to do with poetry almost exclusively; Parnassus is sacred to Phoebus, and Aganippe is the source of Hesiod's river of inspiration, the Permessus. Hermes, Priapus, and Aphrodite are the gods who visit the dying Daphnis in *Id.* 1.77, 81, and 95; Gallus is visited by Apollo, Silvanus, and Pan, 'symbols of poetry, Italy, and pastoral, so that as a trio they represent Italian pastoral poetry'. Animals both wild and tame join the lament for Daphnis in *Idyll* 1; but Gallus is mourned by laurels, 'symbol of Apollo and poetry, and the tamarisk, Virgil's own symbol of unpretentious verse'.[28]

The name 'Lycoris' itself must be the title of a collection of elegies just published by Gallus. Like the later elegists' loves, like Tibullus' 'Delia' and Propertius' 'Cynthia', it seems to have been formed from an epithet of the god of poets—in this case 'Lycian' Apollo.[29] And Gallus imagines 'Lycoris' wandering to the ends of the earth, to the camps and northerly outposts of the Roman empire. Could this be a conceit employed by erotic poets when referring to the publication of their work, to its distribution in the quarters where it was most popular— the Roman army? Officers were notorious for having erotic literature by their bedsides; and it was possible for a Roman poet to address a book just before it became 'public' as if it were eager for a night on the town.[30]

Gallus sees even himself 'under arms of cruel Mars amid the flying weapons and the looming foe' (*Ecl.* 10.44f.)—another conceit of the love elegist. In part it refers to the form of his poetry, for elegy had a long history of 'military' involvement. As early as the seventh century B.C. the Greek poets Callinus and Tyrtaeus had sung their hymns of martial valour in elegiac couplets. Meleager, moreover, brought Eros, with his 'murderous' weapons, to a close approximation of the god of war. The notion certainly carries over to the elegiac poetry of Ovid, who proclaims that 'every lover is a soldier (*militat*), and Cupid has his camp'.[31]

Much of the humour in the poem is undoubtedly lost on us. We can never say, for instance, whether literary puns were intended in the phrases *liber aret* or *Aethiopum versemus ovis* (67f.).

'Closing in on clearings of Parthenius' (57) may refer only to the Arcadian mountain; yet Parthenius was also the mentor of Gallus and the source for much of his amatory material, including above all the poetry of Euphorion of Chalcis, to whom Virgil alludes (we *do* know this from Servius) in verse 50.[32]

Finale

After the final tribute to Gallus (10.72–4), Virgil takes his private leave of a world once dear to him. His words are at once an expression of urgency and determination, mixed with the tenderness of a herdsman toward his flock. The kids have been fed, evening is on its way, and with it comes a harmful shade (75–7). Paying the compliment of imitation to Lucretius, who had mentioned that the shade of certain trees was *gravis* for humans (6.783–5), Virgil adds that *umbra* in general is bad for singers. This 'shade' is equivalent to that retirement from the real world, to that *otium* in which Virgil composed the *Bucolics*.[33] Horace too, probably under Virgil's influence, used *umbra* as a symbol for the poet's retirement.[34]

Virgil determines henceforth to avoid the 'heavy shade' of pastoral. He is *egressus silvis*, his sights are set on something higher and more meaningful—hence the solemn, spondaic tone of *surgamus* (75). The poet must 'arise', must lift himself to the goal which has been set for his life's work. Propertius used the same formula when he called his soul to higher aspirations (2.10.11f.):

> surge anima ex humili iam carmine, sumite vires
> Pierides, magni nunc erit oris opus.

> 'Arise, my soul, from lowly poems; brace yourselves,
> Pierian daughters; now we'll need a mighty voice.'

Virgil's pastoral hero had begun as a lovesick shepherd, a singer of songs which were 'artless' and sung 'in empty earnest' (2.4f.). Shortly thereafter he became the *decus* of the bucolic world, a divine poet (*Eclogue* 5). He appears as a real political hero in *Eclogue* 1, and, as the pastoral world undergoes its final metamorphosis into a world of love elegy, he is seen in the guise of Gallus (*Eclogue* 10). In the meantime, a new hero has been born, and to him the future belongs (*Eclogue* 4). It is *his* career which the poet must pursue to the very end of his life. Between the hopeless plight of the rustic poet in *Ecl.* 2.2 ('nor any hope had he') and the purposeful *surgamus* of the Roman bard in 10 lies a strange, novel world, a proving ground for the development of themes and figures which would culminate in poetry destined to outlive the fame of any hero whom Virgil could have imagined.

Appendix I: Rejuvenation through the Muses

Youth as a special and permanent attribute of the *poet* had first been proclaimed by Callimachus, who characterized himself, though burdened with 'more than a decade', as a *pais* when in the act of fashioning his own *genus tenue* (*Aitia* fr. 1.5f.). In the same introductory section of the *Aitia* (21ff.) his encounter with Apollo as a small boy is set forth: the divine command to 'keep his Muse slender' he intends to follow even in his old age. The poetry he prefers is compared to the song of the cicada, a symbol of the poet himself: 'Let me become the little one, the winged one' (32). As a cicada he would drink heavenly dew and shed old age as the insect sheds his skin: the Muses, he asserts, do not desert the old age of poets whose childhood they have smiled upon (34–8).

The cicada as a literary symbol was not new with Callimachus, nor was the notion of the rediscovery of youth through poetry.[1] His combination of the themes seems to be new, however, especially in that he has made *dew* the restorative agent for himself as poet-cicada. Again, water symbolism in connection with the poet is not new in Greek literature, and is frequent in Callimachus.[2] But when adapted by him to the 'rejuvenated cicada' image, it becomes highly appropriate for the sort of poetry in which Callimachus was pioneering—the 'delicate', *lepton*. At the same time, Callimachus stresses a novel type of 'erotic' motif in poetry, the mutual love between Muse and poet. The motif found favour with Theocritus and his successors in the pastoral-epigrammatic tradition, and was extended by Virgil to include love for all sources of inspiration —Phoebus and Daphnis, the Nymphs and Gallus, even poetry in the abstract.[3]

Appendix II: The Third Eclogue: Palaemon

The judge who appears on the scene rather late in *Eclogue* 3 to arbitrate the poetry contest forms a marked contrast in personality to the two young singers: there is something solemn and oracular in his pronouncements. As he seats himself upon the soft grass, Palaemon's first words direct the poets' attention to nature and to the Spring (55ff.):

> Sing on, as long as we recline on meadow soft,
> for every field now, every tree now bears its fruit,
> now leafs the forest, now's the season full of grace.

Palaemon is dropping no casual, irrelevant, or distracting remark. His is the voice of literary tradition, he it is who sets the scene, who creates the mood proper to a bucolic recitation. He echoes the words of Meleager:[1]

> If foliage rejoices, and the earth bears fruit,
> if herdsman pipes, and woolly flocks are glad,
> if sailormen cast off, and Dionysus dances,
> if fledglings sing, and bees are toiling hard,
> how can a singer not compose a pretty song in Spring?

Palaemon is a judge, the representative of the bucolic genre itself, presiding over the attempt of two new pastoral poets to match their songs with the song of nature. He follows his remarks about the surrounding landscape with an authoritative directive to each of the poets; his authority in this case is that of the Latin Muses themselves. It is Palaemon who knows that 'These turns the Nymphs Camenae love' (59). And when the singers have spent their energies, Palaemon blesses both: each is worthy of the heifer, for each has shown that he understands what it is to be a poet (109f.):

> You're worthy of the heifer, so is he, and so are all
> who either dread a love that's sweet, or suffer bitter loves.

The lover who has felt Meleager's 'bittersweet barb of Eros' has fulfilled the first and most important requirement for the composition of bucolic poetry.[2]

Palaemon's final remark, the closing line of this *Eclogue*, 'Now close the streams, my boys. The meadow's drunk enough', (*claudite iam rivos pueri, sat prata biberunt*), must not be taken simply as a command to the singers to disperse once more to their workaday tasks. Servius, who commented: 'Or, of course, he means allegorically "Leave off singing now, for we've had enough of listening" '. If Servius' suggestion be followed, the 'critic' Palaemon will then appear to have been speaking in terms well suited to his character and to his office. His language is seen here, too, to tend towards the symbolic. In the first place, he addresses the poets as *pueri*, a term of special significance for Virgilian poetry. Their songs (in Servius' 'allegorical' interpretation) are designated 'streams', a conventional symbol for poetry since the time of Pindar, who speaks of his poems as 'Muses' streams' (*Nem.* 7.12) and as 'glorious streams of words' (*Isth.* 7.19).[3] Water and water-sources are used more than once elsewhere by Virgil as a clear expression of poetic activity: Menalcas' singing is characterized as a bringing of shade to springs in *Ecl.* 9.20; water Nymphs become sources of inspiration for Virgil in 7.21 and in 10.1; and he portrays himself as 'unsealing sacred springs' as he writes the *Georgics* (*Geo.* 2.175).

The closing verses of Catullus' sixty-first poem were seen first by Forbiger as the model for *Ecl.* 3.111.[4] Catullus' *virgines*, who have been portrayed as singing the hymenaeal chorus (61.36–40) are ordered to cease their song with the words *claudite ostia virgines / lusimus satis* (231f.: 'Close the doors, my maids. We've sported enough.'). Here the *ostia* are the doors of the wedding chamber; *lusimus* refers to the singing, not only of the girls, but of the poet himself. The primary function of the verses is to provide an appropriate close for the entire poem; the closing of the *ostia* becomes, accordingly, a symbol for the poet's farewell to the bridal pair. His own activity is characterized with the verb *lusimus*. The parallelism in Catullus and in the *Eclogue* consists not only in mere verbal similarity. Virgil may well have come upon his water symbolism through the alternate meaning of *ostia*—'river mouth'—which suggests itself immediately and which may, in fact, explain why Catullus, who was himself well versed in Hellenic literary conventions, chose precisely this word instead of *ianua*, which he had used for the chamber door in verse 76. Virgil, having used the even more obvious *rivos*, carries the water image through to *biberunt* and links it with 'meadows', remaining true to his genre. Just as appropriate was Catullus' *lusimus* for his own genre, where the sportive element is a requisite factor. Both poets have managed to close their poems in words relevant both to the matter of the poem and to poetic activity as it had been characterized in their literary tradition.

NOTES

INTRODUCTION

1. See S. Radhakrishnan, *The Bhagavadgītā*, New York, 1948, pp. 40–2.

2. Introductory *śloka* followed by 13.1–4, translated by Swami Nikhilananda, New York, 1944.

3. Trans. Nikhilananda.

4. *Bhagavadgītā* 13.33, trans. Radhakrishnan.

5. *Bhagavadgītā* 8.9, trans. Radhakrishnan.

6. J. Mascaró, *The Bhagavad Gita*, Penguin, 1962.

7. 'Often I am permitted to return to a meadow', from *The Opening of the Field*, New York, 1960, p. 7.

8. *Dialogus* 9.6 and 12.1f.

9. Curtius 145f. An outstanding example appears in Hesiod, *Theogony* 81–103. See Sperduti 209f. and 224–9. Pindar, who emphasized the poet's *sophia*, also enriched his poetry through natural metaphors as symbols of his own work. See below, pp. 152, 193; Sperduti, 235; and H. Maehler, 66, 77, and 93–8.

10. Cf. Hesiod, *Theogony* 97: 'Happy is he whom the Muses love; a sweet voice flows from his mouth.' See below, pp. 151–2. On nymphs and Muses, see Desport, 244.

11. Sappho fr. 55 (Lobel & Page). Many Greek collections of epigrams in antiquity bore the title *stephanos*, 'Garland'. Flowers as symbols for poems become conventional in the Greek literary tradition with Bacchylides and Pindar: cf. Maehler 59f., 60 note 1, 87 note 8, and 93 note 1. The symbol was recurrent throughout the epigrammatic tradition: cf. Meleager, *AP* 5.147, 12.256, 257, etc.; Crinagoras, *AP* 6.345; Anon., *AP* 7.20; and above all the *Florilegia* of *AP* 4. Cf. Hubaux, *Réalisme* 60f.

12. Archilochus is a cicada in fr. 88A (Diehl). For testimony on insect and honey metaphors, see below, pp. 213 note 1 and 207 note 60. See also Sperduti (above, note 9) 209 and 224f. The insect image crops up (possibly without conscious reference to ancient literary traditions) in modern poets discussing their own work; cf. Robert Frost, 'The Figure a Poem Makes', in *Selected Prose of Robert Frost*, ed. Hyde Cox and E. C. Lathem, New York/Chicago/San Francisco, 1966, p. 18: 'We (poets) bring up as aberrationists, giving way to undirected associations and kicking ourselves from one chance suggestion to another in all directions as of a hot afternoon in the life of a grasshopper.'

13. In defining the 'garden' as the poet's analogy to, or symbol of, his own craftsmanship, I distinguish it sharply from the so-called *locus amoenus*, a literary motif classed as an ingredient of all ancient and medieval pastoral by Curtius pp. 192–202. F. Klingner, *Virgil* points out on p. 60 that *locus*

amoenus is not a literary *terminus technicus* in antiquity, though Curtius has made it so for modern philologists. It signifies nothing more than 'a pleasant place'; the description of such places was open to all, whether or not they were self-conscious pastoral poets. The true significance of pastoral landscapes is barely noticed by Curtius on p. 187, where emphasis falls not upon the landscape, but upon the 'sociological framework' of pastoral, the shepherd's life.

CHAPTER I

1. For an excellent treatment of this poem, its meaning for Theocritus' career, and its pivotal position in the history of Greek literature, see Norman Austin, 'Idyll 16: Theocritus and Simonides', *Transactions and Proceedings of the American Philological Association* 98 (1967) 1–21.

2. The Cyclops' bestial side is represented in Euripides' Satyr drama *Cyclops*. Evidence for Philoxenus' poem in Denys L. Page, *Poetae Melici Graeci*, Oxford, 1962, pp. 423–8.

3. Highly recommended: T. G. Rosenmeyer, *The Green Cabinet: Theocritus and the European Pastoral Lyric*, Berkeley/Los Angeles, 1969.

4. *Ibid.*, 92–7.

5. Ancient and modern discussion of the term *eidyllia* (none of it conclusive) collected in A. S. F. Gow, *Theocritus*, 1, Cambridge 1950, lxxi–lxxii. Not mentioned by Gow is H. Brunn, 'Die griechischen Bukoliker und die Bildende Kunst', *Sitzungsberichte der königlichen bayerischen Akademie der Wissenschaften*, Philosophisch-philologische Classe, 2 (1879) 1–21. Brunn on pp. 20–1, while regarding Christ's *kleine Weise* as an acceptable rendering, emphasizes the pictorial quality of Theocritus' 'genre-pictures' and makes the attractive suggestion that *eidyllia* be translated '*Bildchen*'.

6. S. Nicosia, 49–65.

7. T. B. L. Webster, pp. 82f. The 'satyric' nature of Theocritus' characters was first emphasized by Brunn (see above, note 5) p. 8. G. Lawall, pp. 81–6 suggests on *Idyll* 7 that Lycidas' attire and his smile identify him as a satyr, while Simichidas' name (*simos* = 'snub-nosed') may put him in the same category.

8. Webster, pp. 165f. Cf. Rosenmeyer, pp. 37–40.

9. Sources in Reitzenstein 197–263. See U. von Wilamowitz-Moellendorff, 'Daphnis', *Reden und Vorträge* I[4] 259ff., and Rosenmeyer, pp. 32–5.

10. Servius, *Prooemium ad Bucolica* p. 1.12–13 (Thilo & Hagen): *Alii . . . Apollini Nomio consecratum carmen hoc volunt, quo tempore Admeti regis pavit armenta.* See also Servius' comment on *Ecl.* 5.35, and Euripides, *Alcestis* 568–85.

11. Lawall, p. 2.

12. Ibid., 20.

13. Nicosia 27–38. Cf. Paul Friedländer, *Johannes von Gaza und Paulus Silentiarius: Kunstbeschreibungen justinianischer Zeit*, Leipzig/Berlin, 1912, p. 14: 'Vielleicht soll der Efeu aussen an der Lippe, der Akanthus innen herumlaufen. Aber auch das wird nicht klar bestimmt, und sicher liegt der

Dichter mehr daran, die Ranken um seine poetische Darstellung zu schlingen.'

14. I include here the attempt to link the writing of pastoral to withdrawal into an Epicurean 'garden', as in Grimal, pp. 383-420, and now Rosenmeyer, esp. pp. 65-97. Troxler-Keller, p. 32 draws evidence from Plato and Aristophanes to show that Greek poets in the fifth century B.C. were already speaking metaphorically of their activity as a 'tarrying in the Muses' meadows'. See, for example (with emphasis on the poet as bee), Simonides fr. 88 (Page); Aristophanes, *Birds* 748ff.; and Plato, *Ion* 534 A-B.

15. Hesiod, *Theogony* 32f. On Orpheus as singer, lover, and hierophant, see W. K. C. Guthrie, *Orpheus and Greek Religion* and I. M. Linforth, *The Arts of Orpheus*, Berkeley/Los Angeles, 1941.

16. See W. F. Albright, 'Primitivism in Ancient Western Asia (Mesopotamia and Israel)' in Lovejoy-Boas, pp. 423f.

17. Tablet I, col. 4.2-7, trans. Heidel.

18. Tablet I, col. 4.21-8, trans. Heidel.

19. Tablet II, col. 2.22f., trans. Heidel.

20. Cf. Albright in Lovejoy-Boas, pp. 430f.

21. Translated by Kramer, pp. 110-12.

22. Tablet VI 42-7, trans. Heidel.

23. Frazer, pp. 3-12.

24. For sources, see H. J. Rose, *A Handbook of Greek Mythology*, New York, 1959, pp. 124f. and Frazer, pp. 223-59.

25. Sappho fr. 140 (Lobel & Page); Theocritus, *Idyll* 15.100-49; Bion 1; and variations on the theme in other poets of the bucolic tradition. See Berg, 12ff.

26. See Frazer, pp. 263-87.

27. See E. Maass, *Orpheus*, Munich, 1895; Guthrie 43f.; and M. O. Lee, 'Mystic Orpheus: Another Note on the Three-Figure Reliefs', *Hesperia* 33 (1964) 401-4.

28. I. Trencsényi-Waldapfel notices that the 'death and resurrection' theme is common to *Idyll* 7.72-89 (Daphnis and Comatas) and *Eclogue* 5 (Daphnis dies, Daphnis rises). He suggests that Daphnis is more than merely analogous to Tammuz. The name *Tammuz* was sometimes Hellenized in Syria as *Damis*: confusion with *daphne* ('laurel') produced *Daphnis*: 'Werden und Wesen der bukolischen Poesie', *Acta Antiqua* 14 (1965) 26-30.

29. Callimachus, *Aitia* fr. 1.37f. (Pfeiffer) and *Epigram* 21.5f. Other examples of the Muses' love in Theocritus: *Id.* 5.80 and 11.6. See also Philodemus, *AP* 5.107.8 (where the love relationship has a strong erotic flavour); Anon., *AP* 7.664.4; Leonidas, *AP* 7.715.3f.; and Anon., *AP* 9.191.5.

30. Lawall, 78.

31. Ibid., 100f.

32. Ibid., 74-117. Lawall's interpretation of *Idyll* 7 extends and harmonizes the symbolic approaches suggested by Kühn in *Hermes* 86 (1958) 40-79; van Groningen in *Mnemosyne* 11 (1958) 293-317 and 12 (1959)

24–53; Lasserre in *Rheinisches Museum* 102 (1959) 307–30; and Puelma in *Museum Helveticum* 17 (1960) 144–64.

33. Lasserre (see above, note 32), 325–7; Puelma (see above, note 32), 156; Lawall, pp. 102–8. The wine is four years old (*Id.* 7.147) because, as Lawall ingeniously suggests, Theocritus' literary activity on Cos has lasted four years (p. 122).

34. Lawall, p. 3.

35. E.g. John Keats. Cf. Rosenmeyer, pp. 200f.

36. William Empson, *Some Versions of Pastoral*, New York, 1950.

CHAPTER III

1. Hesiod, *Theogony* 917. See A. Lesky *s.v. Thaleia* in Paully-Wissowa, *Realenzyklopädie der Altertumswissenschaft* 5.1.1205.

2. See above, Chapter I, p. 12.

3. Pausanias 9.35.3; Plutarch, *De musica* 14; J. G. Frazer, *Pausanias's Description of Greece* 5, Cambridge, 1965, pp. 174f.

4. Suetonius, *Life of Lucan* 2. Statius, *Silvae* 1 Prooemium; 2.7.73f. Martial 8.56.19; 14.185. On correspondences in archaic and post-classical tastes, see P. Friedländer's thought-provoking lecture, 'Vorklassisch und nachklassisch', in W. Jaeger, *Das Problem des Klassischen und die Antike*, Teubner, 1933.

5. *E.g.* O. Skutsch, 'Culex 59', *Harvard Studies in Classical Philology* 72 (1967) 309f. (Lucretius). *Loci similes et disputationes* in the edition of A. Salvatore, *Appendix Vergiliana* I (Torino 1957) must be checked carefully; often a passage with only vague similarities will be listed. This is particularly true for 'reminiscences' of the Greek bucolic poets.

6. E. Fraenkel, 'The Culex', *Journal of Roman Studies* 42 (1952) 1–9. For an excellent bibliography on the *Culex*, cf. D. Güntzschel, *Beiträge zur Datierung des Culex*, Münster, 1972.

7. M. Wigodsky, *Vergil and Early Latin Poetry*, Wiesbaden, 1972, = *Hermes Einzelschriften* 24, pp. 23f.; Norden, *Aeneis VI* 16ff.; P. Boyancé, 'Sur le discours d'Anchise (Énéide, VI, 724–51)', *Hommages à Georges Dumézil* (Collection Latomus vol. 45, Brussels, 1960, pp. 60–76.

8. Compare *Ecl.* 4.51 with *Geo.* 4.222, *Ecl.* 5.76–8 with *Aen.* 1. 607–9.

9. *Geo.* 4.171–5, *Aen.* 8.449–53. K. Mras, 'Vergils Culex', *Das Altertum* 7 (1961) 207–13.

10. A. Klotz, 'Zum Culex', *Hermes* 61 (1926) 41.

11. *Theriaca* 164–67. See Salvatore's edition on *Culex* 163ff.

12. For illustrations of the many uses of *manare* in classical Latin, cf. A. Forcellini, *Totius Latinitatis Lexicon* and his remark *sub voce*: '*Mano* dicitur etiam de aliis rebus utcumque fluentibus, serpentibus, et se diffundentibus'.

13. Cicero, *Pro Archia* 18.

14. T. Birt, *Jugendverse und Heimatpoesie Vergils*, Leipzig, 1910, pp. 67–9, 131. Mras (see above, note 9) and Büchner 85 concur.

15. See below, Chapter IV p. 115f. and Chapter VI p. 168.

16. Mras (see above, note 9), 210–12.

17. See the verbal echoes listed in Salvatore's edition.

18. C. Plésent, *Le Culex: Étude sur l'alexandrisme latin*, Paris, 1910, 483f. Plésent also counts an identical number of bucolic caesurae in the *Culex* and the 414 lines selected from *Eclogues* 1, 2, 4, 6, 9, and 10.

19. Duckworth adds that repeat-clusters of metrical patterns and repeated patterns in adjacent lines in the *Culex* are extremely close only to the *Bucolics*: G. E. Duckworth, 'Studies in Latin Hexameter Poetry', *TAPA* 97 (1966) 89–92 (now = *Vergil and Classical Hexameter Poetry: A Study in Metrical Variety*, Ann Arbor: 1969, pp. 82f.). As for elisions, Büchner 79 finds 11 per cent in the *Culex* over against 29 per cent in the *Bucolics*, 49 per cent in the *Georgics*, and 55 per cent in the *Aeneid*; this could easily be interpreted as a development over a 30-year period in the style of one and the same poet. The question of caesura has not been fully investigated, and may never be resolved, since the intonation of any given line of verse depends to a significant degree on individual interpretation. Büchner 80f. divides the occurrence of Virgil's penthemimeral caesurae into two categories (those accompanied, and those unaccompanied, by secondary caesura in the fourth foot), producing figures which make the *Culex* seem out of step with genuine Virgilian work. If the two categories be combined, however, the *Culex* is seen to have one penthemimeral caesura every 18 lines, as opposed to one every 23 lines for the *Bucolics* and the *Aeneid* and one every 45 lines for the *Georgics*. In this connection, W. F. Jackson Knight's observations on fourth-foot texture must be significant (*Accentual Symmetry in Virgil*, Oxford 1939): the percentage of fourth-foot 'homodyne' (coincidence of verse-pulse and word accent) is exactly the same in the *Culex* as in the *Bucolics*. See Wilkinson pp. 118–32.

20. Büchner, p. 87 has dispelled the notion, based largely on vv. 261ff., that the *Culex* is a translation or even an adaptation of a Greek epyllion entitled *Empis*. The gnat does not need to have been originally female to be met by Persephone and heroines (Maass, *Orpheus*, Munich, 1895, pp. 238ff.; Zielinski, *Philologus* 60, 1901, 3), any more than does Odysseus in the model for this passage, *Odyssey* 11.225ff.

21. See the *Loci similes et disputationes* in Salvatore's edition.

22. Plésent (see above, note 18), 112 and 266; G. Jachmann, *Gnomon* 4 (1928) 577.

23. See below, Chapter III p. 105. Gow and Page, *The Greek Anthology: Hellenistic Epigrams* II, Cambridge, 1965, pp. 525f., who consider it unlikely that Meleager's collection contained Theocritean epigrams, point to the strange 'dismemberment' of this poem in *AP* 9. The dislocation could have occurred during a transfer from the *Garland*.

24. The poplars of v. 142 are the sisters of Phaethon. As for the myrtle of 145, Plésent suggested in his edition (Paris 1910) that it was meant to be conscious of the 'fate' of Myrsinus. But if *non nescia fati = fatidica*, the allusion must be to the myrtles before the temple of Quirinus, which had once foretold the relative prosperity of patricians and plebeians (Pliny, *Nat. hist.* 15.120f.)—yet another Roman allusion in the midst of Hellenic themes.

25. See below, pp. 103f.

26. See below, pp. 103–5, 124, 148, 150.

27. H. G. Beyen, *Pompeianische Wanddekoration*, II 1 (1960) 320–47; Hubaux, *Thèmes* 153f.; P. Boyancé, 'Le sens cosmique de Virgile', *Revue des études latines* 32 (1954) 220–49, esp. 232–42.

28. As a copy of a somewhat older Italian or Sicilian mural: cf. P. H. von Blanckenhagen, 'The Odyssey Frieze', *Römische Mitteilungen* des deutschen archäologischen Instituts 70 (1963) 100–46.

29. Beyen (see above, note 27) 347.

30. P. H. von Blanckenhagen and C. Alexander, 'The Paintings from Boscotrecase', *Römische Mitteilungen* Ergänzungsheft 6 (1962); P. Grimal, 'Les *Metamorphoses* d'Ovide et la peinture paysagiste', *Revue des études latines* 16 (1938) 145–61. This sort of painting, with its water-cliff-trees-monument formulae (discussed below, Chapter V pp. 132–4) is reminiscent of the work of Claude Lorraine (1600–82) more than of any other Italian landscape paintings. He was influenced, as were others, by Virgil's 'Arcadian' landscapes; had he also seen ancient sacro-idyllic landscapes? Cf. Kenneth Clark, *Landscape into Art*, Pelican, 1949, pp. 74–9.

31. A discussion of Lucretius' pastoral tendencies can be found in D. H. Gillis, 'Pastoral Poetry in Lucretius', *Latomus* 26 (1967) 339–62. On Lucretius 5.1379–98, cf. Pöschl 53–5 and B. Farrington, 'Vergil and Lucretius', *Acta Classica* 1 (1958) 47.

32. Virgil's use of nature's *imago vocis* and the contrast with Theocritus are eloquently discussed by Damon, esp. pp. 281–90.

33. Hubaux, *Thèmes* 24–34; Clausen 181–96; Otis 26–32; N. B. Crowther, *Classical Quarterly* 64 (1970) 321–7.

34. Otis, pp. 20–4; M. Puelma-Piwonka, *Lucilius und Kallimachos*, Frankfurt a.M., 1949; E. Fraenkel, *Plautinisches im Plautus*, Berlin, 1922; E. W. Handley, *Menander and Plautus*, London, 1968; F. Leo, *Geschichte der römischen Literatur*, Berlin, 1913, 93–211, 405–29.

35. Apropos of Wallace Stevens in *Tradition and Poetic Structure*, Denver, 1960, 108.

36. *AP* 9.205; Gow 1.lix–lxii.

37. Cartault, p. 20; Westendorp-Boerma 52f.

38. Pliny, *Naturalis historia* 28.19; Gow 1.lx n.4.

39. This seems to be the case if the assembly of a Theocritean corpus, adulterated as it was by spurious poems, had to wait for an Artemidorus. Gow (1.lx) points out that even Meleager seems unfamiliar with Theocritus; one epigram, however, must have been included in the *Stephanos* (see above, pp. 100f.). If the poet had been popular, one might have expected at least a definitive edition from his fellow Alexandrians.

40. Donatus, *Vita* 25; Servius, *Vita* 25.

41. I mean the term 'architectural' as it is used by G. E. Duckworth, *Structural Patterns and Proportions in Vergil's Aeneid*, Ann Arbor, 1962, prompted by Virgil's characterization of his own art in *Georgics* 3.12–36 (cf. Duckworth 14). This scholar has discovered patterns in Virgil's poetry which may be even more subtle than what the poet himself had consciously in-

tended; yet the unquestionably frequent occurrence of a proportion which determines beauty of structure in nature (the 'golden section', 1 : 1.618) may be a clue to the creative processes of the human mind itself.

42. Krause, pp. 6f.; E. A. Hahn, 'The Characters in the *Eclogues*', *TAPA* 75 (1944) 196–241; P. Maury, 'Le secret de Virgile et l'architecture des Bucoliques', *Lettres d'Humanité* 3 (1944) 71–147; L. Richardson, Jr., *Poetical Theory in Republican Rome* (New Haven 1944) 121; G. E. Duckworth, 'The Architecture of the *Aeneid*', *AJP* 75 (1954) 2ff.; Otis 128–43.

43. Cf. Klingner, *Virgil* p. 108.

44. Cf. E. A. Fredricksmeyer, 'Octavian and the Unity of Virgil's First Eclogue', *Hermes* 94 (1966) 214. O. Skutsch, who has discovered most of the significant numerical structure in the *Bucolics*, offers a somewhat different explanation for the lack of symmetry here (*Symmetry* 157). Further observations on mathematical structure in the *Bucolics* in Duckworth (see above, note 42) 21f. and 39f.

45. Van Sickle, 493–501.

46. Polybius 4.20; G. Jachmann, 'L'Arcadia come paesaggio bucolico', *Maia* 5 (1952) 161–74.

47. Cf. Snell, 'Arcadia: The Discovery of a Spiritual Landscape' in *Discovery of the Mind*.

48. Cf. 1.54, 2.21, 7.13.

49. Cf. J.-G. Préaux, 'Constatations sur la composition de la 4ᵉ bucolique de Virgile', *Revue belge de philologie et d'histoire* 41 (1963) 63–79.

50. O. Skutsch, 'The Original Form of the Second Eclogue', *Harvard Studies in Classical Philology* 74 (1970) 95–9.

51. Skutsch, *Symmetry* 169.

52. See below, p. 125 n. 34.

53. More elaborate reasons for accepting the chronological priority of 9 over 1, and of both over 4 and 6, are given below, Chapter V 143f. and Chapter VI 170f. Skutsch, *Symmetry* 157, argues that 9 actually determines the structure of 1.

54. Bayet 277–99.

55. Cartault, p. 34, Rose, p. 151, Holtorf, p. 213. Further reasons for accepting the three 'commissioned' poems 6, 8, and 10, all heavily influenced by Gallus' love elegy, as the latest are given below, Chapter VII 183ff.

56. See also below, pp. 129f.

57. Powell fr. 1.1–6. The model was first seen by C. Weymann *apud* E. Pfeiffer 20.

58. Klingner, *Studien* 191f.

59. *AP* 12.127, 164; *AP* 7.100. Cf. Hubaux, *Réalisme* 38–48.

60. *AP* 7.196; 12.127; 12.89.5; 12.163–65; 12.128; 5.146; 9.745; 1.1.14f.; 4.27; 12.158; 12.117; and 12.127 again, which Hubaux calls the major inspiration for *Eclogue* 2. Cf. Hubaux, *Réalisme* 49–81. Notice too the Lucretian echo in *Ecl.* 2.51 (again from 5, verse 889 *molli vestit lanugine malas*).

61. Cf. Klingner, *Virgil* pp. 40f.

CHAPTER IV

1. Servius, *Prooemium ad Bucolica; Vita Probiana* 13. A recent survey of 22 'superior' English pastoral poems by 18 poets indicates 29 as the median age, and 31.36 as the mean age, of the pastoral poet. Years of 'maximum productivity' occur between the ages of 25 and 29: H. C. Lehman, *Age and Achievement*, Princeton, 1953, pp. 105, 118.

2. Pöschl, p. 74.

3. E. A. Schmidt, 'Hirtenhierarchie in der antiken Bukolik', *Philologus* 113 (1969) 189f.

4. An outstanding example is seen in the contrast between *Eclogue* 3 and its Theocritean model, *Idyll* 5. Cf. Fantazzi 177.

5. The cave as a place of worship in Greece is attested from Minoan times onward: cf. Nilsson 261-64. A full treatment of the rôle played by caves in the Greek religious tradition, together with a fine analysis of their effect upon the imagination of the pious Hellene, is to be found in Porphyry, *De antro nympharum*.

6. Philochorus, *FGH* 328 F 219 = A. Gellius 15.20.5. Satyrus' *Bios* in *Ox. Pap.* 9 (1912) 1176, fr. 39 col. 9.4-19. Cf. *Genos Euripidou kai bios* 61-4 (Nauck).

7. Pausanias 7.5.12.

8. Pausanias 9.29.6.

9. See above, p. 11.

10. *De architectura* 5.6.9. Cf. Grimal, pp. 254-353.

11. Webster, pp. 163f. and 'Menander: Production and Imagination', *Bulletin of the John Rylands Library* 45 (1962) 244-50.

12. Rothstein, p. 24 *ad* 3.3.37. Wimmel 247.

13. Kambylis, pp. 167-70. See below, p. 124f.

14. Cartault, pp. 156f. and E. Pfeiffer, p. 61.

15. R. Merkelbach, *Roman und Mysterium in der Antike*, Munich, 1962, pp. 192ff.

16. Murley *passim*; Parry 15; Lawall, p. 117.

17. Phaedrus 230 C, 258 E, 262 D. Murley 284 calls attention to Cicero's symbolic interpretation of the plane tree in the *Phaedrus*. The Muses' shrine had not been mentioned in connection with the plane tree when the site was chosen in *Phaedrus* 229 A-230 C. An altar of the Muses did, however, exist on the site of the dialogue, near the spot on the Ilisus where Boreas had carried off Orithyia (Pausanias 1.19.5), and is included in Socrates' final remarks probably to lend higher significance to the locale. But the verb *katabainein* seems to presuppose a descent which had not been indicated in the earlier description of the place. Had Plato purposely allowed the plane-tree site to undergo a metamorphosis at the end of the dialogue, and to assume the aspects of a Muses' *cave*? Rothstein *ad* Prop. 3.3.27 has certainly understood 278 B to refer to a cave-like area, and has been followed in this interpretation by Wimmel 247 and by Kambylis, p. 164. I am grateful to my colleague John D. Moore for his ingenious suggestion that the very word for 'plane tree' (Gr. *platanos*) held mystical significance for a philosopher who had dubbed himself *Platon*.

18. Reitzenstein 196ff.; Rohde, *Geschichte* 86f. Cf. Callimachus, *Epigram* 22; Theocritus, *Id.* 1; 5.20; 6.1–5, 44 (Daphnis as poet); 7.73–7 (Daphnis as lover); 8 (poet); *Epigrams* 2, 3, 4.14, 5 (Daphnis' music); Zonas, *AP* 9.556 (beauty); Glaucus, *AP* 9.341; Meleager, *AP* 7.535 and 12.128. For the pre-Theocritean origins of the Daphnis-figure, see above, 12ff. and the testimonia and related controversies reported by Desport, pp. 108–11. The *Sikelika* of Timaeus (cited by Parthenius, *Erotic Passions* 29) represented Daphnis simply as a beautiful Sicilian shepherd-musician. This was undoubtedly the form in which he was known and developed by the Alexandrian poets, and by Virgil through his association with Parthenius.

19. The source for this passage, according to Hubaux, *Réalisme* 59f., is to be found in Meleager, *AP* 12.128; the epigram follows immediately upon an Alexis-epigram in the Strato collection.

20. Cf. Theocritus, *Epigram* 4.14 and Meleager, *AP* 12.128.

21. Meleager, *AP* 12.127.3f.; 12.86.4; Moschus, 7.7.

22. *AP* 5.179. Cf. Theocritus *Id.* 7.118f.; *AP* 12.45, 166, etc.

23. Pointed out by Hubaux, *Réalisme* 106f. with special reference to Meleager, *AP* 7.535. Cf. *AP* 7.8–10; Bion 1; *Epitaphios Bionos*; Plato, *AP* 7.670; Antiphanes, *AP* 9.84.6.

24. Meleager effects the apotheosis of his beloved, *AP* 12.68.5. Empedocles immortalizes himself, *AP* 9.569; compare the 'apotheosis' of Epicurus in Lucretius 5.8f., the formal model for *Ecl.* 5.64. Ptolemy's deification: Antipater of Sidon, *AP* 7.241. A shepherd becomes immortal through song in Callimachus, *Epigram* 22. Bion sings his way to resurrection in the *Epitaphios Bionos* 119–26. Cf. further Euripides, *Phoenissae* 1728–31 (Oedipus' immortality through the Muse). *Tollemus ad astra* is reminiscent of Cicero, *Pro Archia poeta* 22: *In caelum huius proavus Cato tollitur*, i.e. through the poetry of Ennius. Cicero goes on to suggest (30) that celebration in poetry constitutes the finest sort of immortality. Cf. also Catullus 6.16f. and Cicero, *Philippic* 2.42.107 end.

25. E.g. *AP* 16.188–90. Compare the *Priapea* in the *Appendix Vergiliana*. *Ecl.* 5.58–73 is reminiscent of the peaceful qualities of Dionysus emphasized by the chorus in Euripides, *Bacchae* 417–20.

26. *Ecl.* 3.62; 3.84; 3.90; 7.21; 9.56; and 6.9–10. Compare this last with *AP* 9.191.5.

27. Parry, 11; Lawall, 20.

28. Snell, p. 290 (tr. T. G. Rosenmeyer). Cf. W. Berg, 'Daphnis and Prometheus', *TAPA* 96 (1965) 11–23, on *PV* and *P. Oxy.* 2245.

29. Rohde, *Ecloge* 132–9; Herrmann 112–17; Desport 123.

30. Desport, pp. 95–108 and 233f. Mountains: 2.5, 6.29f., 8.22–4. Forests: 1.5, 2.5, 6.11, 8.22, 10.8.

31. E.g. Theocritus, *Id.* 7.92; Virgil, *Ecl.* 9.19, 10.1, 7.21; Horace, *Odes* 2.19.3. Cf. Desport, p. 244 and W. F. Otto, *Die Musen* (Darmstadt 1954), pp. 20, 23.

32. U. von Wilamowitz-Moellendorff, *Hellenistische Dichtung* II, Berlin, 1924, p. 93 n. 3; Voigt, *Roschers Lexikon* 1.1082; Maas 375ff.; Kroll 30ff.; and Plutarch, *Quaestiones conviviales* 8, proem.

33. Troxler-Keller, pp. 56–61. P. Boyancé, 'Properce', *Fondation Hardt Entretiens* 2 (1953) 198ff. Cf. Sihler, *AJP* (1905) 1ff. and E. J. Jory, 'Associations of Actors in Rome', *Hermes* (1970) 224–36.

34. Cf. Pindar, fr. 179 Snell; *Olymp.* 6.86f.; *Nem.* 4.94; 7.77. Simias, *Ovum* 1–4. Alcaeus of Messene, *AP* 7.1. Meleager, *AP* 12.257.5–8. Virgil, *Culex* 2.

35. *AP* 7.9.5f. Cf. Rohde, *Forma* 50. Gow and Page, *The Greek Anthology: Hellenistic Epigrams* II 225, believe the invention of the elegiac couplet is meant.

36. 3.62, 104; 4.57; 5.9; 6.3, 11, 29, 66, 73, 82; 7.22, 62, 64; and 10.21. On *Ecl.* 4.10, see below, p. 167 Cf. Pöschl, 106: 'Apollo ist das göttliche Vorbild, an dem sich die Dichtkunst des Hirten orientiert . . .'

37. Lucretius 4.580ff. Cf. Damon 287f.

38. That Meliboeus is unaware of any danger to the kids was suggested by Servius *ad loc.*: . . . *aut quia in capro est spes haedorum, aut intellegimus istum* (sc. *Meliboeum*) *haedos prodidisse, sed nescire, quod tamen ille quasi divinus indicat.*

39. F. Pfister, 'Epiphanie', *RE* Supplementband 4 277–323. On p. 280 Pfister mentions a few formulaic verbs from Hellenistic authors and from the New Testament which seem to correspond to Meliboeus' *aspicio* and *contra videt*, esp. Apollonius, *Argonautica* 4.1551–8. P. 319: response of animals. Other testimony, esp. for Roman literature, in Pöschl 130 n. 41.

CHAPTER V

1. P. H. von Blanckenhagen, 'The Odyssey Frieze', *RM* 70 (1963) 100–46; P. H. von Blanckenhagen and C. Alexander, *The Paintings from Boscotrecase*, *RM* Ergänzungsheft 6 (1962) 24f., 57; Phyllis W. Lehmann, *Roman Wall-Paintings from Boscoreale in the Metropolitan Museum of Art* (New York 1953); A. Rumpf, 'Classical and Post-Classical Greek Painting', *JHS* 67 (1947) 18ff.

2. Compare the landscaped backgrounds for the Icarus-scenes from Pompeii: C. M. Dawson, *Romano-Campanian Mythological Landscape Painting* (*Yale Classical Studies* 9, 1944). The term 'sacro-idyllic landscape' was coined by M. Rostovtzeff, who first described the genre: *RM* 26 (1911) 1ff.

3. Jachmann, *Technik* 113; see also Martin, 100.

4. *Monumenti della pittura antica scoperti in Italia* Sec. 3, Pompeii fasc. 2, plate 1.

5. House no. 19 in *Mon. della pittura* Sec. 3, Pompeii fasc. 2, text p. 32, fig. 25.

6. Paul Herrmann, *Denkmäler der Malerei des Altertums*, Series 1 (Munich 1904–31) plate 172a.

7. A. Maiuri, *Roman Painting* (Geneva, Skira 1959) p. 122.

8. My interpretation of *Eclogue* 9 owes a great deal to the work of these scholars: Jachmann, *Technik* 114; Martin 98–100; F. Leo, 'Vergils erste und neunte Ecloge', *Hermes* 38 (1903) 17; and especially Oppermann 205–211.

9. Martin, 98. Leo, 17.

10. Krause, p. 24; Cartault, p. 361; Rohde, *Forma* 24.

11. *Nymphas* refers to the Nymphs' lament in 5.20ff.; the remainder is a citation, almost word for word, of the preparation of Daphnis' gravesite (5.40). On the likelihood that 9 was composed not long after 5, cf. Klingner, *Ekloge* 241.

12. Oppermann, 205f.

13. The *astrum* is that of the dead Julius Caesar, but has actual significance only if the destiny and responsibility of Octavian is included in the image, for the star *processit*, i.e. its influence expands continually, its effect will be felt most fully in coming generations: *carpent tua poma nepotes*. So also Klingner, *Studien* pp. 242f. and Holtorf, p. 40. The *astrum* cannot be the comet mentioned in Suetonius, *J. Caesar* 88, for its effect is not passing, but enduring; it is the planet Venus (cf. *Dionaei Caesaris*), the ancestral star of the *gens Iulia* (cf. *Aeneid* 8.680f.). See Servius *ad Aen.* 2.801, Propertius 4.6.59 *Idalio miratur Caesar ab astro*, and Herrmann, pp. 116f.

14. The numerous passages which describe a specifically agricultural activity or milieu are listed in Cartault, pp. 459f. and in Hubaux, *Réalisme* 81–9.

15. Hubaux, *Réalisme* 84, calls *Ecl.* 9.46–50 an *arrière-plan géorgique*. Surely *Ecl.* 10.36 *aut custos gregis aut maturae vinitor uvae* refers to Virgil's dual preoccupation at the time of the composition of the tenth *Eclogue*.

16. Cf. Klingner, *Virgil* pp. 154–8.

17. See above, Chapter I pp. 22–5.

18. See above, p. 23.

19. For references to the belief, both ancient and modern, that awesome powers walk at midday, cf. Gow II 4 *ad Id.* 1.15ff.

20. C. P. Segal, '*Tamen cantabitis, Arcades*—Exile and Arcadia in *Eclogues* One and Nine', *Arion* 4 (1965) 237–66, esp. 250.

21. I am grateful to T. B. L. Webster for his suggestion that *silet* is another signal for the epiphany *manquée*, and for two references to 'pre-epiphany silence' in Attic tragedy: Sophocles, *Oedipus at Colonus* 1623 and Euripides, *Bacchae* 1084.

22. *AP* 7.261.3: cf. S. Tugwell, 'Virgil, *Eclogue* 9.59–60', *CR* 77 (1963) 132f. Servius' attempt to identify Bianor with the founder of Mantua is an inept example of the ancient (and modern) quest for biographical detail in this poem. Virgil himself gives the name of Mantua's founder as 'Ocnus' in *Aen.* 10.198–201.

23. *AP* 4.2.11; *AP* 9.423. A. S. F. Gow and D. L. Page, *The Greek Anthology: The Garland of Philip and Some Contemporary Epigrams* II Cambridge, 1968, p. 197.

24. *AP* 9.295 and 10.101.

25. *AP* 9.273, 9.308, *Anthologia Planudea* 276, and *AP* 7.49.

26. *AP* 10.18.

27. See above, pp. 22–5.

28. For the probability that the real events which serve as a background for the ninth and the first *Eclogues* are the dispossessions occurring *before* the Perusian War (Appian 5.51) under the administration of the *triumviri agris dividundis* of 41 B.C., cf. Bayet, 271ff.; Rose 78ff.; and Holtorf 223.

29. Klingner, *Studien* pp. 240-3.
30. Cf. Maehler, 67, 77, and 93-8.
31. Esp. fr. 1.51f. Diehl.
32. *Olympian* 2.85f.
33. 9.3; compare Pindar, *Paian* 6.6.
34. 10.39 and fr. 5 Snell.
35. 3.85.
36. Cf. J. V. Cunningham, pp. 107ff.
37. Cf. Clausen, 191.
38. Cf. Ecl. 4.20 *colocasia*, which is *hapax legomenon*, and his attempt to introduce *spelaeum* (*Ecl.* 10.52) into the Latin language: Norden, *Aeneis VI* 119 *ad Aen.* 6.10.
39. Cf. Rose, 127: '. . . it is a common figure of speech to say that a poet does that which he describes someone as doing'. Martin, 104: 'Es gab also einen Topos in der römischen Dichtung, nach dem durch den Inhalt des Gedichtes die Art des Dichtens selbst angegeben wurde'.
40. See above, Chapter III p. 125 note 34. The symbolism of *Ecl.* 10.71 was not lost on Servius: *allegoricos autem significat se composuisse hunc libellum tenuissimo stilo*.
41. Wimmel, 82.
42. *Studien* p. 233.
43. W. F. Jackson Knight, 'Virgil's Secret Art', *RCCM* 6 (1964) 122f.
44. Translated from Rohde, *Ecloge* 121.
45. As O. Skutsch, *Eklogen* 200f. and Pöschl, pp. 9-13 have shown, the name 'Tityrus' occurs in this *Eclogue* for its euphonic effect within the initial verses of the poem; its appearance holds no deeper significance.
46. Martin, 105.
47. Cf. *Idylls* 6.6-19 and 11.
48. Similarly now B. F. Dick, 'Vergil's Pastoral Poetic', *AJP* 91 (1970) 283-7.
49. Desport, p. 119; Martin, 103.
50. Martin, 103. Compare the epiphany of Daphnis in *Ecl.* 7.7f. (see above, pp. 129-31). The god Pan manifests himself to the poet according to the same formula in *Ecl.* 10.26.
51. See above, p. 145 and note 39.
52. Pöschl, pp. 46-55.
53. Desport, pp. 22f. and 55.
54. Martin, 104.
55. Compare the 'poetic' function of the river Eurotas, *Ecl.* 6.82f., and the symbolic use of the river Permessus in the Gallus scene, *Ecl.* 6.64. In the latter passage Virgil is imitating Callimachus' account of his own consecration as poet in the *Aitia*: cf. Wimmel, 227, 234ff.
56. See below, note 60.
57. Kambylis, pp. 113-16. On the kinship of the Mantis and the poet, who are both full of the divine and the holy, cf. Plato, *Ion* 534 A-B. Poets and prophets are grouped in the same category in Homer (*Od.* 17.384-6) and Empedocles (*Vors.* 31 B 146). Ingrid Löffler, 'Die Melampodie:

Versuch einer Rekonstruktion des Inhalts', *Beiträge zur klassischen Philologie* 7 (1963) 14ff., suggests that priests and seers were the first authors of epic poems.

58. Kambylis, pp. 66f. shows that the scholia to the *Aitia* (*Pap. Oxy. ined. a*, fr. 1, in Pfeiffer vol. II under 'Addenda et corrigenda ad vol. I', 102ff.), together with considerations for the internal structure of the *Aitia* prologue, prove Callimachus to have originated this unorthodox version, which was followed by Alcaeus of Messene, *AP* 7.55.5f.; Antipater of Thessalonica, *AP* 11.24.1-6; and Archias or Asclepiades, *AP* 9.64.

59. If this is the sense of Book 7, fr. 1.217 (*nos ausi reserare*), imitated by Virgil in *Geo.* 2.175: G. Pascoli, *Epos* 2 (Livorno 1911) 34; J. H. Waszink, 'The Proem of the *Annales* of Ennius', *Mnemosyne* Ser. 4 vol. 3 (1950) 225f.; and Kambylis, p. 194. Cf. however O. Skutsch, *Studia Enniana*, London: 1968, p. 124.

60. Bees and poets: for examples in Simonides, Pindar, and Bacchylides, cf. Maehler 91 and 94; in Aristophanes and Plato, Troxler-Keller, pp. 31ff.; in Callimachus, Varro, and Lucretius, Wimmel 112ff.; in Horace, Troxler-Keller, pp. 153ff., who writes that pungent *thyme* in connection with the bee-poet metaphor is attested only in Simonides, fr. 43 Diehl, and in Horace, *Ode* 4.2.27ff. This is not the case: cf. Dioscorides, *AP* 7.708.6. Furthermore, Daphnis, whose connection with poetry is discussed in Chapter IV above, pp. 123-30, is said by Virgil to have honour 'as long as thyme is food for bees, and dew for crickets' (*Ecl.* 5.77). Further examples of the bee-and-honey symbol from Hellenistic poetry: Theocritus, *Id.* 8.83, 7.78-89 (cf. Desport 114f.); Callimachus, *Hymn* 2.110; Anon., *AP* 7.12.1; *AP* 9.187. 1f., 190.1f., and 505.6. General discussion of the bee's relationship to the Muses in Olck, *RE* vol. 3 part 1, 447 s.v. *Biene*. W. Wili, *Horaz und die augusteische Kultur*, Basel: 1948 p. 257: 'Das Tierchen war also nur für die Nichtwissenden klein, für den Dichter war es liebliches signum musischer Begabung'.

61. O. Skutsch, *Eklogen* 198f.

CHAPTER VI

1. *Geburt des Kindes*. Norden's foremost precursor in the search for ancient oriental and Egyptian sources for the fourth *Eclogue* was F. Boll, *Aus der Offenbarung Johannis*, Berlin: 1914, pp. 13f. and *Sulla quarta ecloga* (see Bibliography).

2. *Oracula sibyllina* 3 (ed. J. Geffcken), Leipzig, 1902. Norden, *Geburt* 50, 138, 142, 147-57.

3. *Geburt* 149.

4. Jachmann, *Ekloge* 23f.

5. *Orac. Sibyll.* 3.652. The 'king sent from the sun' was believed by Norden and his followers to refer to a descendant of Apollo Helios; hence *Ecl.* 4.10 *tuus iam regnat Apollo.* Jachmann, *Ekloge* 41ff. shows that 'from the sun' can only mean 'from the sunrise', i.e. 'from the East'.

6. Jachmann, *Ekloge* 21.

7. Ibid., 56ff.

8. Ibid., 19f., 40f.

9. Ibid., 50f., 60.

10. E. Pfeiffer, p. 90.

11. Rose, pp. 196ff. presents all the conclusive arguments against identifying the *puer* with a son of Pollio.

12. Boll, 17; Jachmann, *Ekloge* 54. Cf. also Carcopino 125ff., who maintains that Pollio could have been consul *de facto* and *de iure* only after the Peace of Brundisium, and not in January of 40 B.C.

13. Rose, p. 188; cf. R. Syme, *The Roman Revolution* 2nd ed., Oxford, 1952 p. 220.

14. 'Virgil's Messianic Eclogue', *CR* 22 (1908) 150f.

15. Hubaux, *Thèmes* 73f.

16. Desport, p. 237.

17. Cf. Rosenmeyer, pp. 266f. on the function of the *adynaton* in pastoral.

18. For the ultimate source of these images, see below, note 36.

19. Examples from Virgil and his Hellenic models: see above, Chapter I note 29 and Appendix I note 3.

20. Desport, p. 229.

21. Virgil calls Pollio the *lector* of his Muse in *Ecl.* 3.85. Since *lector* can mean 'one who reads aloud', it might be suggested that Pollio had been the one who actually 'published' Virgil's early poetry, and who first brought it to the attention of Octavian.

22. Virgil, *Ecl.* 3.86; Horace, *Ode* 2.1, *Serm.* 1.10.42f., 84f.; Pliny. *Epist.* 5.3.5f.; Tacitus, *Dialogus de oratoribus* 21; Cartault 22–30.

23. Catullus 12.6f.

24. Cartault, p. 20.

25. 'Catulls Peleus-Epos', *Studien* 156–224.

26. Klingner, *Studien* pp. 191–204 and 213–16.

27. Ibid., 191–204.

28. Putnam, 200.

29. F. Klingner, *Römische Geisteswelt*, 4th ed., 270–2.

30. Klingner, *Studien* pp. 187–212; Otis, pp. 27–9 and 100; and Putnam *passim*.

31. Klingner, *Studien* pp. 208–10 and Otis, p. 208.

32. Klingner, *Studien* pp. 161, 187, 207.

33. Catullus 64.22f., echoed in *Ecl.* 4.5 *magnus ab integro saeclorum nascitur ordo*. G. Pasquali, 'Il Carme 64 di Catullo', *Studi Italiani* 1 (1920) 17 was of the opinion that 64.38–42 actually refers to a return of the Golden Age. It should be noted that Virgil has modelled some of the symptoms of his own Golden Age on precisely these verses (*Ecl.* 4.40f.).

34. Compare Catullus 64   with   *Eclogue* 4
      51 heroum virtutes   26 heroum laudes et facta
                                                              parentum
         78 electos iuvenes simul et decus   35 delectos heroas
      323 o decus eximium magnis   11 decus hoc aevi
            virtutibus augens

348 virtutes claraque   27 virtus
     facta   54 tua facta
357 magnis virtutibus   17 patriis virtutibus

35. Herrmann, pp. 62–6: 4.6 from 64.398; 4.7 and 49 from 64.23a–b; 4.13 and 31 from 64.295 and 397; 4.15f. from 64.405–8 and 384ff.; 4.17 from 64.323ff.; 4.35ff. from 64.4, 6, and 344f.; 4.40f. from 64.38ff.; 4.46f. from 64.321f., 326f., etc., and 382f.

36. 4.38 *nautica pinus* seems to be inspired by 64.1 *vertice pinus*: in both cases, *pinus* is the last word of the line. 4.5 *integro saeclorum nascitur ordo* echoes 64.22 *optato saeclorum tempore nati. Teque adeo*, which begins 4.11, is from 64.25 *teque adeo*, which also begins a line; the same for *irrita*, the initial word of 4.14 and of 64.59, and for *delectos heroas* (4.35) and *electos iuvenes* (64.78). Furthermore, not only *delectos heroas*, but the entire reference to the Argonauts (4.34f.) as well as the use of Thetis (4.32), must have been inspired to some extent by Catullus 64. *Munuscula* (64.103) is used by Virgil for the first and only time in 4.18 (Holtorf 166). 64.353f. *praecerpens messor aristas . . . flaventia demetit arva* was surely in Virgil's mind when he wrote *molli paulatim flavescet campus arista* (4.28). The proximity of *quercus* and *sudanti cortice* in 64.106 will have suggested 4.30 *quercus sudabunt*; this Catullan verse has also influenced the 'golden' passage of *Ecl.* 8.52–6 (see above, 160), where *quercus* and *corticibus sudent* again occur in close proximity (53f.). Finally, the position of *lana* (4.42) and *vellera* (4.44) directly before the verses of the *Parcae* (4.46ff.) must have been influenced by *lanae vellera* (64.318f.), which occurs just before the Parcae begin to speak in Catullus 64.323ff.

Borrowings from Catullan poems other than 64 include 4.6 *iam redit et virgo* (from 62.4 *iam veniet virgo*), 4.49 *magnum Iovis incrementum* (cf. 34.6 *magna progenies Iovis*), and 4.8–10 *tu . . . Lucina* (34.13 *tu Lucina*). Another borrowing seems indicated by the 'laughing infant' motif in 4.60ff.; cf. Catullus 61.216–20 *matris e gremio suae . . . dulce rideat ad patrem*.

37. Herrmann, pp. 67ff.

38. E. Linkomies, 'Vergils vierte Ekloge', *Arctos* 1 (1930) 168ff., 187.

39. W. F. Jackson Knight, *Roman Vergil*, London, 1944, pp. 271f.

40. G. E. Duckworth, 'Variety and Repetition in Vergil's Hexameters', *TAPA* 95 (1964) 17–22: 'The unusually high percentage in *Eclogue* IV both of the first pattern and the first eight patterns resembles closely the procedure of Catullus, as does the distribution of spondees and dactyls in the first four feet, and the high proportion of spondees in the fourth foot' (22). Cf. also Wilkinson 194.

41. Among them Norden, *Geburt* and Jachmann, *Ekloge* 49.

42. Otis 128f. discusses the poems according to 'Theocritean', 'Roman-Theocritean', and 'non-Theocritean' categories.

43. 3.9 *Nymphae risere*, 6.23 *dolum ridens* sc. *Silenus*. Note the description of early Italian song in *Geo.* 2.385ff.: *nec non Ausonii, Troia gens missa, coloni/ versibus incomptis ludunt risuque soluto*; the *ludus* and *risus* of rustic poetry are also brought together by Lucretius 5.1397f. In the *Georgics* Virgil designates his pastoral poems by referring to himself as *carmina qui lusi pastorum* (4.565).

44. E. Pfeiffer, p. 108.

45. Herrmann 72.

46. See above, Chapter IV, note 36.

47. *Id.* 5.79 *Paian*, 82f.; *Id.* 6.27 *Paian*; *Id.* 7.100f.

48. Rose, p. 193; Jachmann, *Ekloge* 60.

49. I follow Servius, Sabbadini, and one older MS tradition (M1, b) in preferring *nascentem* to *crescentem*. Parallelism in the two passages seems intentionally close.

50. Noted by Servius *ad* 4.19: *Mire autem puerum laudat ex ipsis muneribus: nam hederae indicant futurum poetam.*

51. To the best of my knowledge, this solution to the problem of the *puer*'s identification has never before been proposed. Very much akin, however, to my suggestion was the theory of Ruggero della Torre, who believed that the *puer* was Virgil's poetry, and especially the *Aeneid*: 'Il *puer nascens*, non è che opera di Virgilio' (35); 'Il *puer* è nella cuna, quando l'Eneide è in germe nelle bucoliche' (77). The *puer*'s father is Virgil, his mother the Muse (184); this I believe to be correct. Della Torre's work is more apologetic than scholarly, and is based upon his careful reading and thorough knowledge of Virgil, upon his own emotional reactions to the poet, and above all upon his Italian patriotism. He believes that Virgil meant his readers to derive the *virtus* assigned to the *puer* from a reading of his own works 'sempre guidata da nobili ed alti fini' (184). The *puer*'s *regnum* is not political, but spiritual: he is the making of the Roman citizen, the bestower of peace of soul (59–62). Della Torre did not investigate the Greek or Roman literary sources for *Eclogue* 4, and therefore missed seeing the influence of Catullus 64. He eliminated Pollio's rôle altogether by accepting Schaper's emendation of 4.12, substituting *orbis* for *Pollio*.

52. Della Torre 61f., who cites *di patrii* as a common parallel; cf. also *Geo.* 1.52 *patrios cultus.* See below, note 57.

53. The transposition of 4.23 after 4.20 now seems certain: cf. G. E. Duckworth, 'The Cradle of Flowers', *TAPA* 89 (1958) 1–8.

54. And like Daphnis, who showed characteristics of Apollo and Bacchus in *Eclogue* 5, the *puer* seems here to be represented in the tradition of the infants Apollo and Dionysus. Cf. the blooming of Delos with flowers for Apollo at his birth, *Hymn. Hom.* 3.135–9, and Euripides, *Iph. Taur.* 1234–8. Euripides represents ivy covering the infant Dionysus spontaneously in *Phoenissae* 649–56; the chorus goes on directly to tell of the *drakon* which Cadmus slew (657ff.). Could Virgil have been thinking of this Euripidean passage when he wrote *occidet et serpens* (*Ecl.* 4.24)? Jeanmaire 29 calls attention to the specifically Dionysiac quality of one for whom ivy, grapes, milk and honey appear, comparing Euripides, *Bacchae* 142ff.

55. See above, Chapter V pp. 137–8. The absence of any reference in the *Bucolics* to the third *Georgic* may be attributable to the fact that Nicander, Virgil's predecessor in the 'georgic' genre, had excluded stock-raising from the two books of his *Georgika*; this work, together with the *Melissourgika*, probably constituted the three works of Nicander which Virgil had adopted as a framework for the *Georgics*. On the contents of Nicander's *Georgika*,

see A. S. F. Gow, *Nicander*, Cambridge: 1953, p. 209; on the *Melissourgika*, Lesky, p. 754.

56. Cf. Cartault, p. 248, Holtorf, p. 167.

57. Polybius 15.4.11, of Publius Scipio. Similarly Polybius 31.24.5, where Scipio's activity is said to consist in 'speaking and doing what is worthy of his ancestors'. Among the manuscripts of Virgil surviving the end of antiquity, only the *Codex Romanus* preserves the reading *parentum* for *Ecl.* 4.26. All others show the singular *parentis*, which fits the Constantinian/ Eusebian interpretation of the poem: the *parens* is of course God the Father. This reading, adopted universally in the Middle Ages, is usually understood by modern exegetes to signify a prominent political figure who might qualify as the child's father; the choice is usually among Octavian, Pollio, and Antony. *Patriis virtutibus* (17) is then taken to refer to a particular 'father's' virtues (but see above, p. 171). The reading *parentum*, and only *parentum*, fits what I believe to be the original sense of the *Eclogue*. Sabbadini suggests in his edition that *parentis* and *parentum* represent a 'double recension' of the poem by Virgil himself.

58. *Epigram* I (Ernout p. 193).

59. The idea that reading and literature in general are conducive to *virtus* is found in Cicero, *Pro Archia poeta* 15, who cites such illustrious examples as (again) Scipio Africanus, Laelius, L. Furius, and Cato Censorius.

60. Cicero, *Epistulae ad familiares* 6.18 end.

61. Cf. Aeneas' words to his men, *Aen.* 10.295f. *inimicam findite rostris/hanc terram, sulcumque sibi premat ipsa carina.*

62. Herrmann, p. 65 note 2.

63. See below, Chapter VII p. 179f.

64. Della Torre 182: 3.58 *incipe Damoeta*, the refrain in 8, *incipe Maenalios mecum mea tibia versus*, and 9.32 *incipe si quid habes*. Cf. also 6.26 *simul incipit ipse*, *Geo.* 1.5 *incipiam*, *Geo.* 3.295 *incipiens edico*, and *Aen.* 2.13 *incipiam*.

65. Note the echo of Catullus' final statement of 64 in the last line of *Eclogue* 4: *nec dignantur* (64.407)—*nec dignata est* (4.63); cf. Linkomies, 171–3.

66. Lovejoy-Boas, pp. 1–102, 421–46.

67. H. P. L'Orange, 'Ara Pacis Augustae: La zona floreale', *Institutum Romanum Norvegiae: Acta* 1 (1962) 7–16.

CHAPTER VII

1. Hubaux, *Thèmes* pp. 13–19.

2. Cf. Wimmel, 132ff.

3. For the suggestion that the *triumviri agris dividundis* had rotated their chairmanship so that Pollio (41 B.C.) had been succeeded by Varus (40 B.C.), and that Virgil owed at least the latter a political favour, cf. Bayet 271–80.

4. Otis, p. 132.

5. All the evidence to show that Virgil did not mourn Caesar in Daphnis is presented in Rose, 130–4. See also Berg 20–3.

6. See above, Chapter III, note 42.

7. Cf. Rosenmeyer, 33.

8. *P. Oxy.* 2079. Cf. R. Pfeiffer, 322ff.

9. Wimmel, 142–7.

10. Wimmel, 147.

11. Some of the more interesting investigations: F. Skutsch, *Aus Vergils Frühzeit*, Leipzig: 1901, 28–49, believed that Silenus sings a list of Gallus' poems. O. Skutsch, *Eklogen* 193–6 finds the catalogue a list of Alexandrian themes. Z. Stewart, 'The Song of Silenus', *HSCP* 64 (1959) 179–205, who thinks Virgil alludes to ten different literary *genera*, provides a full bibliography for all interpretations of *Eclogue* 6 as a *Kataloggedicht*. J. P. Elder, '*Non iniussa cano:* Vergil's Sixth Eclogue', *HSCP* 65 (1961) 109–25, finds that *Eclogue* 6 is meant to demonstrate Virgil's virtuosity in bucolic poetry, and is a statement of his 'credo of poetics' for the pastoral genre.

12. F. Skutsch, *Fruhzeit* 45f., Büchner 201.

13. Wimmel, 147 note 1.

14. See above, Chapter V, p. 153f.

15. The brilliance of Virgil's technique of dramatic representation throughout Silenus' song was the object of Servius' ingenuous admiration *ad Ecl.* 6.62: 'Mira autem est canentis laus, ut quasi non factam rem cantare sed ipse eam cantando facere videatur'. Cartault 286 saw that the myths in Silenus' song could all have been developed into *epyllia*, and suggested that Virgil was actually experimenting with this genre.

16. And probably was so extended, as Wimmel, 144f. has suggested, by Gallus or another poet.

17. Otis, pp. 125–7.

18. Cartault, p. 286.

19. See above, p. 153f. Fantazzi, 190 (on *Eclogues* 8 and 10): 'The crude eroticism of the Sicilian shepherds gives place to a more tenuous idealization of love'.

20. Otis, pp. 104–20. In this connection attention may be called to Putnam's article, which stresses the fact already emphasized by Klingner (see above, 162–4) that the epyllion was used for the first time by Catullus to convey the poet's deep personal feelings. It is further suggested that the one figure above all with whom the poet identifies himself is Ariadne, whose lover's complaint against Theseus expresses the poet's own tragic disappointment with Lesbia. Only through the use of another person could Catullus convey his full range of emotions, and 'the only way Catullus could describe his situation in detail, and not in the bitter brevity of epigram, was through the long epic tale' (Putnam 200). Putnam further remarks that if Catullus had lived a generation later, in the Augustan age, he might have expressed his feelings in the first person through the love elegy. This genre, however, though influenced greatly by Catullus himself, had not yet been developed in his time. The pioneer, of course, in Latin love elegy was Cornelius Gallus: cf. F. Jacoby, 'Zur Entstehung der römischen Elegie', *Rheinisches Museum* 60 (1905) 67ff. I believe that Virgil's achievement in *Eclogue* 8, the 'psychologizing' (to use Otis' expression) of a moment of deep emotion through the use of the first person, can only be understood

in terms of what Virgil had learned from the love elegies of Gallus. The influence of the elegist upon the eighth *Eclogue* was suggested for the first time by J. Perret, *Virgile: Les Bucoliques*, Paris, 1961, 85.

21. Fantazzi, 181.

22. See above, Chapter IV, p. 121.

23. Cf. Desport, pp. 48–51.

24. *Nemean* 8.49; compare *Nemean* 4.3f. Cf. Maehler 81 note 4; E. E. Beyers, 'Vergil: *Eclogue* 7—A Theory of Poetry', *Acta Classica* 5 (1962) 41f.; and Pöschl 51–3, who gives further examples from Pindar, Hesiod, Catullus, Ovid, and others, along with a bibliography on the Greek conception of poetry as *Heilgesang*.

25. Cf. W. Steidle, 'Zwei Vergilprobleme', *Innsbrucker Beiträge zur Kulturwissenschaft* 7–8 (1962) 323–34.

26. Cf. O. Skutsch, *Eklogen* 198f.

27. Klingner, *Virgil* pp. 172f. cites Propertius 1.8 and Tibullus 1.10.7–14 as close parallels.

28. Kidd, 55f.

29. Klingner, *Virgil*, p. 167.

30. As Horace does in *Epistula* 1.20. Cf. the Parthian shock at finding Milesian tales in Roman officers' quarters: Plutarch, *Crassus* 32. Prop. 1.8a is modelled upon *Ecl.* 10 (or upon Gallus) to such an extent that, if such literary symbolism were found in either poem, the other could be similarly interpreted. Verbal parallelism between 1.8a.1–8 and *Ecl.* 10.46–9 is evident, and Klingner, *Virgil* 172f. notes the similarity in content between both poems. The *propempticon* of Ovid, *Amores* 2.11 (12) is another candidate.

31. *Amores* 1.9.1; compare 2.12 (13). Cf. J. J. Hartmann, 'Ad Vergili eclogam X', *Mnemosyne* 40 (1912) 222–8; Kidd 60f. cites Meleager, *AP* 5.180, 198, and 215.

32. Cf. above, Chapter III, pp. 105f.

33. Della Torre, 201; Smith, 303f. Cf. *Geo.* 4.564 *studiis florentem ignobilis oti.*

34. E.g. *Ode* 1.32.1, *Epist.* 2.2.77f. For discussions of the significance of *umbra* for Augustan poets in general, cf. Pöschl, 21–3 and note 25; Smith, 301–4.

APPENDIX I

1. Already in Hesiod attention is called to the song of the *tettix* (*Erga* 582ff.). Archilochus describes himself as a *tettix* in fr. 88A Diehl. Callimachus also seems to be recalling Plato, *Ion* 534 B, as well as the relationship of the cicada to the Muse in *Phaedrus* 230 C and 262 D. Cf. Wimmel 225 note 1. Poetizing cicadas are rife in the Greek Anthology, e.g. Leonidas, *AP* 6.120 (plus dew); Anyte or Leonidas, *AP* 7.190; Mnasalcas, *AP* 7.192; Meleager, *AP* 7.195f. (cf. Hubaux, *Réalisme* 49–51); Posidippus, *AP* 12.98.

Rejuvenation: a similar idea occurs, as R. Pfeiffer 328f. has pointed out, in Euripides, *Herakles* 637–700, where the chorus of old men finds, if not rejuvenation, at least a substitute for youth in singing the praises of Herakles.

Cf. also H. Parry, 'The Second Stasimon of Euripides' *Heracles* (637–700)', *AJP* 86 (1965) 371. Aristophanes, *Frogs* 340–56, has the chorus of initiates, who know the Muses' *orgia*, find rejuvenation.

2. Pindar, *Olympian* 10.10; *Pythian* 4.299, 5.99, 8.57; *Isthmian* 6.74, 7.19; Nemean 7.12; fr. 94b Snell 76f.; Aristophanes, *Frogs* 1005, Plato, *Ion* 534 A–B; Callimachus, *Epigram* 28.3f.; *Hymn* 2.108–12; etc.

3. Theocritus, *Idylls* 5.80, 7.95, 9.31ff., 11.6. Philodemus, *AP* 5.107.8; Leonidas, *AP* 7.715.3f.; Anon., *AP* 7.664.4, 9.191.5; Callimachus, *Aitia* fr. 1.37f., *Epigram* 21.5f. Virgil, *Ecl.* 3.62, 5.52, 6.10, 7.21, 10.72; *Georgics* 2.476; 3.292.

APPENDIX II

1. *AP* 9.363.19–23. Its authenticity is contested by H. Ouvré, *Méléagre de Gadara*, Paris, 1894, 241f. Meleager's authorship is upheld, however, by Reitzenstein 103, by L. A. Stella, *Cinque poeti dell' Antologia Palatina*, Bologna, 1949, 161–4 and by Webster 213. For the thought, compare Lucretius 5.1395–8. The Greek literary tradition seems to have developed a consciousness of the relationship between poetic activity and renewal in nature long before Meleager, owing probably to the part played by poets and musicians in religious ritual commemorating the coming of Spring: cf. Aristophanes, *Clouds* 311–13.

2. Meleager, *AP* 12.109.3, continuing the tradition of Sappho, fr. 130 LP. Hubaux, *Réalisme* 101f. discusses the development of the 'bitter' character of love in the epigrammatic tradition, especially in Meleager. Add to his list Archias, *AP* 5.59.1 and Meleager, *AP* 5.163.3f. The pains of love are found desirable and decidedly civilized as early as Euripides, fr. 897 Nauck 2 (6–8).

3. See above, Appendix I note 2. For water as a symbol among the Romans for poetry (e.g. Propertius 2.10.25 and 3.3) cf. F. A. Todd, *De Musis in carminibus poetarum Romanorum commemoratis*, Jena, 1903 p. 24; Maas, 375ff.; Kroll, 28f.; and Wimmel, 217–27. Dew as a symbol for poetry is already present in Pindar, *Pythian* 5.99.

4. A. Forbiger, *P. Vergili Maronis Opera*, 4th ed. 1, Leipzig: 1872 p. 63 *ad loc.*

BIBLIOGRAPHY

The following list includes only those works which are mentioned more than once. Complete bibliographical data on other works cited will be found in the appropriate notes.

AP: Anthologia Palatina (The Greek Anthology)

BAYET, J., 'Virgile et les triumvirs "agris dividundis" ', *Revue des études latines* 6 (1928) 271–99.

BERG, W., 'Daphnis and Prometheus', *Transactions and Proceedings of the American Philological Association* 96 (1965) 11–23.

BOLL, F., *Sulla quarta ecloga di Virgilio; Memorie della R. Accad. delle scienze dell' istituto di Bologna*, cl. di sc. mor. Ser. 2, 5–7, 1923.

BRUNN, H., 'Die griechischen Bukoliker und die bildende Kunst', *Sitzungsberichte der königlichen bayerischen Akademie der Wissenschaften*, Philosophisch-philologische Classe, 2 (1879) 1–21.

BÜCHNER, K., *P. Vergilius Maro, der Dichter der Römer*, Stuttgart, 1961.

CARCOPINO, J., *Virgile et le mystère de la IV. éclogue*, Paris, 1930.

CARTAULT, A., *Étude sur les Bucoliques de Virgile*, Paris, 1897.

CLAUSEN, W., 'Callimachus and Latin Poetry', *Greek, Roman and Byzantine Studies* 5 (1964) 181–96.

CUNNINGHAM, J. V., *Tradition and Poetic Structure*, Denver, 1960.

CURTIUS, E. R., *European Literature and the Latin Middle Ages*, translated from the German by W. R. Trask, New York, 1953.

DAMON, P. H., 'Modes of Analogy in Ancient and Medieval Verse', *University of California Publications in Classical Philology* 15 (1961).

DESPORT, MARIE, *L'incantation virgilienne*, Bordeaux, 1952.

DUNCAN, ROBERT, *The Opening of the Field*, New York, 1960.

FANTAZZI, C., 'Vergilian Pastoral and Roman Love Poetry', *American Journal of Philology* 87 (1966) 171–91.

FRAZER, J. G., *Adonis, Attis and Osiris* 1 = *The Golden Bough* part IV, 1, 3rd ed., London, 1914.

GOW, A. S. F., *Theocritus*, Cambridge, 1950.

GRIMAL, P., *Les jardins romains à la fin de la république et aux deux premiers siècles de l'empire*, Paris, 1943.

GUTHRIE, W. K. C., *Orpheus and Greek Religion*, 2nd ed., London, 1952.

HEIDEL, A., *The Gilgamesh Epic and Old Testament Parallels*, 2nd ed., Chicago, 1949.

HERRMANN, L., *Les Masques et les Visages dans les Bucoliques de Virgile*, Brussels, 1930.

HOLTORF, H., *P. Vergilius Maro: die grösseren Gedichte* 1, Freiburg, 1959.

HUBAUX, J., *Le réalisme dans les Bucoliques de Virgile*, Liége, 1927.

—, *Les thèmes bucoliques dans la poésie latine*, Brussels, 1930.

JACHMANN, G., 'Die vierte Ekloge Vergils', *Annali della scuola normale di Pisa* (lettere, storia, e filosofia) 21 (1952) 13–62.

—, 'Die dichterische Technik in Vergils Bukolika', *Neue Jahrbücher für das klassische Altertum, Geschichte, und deutsche Literatur* 49 (1922) 101–20.

JEANMAIRE, H., *Le messianisme de Virgile*, Paris, 1930.

KAMBYLIS, A., *Die Dichterweihe und ihre Symbolik*, Heidelberg, 1965.

KIDD, D. A., 'Imitation in the Tenth Eclogue', *University of London Bulletin of the Institute of Classical Studies* 11 (1964) 54–64.

KLINGNER, F., *Studien zur griechischen und römischen Literatur*, Zürich/Munich, 1964.

—, *Virgil*, Zürich/Stuttgart, 1967.

KRAMER, S. N., *Mythologies of the Ancient World*, Garden City, 1961.

KRAUSE, E., *Quibus temporibus quoque ordine Vergilius eclogas scripserit*, Berlin, 1884.

KROLL, W., *Studien zum Verständnis der römischen Literatur*, Stuttgart, 1924.

LAWALL, G., *Theocritus' Coan Pastorals*, Harvard, 1967.

LESKY, A., *Geschichte der griechischen Literatur*, 2nd ed., Bern/Munich, 1963.

LINKOMIES, E., 'Vergils vierte Ekloge', *Arctos* 1 (1930) 168–87.

LOVEJOY, A. O., and BOAS, G., *Primitivism and Related Ideas in Antiquity* I, Baltimore, 1935.

MAAS, E., 'Untersuchungen zu Properz', *Hermes* 31 (1896) 375–434.

MAEHLER, H., *Die Auffassung des Dichterberufs im frühen Griechentum bis zur Zeit Pindars*, *Hypomnemata* 3, Göttingen, 1963.

MARTIN, J., 'Vergil und die Landanweisungen', *Würzburger Jahrbücher* 1 (1946) 98–107.

MURLEY, C., 'Plato's *Phaedrus* and Theocritean Pastoral', *Transactions and Proceedings of the American Philological Association* 71 (1940) 281–95.

NICOSIA, S., 'Teocrito e l'arte figurata', *Quaderni dell' Istituto di Filologia Greca della Università di Palermo* 5 (1968).

NIKHILANANDA, SWAMI, *The Bhagavadgītā*, New York, 1944.

NILSSON, M. P., *Geschichte der griechischen Religion* I, 2nd ed., *Müllers Handbuch*, Munich, 1955.

NORDEN, E., *Die Geburt des Kindes: Geschichte einer religiösen Idee*, Leipzig, 1924.

OPPERMANN, H., 'Vergil und Octavian', *Hermes* 67 (1932) 197–219.

OTIS, B., *Virgil: A Study in Civilized Poetry*, Oxford, 1963.

PARRY, A., 'Landscape in Greek Poetry', *Yale Classical Studies* 15 (1957) 3–29.

PFEIFFER, E., *Virgils Bukolika*, Stuttgart, 1933.

PÖSCHL, V., *Die Hirtendichtung Virgils*, Heidelberg, 1964.

PUTNAM, M. C. J., 'The Art of Catullus 64', *Harvard Studies in Classical Philology* 65 (1961) 165–205.

RADHAKRISHNAN, S., *The Bhagavadgītā*, New York, 1948.

REITZENSTEIN, R., *Epigramm und Skolion*, Giessen, 1893.

ROHDE, G., 'De Vergili eclogarum forma et indole', *Klassisch-Philologische Studien* 5 (1925) 1–69.

—, *Studien und Interpretationen zur antiken Literatur, Religion, und Geschichte*, Berlin, 1963.

ROSE, H. J., *The Eclogues of Vergil*, Berkeley, 1942.

ROSENMEYER, T. G., *The Green Cabinet: Theocritus and the European Pastoral Lyric*, Berkeley/Los Angeles, 1969.

ROTHSTEIN, M., *Die Elegien des Sextus Propertius* 2, Berlin, 1924.

SKUTSCH, O., 'Zu Vergils Eklogen', *Rheinisches Museum* 99 (1956) 193–201.

—, 'Symmetry and Sense in the Eclogues', *Harvard Studies in Classical Philology* 73 (1968) 153–69.

SMITH, P. L., '*Lentus in umbra:* A Symbolic Pattern in Vergil's *Eclogues*', *Phoenix* 19 (1965) 298–304.

SNELL, B., *Discovery of the Mind*, translated by T. G. Rosenmeyer, New York, 1960.

SPERDUTI, ALICE, 'The Divine Nature of Poetry in Antiquity', *Transactions and Proceedings of the American Philological Association* 81 (1950) 209–40.

TORRE, R. DELLA, *La quarta egloga di Virgilio commentata secondo l'arte grammatica*, Udine, 1892.

TROXLER-KELLER, IRENE, *Die Dichterlandschaft des Horaz*, Heidelberg, 1964.

VAN SICKLE, J. B., 'The Unity of the *Eclogues*: Arcadian Forest, Theocritean Trees', *Transactions and Proceedings of the American Philological Association* 98 (1967) 491–508.

WEBSTER, T. B. L., *Hellenistic Poetry and Art*, London, 1964.

WESTENDORP-BOERMA, R. E. H., 'Vergil's Debt to Catullus', *Acta Classica* I (1958) 51–63.

WILKINSON, L. P., *Golden Latin Artistry*, Cambridge, 1963.

WIMMEL, W., 'Kallimachos in Rom', *Hermes* Einzelschriften 16, 1960.

INDEX

Adonis, 11, 13, 18–20
adynaton, 160, 185, 208 n. 17
Aeneas, 19, 137, 149, 170, 174, 186
Aeschylus, 123
Aganippe, 188
Aion, 155–7
Alcaeus of Messene, 204 n. 34, 207 n. 58
Alexandrian poetry, 8, 96, 106, 182
amomum, 159, 172
Anchises, 13, 19f., 97, 170
Antipater of Sidon, 105, 203 n. 24
Antipater of Thessalonica, 207 n. 58
Antiphanes, 203 n. 23
Anyte, 213 n. 1
Aper, M., 4
Aphrodite, 13, 18–20, 22, 188. *See also* Venus
Apollo, 12 (Nomius), 15, 24, 95, 109, 118, 125–7 (Nomius), 130 (Nomius), 148, 150, 167, 181, 188, 191, 207 n. 5, 210 n. 54
Apollonius, 174, 204 n. 39
Appendix Vergiliana, 97
Ara Pacis, 177
Aratus, 23, 157, 165
Arcadia, 109f., 150, 186f., 189
Archias, 105, 207 n. 58
Archilochus, 5
Argonauts, 95, 162, 174, 209 n. 36
Arion, 160
Artemidorus, 107
Asclepiades, 207 n. 58
Astarte, 17
Attis, 19f.
Augustine, 155

baccar, 169, 172
Bacchus, *see* Dionysus

Bacchylides, 144, 207 n. 60
Balbus, Cornelius, 159
bee symbolism, 5, 23f., 119f., 150f., 153, 197 n. 14, 207 n. 60
Bhagavadgītā, 1–3
Bianor, 133, 141f.
Bion, 21f., 107, 152
Brundisium, Peace of, 158f., 208 n. 12
Burina, 22–4

Caesar, Julius, 99, 180, 205 n. 13
Caesar Octavianus (Augustus), 99, 109, 117, 131, 137, 143, 156f., 166, 170–2, 205 n. 13
Callimachus, 10, 22, 24 (*Aitia*-prologue), 106f., 117, 120f., 124f. (*Epigr.* 8, *Iamb.* 1), 145f., 151–3 (*Hymn* 2), 166 (*Aitia*), 181 (*Aitia*-prologue), 191
Calliope, 176
Calvus, 106, 182
Catullus, 100 (64), 106f., 111 (64), 113 (64), 145, 162–7 (64), 175–7 (64), 182f. (64), 185, 193f. (61), 212 n. 20
Catulus, Q. Lutatius (Maior), 105
cave symbolism, 24, 95, 116–20, 151, 202 n. 17
cicada symbolism, 5, 23f., 102, 114, 119f., 141, 150, 191, 213 n. 1
Cicero, 106, 120, 165, 174
Cinna, C. Helvius, 105, 182
Claudian, 99
Constantine, 211 n. 57
Crassus, Canidius, 159
Cremona, 140, 142
Crinagoras, 195 n. 11
Culex, 94–102
Cybele, 19